HOW TO
SOLVE THE
MISMANAGEMENT
CRISIS

Diagnosis and Treatment of Management Problems

HOW TO
SOLVE THE
MISMANAGEMENT
CRISIS

Diagnosis and Treatment of Management Problems

ICHAK ADIZES, Ph.D.

Adizes Institute, Inc.
and
Graduate School of Management
UCLA

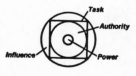

 Institute, Inc.
The Institute for Managerial Development
2001 Wilshire Boulevard
Santa Monica, California 90403
(213) 453-5593; TLX 664929 Adizes USA

First Printing 1979/Dow Jones-Irwin
Second Printing 1980/MDOR Institute
Third Printing 1981/ADIZES Institute
Fourth Printing 1983/ADIZES Institute
Fifth Printing 1985/ADIZES Institute

This publication is designed to provide accurate and
authoritative information in regard to the subject matter
covered. It is sold with the understanding that the
publisher is not engaged in rendering legal, accounting, or
other professional service. If legal advice or other expert
assistance is required, the services of a competent
professional person should be sought.

*From a Declaration of Principles jointly adopted by a Committee
of the American Bar Association and a Committee of Publishers.*

ISBN 0-937120-00-6
Library of Congress Catalog Card No. 78–59225

Printed in the United States of America

5 6 7 8 9 0 K 6 5

To Tchia, Topaz, and Shoham
my companions in life

Preface

Have you ever known executives who graduated from leading schools of management but as managers you felt they
were mismanaging? They "shot from the hip" or procrasti-
nated in making decisions, or were bureaucratic in the sense
of "going by the book"? They knew their management theory;
they knew they had to plan and organize and motivate and
control but somehow on one or more of these functions they
failed? Their *style* of managing was inadequate?

Have you ever read a textbook about management principles and found it made excellent sense; it was simple and
exciting? But what appeared so simple in the book was in
fact highly complicated, and in reality things did not work
out according to those rational and obvious principles?

If you are a top executive you probably have had frequent
"loneliness blues"—no one to talk to about the burdens of
responsibility, no one to share in the decision making. And
whether or not you feel comfortable with your decisions, you
are responsible for them.

Most management books describe what I call the "textbook manager"—a "model person" who excels in performing

all the roles of management. These books ignore differences in personal styles. Furthermore, in my opinion, they oversimplify the complexity of the managerial task. These textbooks by and large focus on an individual—what a manager should do.

The aim of this book is to present a view of the *managerial process* as a team process and to provide the reader with the tools for diagnosing and treating mismanagement. The book will provide the tools for composing teams and for rejuvenating organizations to counter their tendency to age and become bureaucratized. These tools have been used successfully by me and by my associates at MDOR to improve the effectiveness and efficiency of organizations while simultaneously facilitating the personal growth of the people in the organizations who used the methodology presented in this volume.

May 1979   ICHAK ADIZES

Acknowledgments

The people who helped me with the manuscript and with ideas are too numerous for me to name all of them. The following is a list of the most significant contributors to whom I owe much gratitude.

First, I thank Kirby Warren of Columbia University, who encouraged and prodded me into writing this book. His comments on the final draft improved the content and presentation.

My research assistants over the years, Uma, Avi Nachlieli, Gad Caspi, Gene Neiman, Earl Schub, Amram Haisraeli, and Susan Ehrhart, were helpful with comments, criticisms, and library research. Bill Grieb from MDOR Institute collated the raw material and edited an early version of this book. Without that early, messy, starting version I probably would have never gotten to this one. I owe him special thanks.

Among my colleagues, Jim Taylor, Jim Jackson, Bob Tannenbaum, and Warren Schmidt from UCLA and Will McWhinney and Moshe Ben Bassat from MDOR Institute were very helpful in reading parts of the manuscript and making valuable comments.

Marla Rabin, Ruth Dordick, and Reta Singer slaved over the typing and keeping the footnotes in order. Rhoda Blecker edited the book into a readable form. The UCLA Academic Senate Research Committee, The UCLA Institute of Industrial Relations, and MDOR Institute financially supported the typing and editing of the manuscript. A sabbatical leave from the UCLA Graduate School of Management made it possible for me to complete my work on the book.

To them all—my gratitude!

An article on this model appeared under the title "Mismanagement Styles" in the *California Management Review,* vol. 19 (Winter 1976), no. 2. I thank them for the right to reprint passages of the article in this book.

I. A.

Contents

Part I   THE TRAP

    1. Introduction, 3

Part II   MISMANAGEMENT STYLES

    2. P———: The Lone Ranger, 13
    3. −A——: The Bureaucrat, 24
    4. ——E−: The Arsonist, 37
    5. ———I: The Superfollower, 55
    6. ————: The Deadwood, 71
    7. PAEI: The Textbook Manager, 81
    8. Organizational Styles, 92

Part III   WHAT TO DO ABOUT IT?

    9. What, Then, Is a Good Manager? 131
  10. Developing and Training a Good Manager, 149
  11. Fitting a Personal Style to Task Demands:
      Building the Managerial Mix, 174
  12. Organizational Therapy, 197

Part IV   OUT OF THE TRAP

  13. Once Again and for the Last(?) Time:
      What IS Management? 215
  14. An Introduction to the Adizes Management
      Method, 231

Appendix: Variations on the Theme (Performing Several
      Roles—but Not All of Them!), 253

Index, 277

Part I

THE TRAP

Chapter 1

Introduction

I remember how the idea for this book was conceived. One afternoon a door-to-door salesman for *Encyclopaedia Britannica* came to sell me the newest edition, 30 volumes of the accumulated human knowledge. "What do you do, sir?" he asked. "I teach management," I replied. "Well," he said, "let's see what the encyclopedia has to say about the subject."

So we looked. With increasing uneasiness on his part and bewilderment on my part, it soon became apparent that there was no such term in the encyclopedia. There was management science, which is mathematical models for decision making, and organizational behavior, which is the sociology of organizations, but plain simple *management,* what millions of people around the world do day in and day out, was totally excluded.

It made me stop and think. What *is* management? In Yugoslavia, if one manages as we do in the United States, he or she could be criminally prosecuted and even sent to prison.[1] To manage, as we know it, is illegal there. Management in Yugoslavia *recommends* to the workers what can be done, and it is the "subordinates" who make the final decisions.

In Israeli kibbutzim a manager (the secretary of the kibbutz) supervises for a few years and then goes back to the daily tasks, such as milking the cows. As a matter of practice, the managerial task is rotated. The Israelis negate professional management, and if one tries to actually manage others, that is, tell them unilaterally what to do, he or she can easily be recalled by the electorate.

From textbooks we learn that management plans, decides, organizes, controls, and motivates. However, there are organizations where management is not supposed to perform some of those functions. Several years ago I did some research on the management of artistic organizations, opera, dance, theater, etc. After visiting the major opera houses, ballet companies, theaters, and museums, I became aware that managers cannot manage the artists as, let us say, one can manage workers. They cannot plan, organize, and control like the textbooks prescribe.[2] An administrator in a theater serves and administers *for* the artistic director. I once noted the same phenomenon in the health and educational systems. Here, the administrators do not perform all the functions of management. They do not decide policy matters since the physicians and the educators have input on the subject as well.

So what is management really? What does it do? Can any system really do without management? I have found in my previous research reported elsewhere that management cannot be eradicated.[3] In spite of the laws in Yugoslavia, management manages, and the same holds true in Israel. It appeared to me that management must perform some functions that neither the law nor social pressure can eliminate.

In determining what these functions might be, I found that management has to perform four roles: producer, administrator, entrepreneur, and integrator. Each role is *necessary* and the four together are *sufficient* for good management. By "necessary" I mean that if any one role is not performed, a certain pattern of mismanagement can be identified. This book describes the four roles and explains how to diagnose mismanagement patterns.

I have concluded that one individual *alone* cannot perform all four roles. Those who are outstanding with respect to ideas and planning are usually weak on implementation; others who excel in implementation might be poor motivators; those who excel in motivating might have problems running a tight ship; and those who are capable of running things smoothly usually are weak in introducing changes and accepting new ideas. Effective management of a growing organization is *too complicated* for any *one* individual to handle alone. The four roles are in conflict and no one person can perform them simultaneously. When an individual attempts to do so, the result is generally mismanagement. The conclusion I have arrived at is that for good management to happen, *complementary staffing* is necessary, which means acknowledging differences in style and opinion and accepting conflict as an inevitable and desirable facet of managing.

MANAGEMENT ROLES

The necessary and sufficient roles that need to be performed for the long-run effective and efficient operations of an organization are: to produce, to administer, to be an entrepreneur, and to integrate.

The Producer (P)

A manager is expected to achieve results or produce services equal to or better than those of the competition. In order to perform this function, a manager needs knowledge of his or her field, whether it is marketing, engineering, accounting, law, or any other discipline, and must have the necessary drive to see that the final results are produced.

The Administrator (A)

A manager should have more than drive and knowledge. Being productive as an individual and having the functional knowledge of a particular discipline or technology do not necessarily enable one to produce commensurate results in managing a group of people. In this role managers schedule, coordinate, and verify implementation. They are administrators and see to it that the system works as it was designed to work.

The Entrepreneur (E)

Management is more than producing and administering, however. It entails a higher degree of discretion in setting goals, strategic planning, and policymaking. This discretionary decision making involves entrepreneurship. In a changing environment, a manager must use judgment and be able to change the goals and the systems by which they are implemented. To perform this role, the manager must be an organizational entrepreneur. Unlike administrators who are given certain plans to carry out and certain decisions to implement, entrepreneurs have to generate their own plan of action. They have to be self-starters. Managers who perform the entrepreneurial role have to be creative to identify new courses of action and be willing to take risks. If they are not creative, they will be unable to perceive new possibilities; if they cannot take risks, they may not be able to take advantage of opportunities.

But, even together, these three roles are insufficient for adequate managerial functioning. Many organizations that were managed by excellent achiever-administrator-entrepreneurs (usually their founders) "nose-dived" when this key individual died or for some reason had to be replaced. An organization's life span is longer than the life span of any individual within it. Thus, for an organization to be continuously successful over time, an additional role has to be performed.

The Integrator (I)

The fourth essential role of management is integration. By integration I mean the process by which individual risks become group risks, individual goals are harmonized into group goals, and ultimately individual entrepreneurship emerges as group entrepreneurship. When a group can operate on its own with a clear direction and is able to successfully choose new directions without depending exclusively on any one individual, then the integrating role has been performed adequately. A good integrator becomes dispensable; the integrated team can survive without him or her.

MISMANAGEMENT

I have found that whenever a role has not been performed, a style of mismanagement can be identified. By "style" I mean a repetitive set of behaviors that predictably occur in response to specific situations. Thus, when a person displays a style, it means we can predict how the person will act if the situation is known.

A task is one type of a situation, and each task has qualities that are distinctly its own. Thus, particular tasks require particular styles of behavior from people. A sales job needs people who have a certain style of behavior that is different from the style an accountant might have.

The classical "functions of management" approach assumes that all people have the same style and ignores the fact that different people organize, plan, and control differently. To me, the important point is whether the managerial style and the manager's job fit together well. A style mismatched with a task might well be one of the reasons why organizations are mismanaged.

During my research I discovered that the four roles **P, A, E,** and **I,** can also be used to describe and analyze organizational life cycles and that the behaviors of organizations change over the life cycle. At any given time one managerial role is more prominent than the others. This means that one can predict "passages" (to use Gail Sheehy's expression) in organizational life and prepare for them.

VALUE OF STUDY

Determining the relationships among **P, A, E,** and **I** roles is a very valuable approach to diagnosing management effectiveness. First, it can be used in executive staffing and search. Since I claim that no one manager has all the personality traits necessary to successfully manage an organization, this methodology provides a framework for establishing a mix of complementary styles necessary for managing the organization.

Second, the **PAEI** model can be used as a predictive tool. Once a *pattern* in the behavior of a manager is identified and verified, it is possible to predict other variables in the pattern and thus the person's behavior.

My associates at MDOR and I have used the model described in this book and have found that predictive tools are quite powerful. They give us the ability to "x-ray" and analyze an organization. One can look at the total organization or the style of the individual manager and predict how the various departments will operate within the organization: Will there be turnover of employees? How much training and of what type is taking place? How are people promoted and for what reasons? Who might be the next president of the company and why? Who is in conflict with whom? Which conflict is desirable and which must be eliminated?

METHODOLOGY AND SOURCE OF DATA

The methodology used in accumulating data for this book was that of participant observations: As an agent for organizational change I worked with managers and recorded what I saw. Extensive use of interviews was made as well. The companies I worked with and observed range from $1 million to $1 billion in sales and employ from 80 to 15,000 people. They are involved in various technologies including aircraft, insurance, banking, the performing arts, museums, government agencies, and others and are in both the profit and not-for-profit sectors.

Since my work as an organizational therapist frequently takes me to different countries, I have been able to compare notes and share my observations with both domestic and foreign executives. In addition, the model has been presented to top executives in various executive programs around the world. Thus, the model and its findings have been verified by hundreds of practicing managers in the field as being universal in nature and unbounded by cultural or technological biases.

The focus of this research differs from psychologists such as Maslow, McCleland, and Reading, who describe needs and try to predict behavior from them. I am interested not in *why* a given behavior occurs but in *what* behavior occurs and *how* it affects the organization. This study concentrates on the manager's style as a determinant for predicting the behavior of the organization, and an attempt is made to prescribe what needs to be done.

Another methodological point: Several attempts have been made in the past to classify and codify managerial behavior (Blake and Mouton, Reddin, M. Maccoby, Fielder, and others) using one-, two-, or three-dimensional analysis. These studies and theories, however, focus on an individual, his or her behavior, and its effectiveness. The management and leadership literature focuses on an individual similarly to microeconomic theory, which focuses on one individual, the entrepreneur, or "the firm" to personify the complex decision-making process in an organization.

The same individualistic approach can be seen in management theory which has traditionally looked at one predominant aspect of management. F. Taylor, a pioneer in the field, was concerned primarily with productivity, specialization, and efficiency (the **P** role). Fayol and Urwick, on the other hand, were concerned with the organizational structure —authority, span of control, delegation of authority, and staff-line relationships (the **A** role). N. Weiner focused on the dynamics of change and subsequently introduced cybernetics (the **E** role). E. Mayo considered the human aspect, and behavioral science and the study of individuals in organizations became the dominant focus of management theory (the I role). Essentially, all of them considered what the individual manager does in one of the four roles of management described above as the total management process, i.e., it includes the other three roles.

The "general management" theoreticians like Drucker, Newman, and Koontz tried to put efficiency (P), structure (A), change (E), and the human element (I) together into a whole, which they called the process or functions of management. However, they basically remained with the past focus of inquiry: the individual manager.

My contribution is I believe that all the four roles have to be performed but it has to be done by several people. For good management one needs to bring together people who act and think differently. Instead of talking about *the manager* planning, organizing, etc., we should talk about the *managerial team* performing these functions. *The roles of producer, administrator, entrepreneur, and administrator have to be performed by a complementary team since no one person can be responsible for them all.* The why and how to do it make up the content of this book.

NOTES

1. Ichak Adizes, *Industrial Democracy: Yugoslav Style* (initial publication, New York: Free Press, 1971; reprinted softcover, Los Angeles: MDOR Institute, 1977).

2. Ichak Adizes, "Administering for the Arts" in *California Management Review* 15 (1972), no. 2.

3. Ichak Adizes and Elizabeth Mann Borgese, *Self-Management: New Dimensions to Democracy* (Santa Barbara, Calif.: ABC/CLIO, 1977).

Part II

MISMANAGEMENT
STYLES

Chapter 2

P---: The Lone Ranger

THE ROLE OF PRODUCING RESULTS

A person who is committed to his or her discipline and his or her work, and has the know-how of his or her field, is invaluable to an organization. He or she is industrious and an excellent producer of results.

As a **P**—producer—he sells, engineers, runs the production system, or effectively completes research assignments. He is committed to getting the job done. Any organization needs managers who are action-oriented and results-oriented, who can be relied upon to perform well.

A producer of results, a person who performs well in his tasks, has a strong need to achieve, to get results. He is impatient with postponed gratification. As a salesman, he wants to close a deal as soon as possible. As an engineer, he can't wait to hear the machines humming. As a tennis player, he seldom warms up long before suggesting "Let's play" and he usually pays close attention to the score.[1]

To be a producer of results, a person must have a strong achievement need and also know what he is doing. The knowledge component is present in all of the four roles (**PAEI**)—pronounced like *pie*—but let us confine ourselves here to the effect of knowledgeability on producing results. To produce results, one must know the technology of a discipline—one must know what needs to be controlled and how to control it.

Technology should be understood in the broad sense of the word. Every discipline has a technology. In marketing, it is the buyers, competitors, channels of distribution, and so on. In production, it is the machines, the raw materials, the human operatives, and so on.

Often one hears the claim that a good manager can manage anything, that he or she can move from one technology to another and succeed. One claim goes, "From shoes to bubble gum, there is no difference." One merely needs to have the know-how to plan, organize, etc. This claim needs a little modification. One can manage any technology *after some time.* But first the manager has to learn the differences in its technology: What makes the organization "tick"? How do its markets operate? What is unique to its production system? Many organizations in the arts have had severe problems being "artistic" because of the notion that a good manager can manage anything. They had on their boards of directors people whose experience was exclusively in business, and who tried to run a theater as they would have run, let us say, a soap company. "All you have to do," these people claimed, "is produce what the clients want, budget the production, and sell."[2]

But without knowledge of the technology necessary to produce results, a manager's ability to make decisions is impaired. Errors may be made in the what, when, and how of decisions. The timing of actions and the degree of effort that is put into them may be faulty.[3]

The manager who is not knowledgeable but has the drive to achieve cannot be a complete producer. Instead he is almost a drone, stumbling ineptly from task to task, working hard, but never quite providing useful results. He wants to achieve, but since his know-how is limited, he makes mistakes. The side effects of his mistakes can be so devastating that he ends up with more work to do than he began with—and he again performs ineptly. So the harder he works, the further behind he gets. The result is that he is going full speed backward.

On the other hand, a manager who is knowledgeable but has no motive to achieve will often end up in a staff-type position. He is in his office all hours of the day, working, reading, learning, considering. When one asks the staff person a question, he will produce an extremely well-qualified answer. He is usually very knowledgeable in his field, but he is just not interested in getting things done. He likes the analytical and intellectual part of an operation, a mechanism, a technology, or a system, but he doesn't like getting his hands dirty. He is bored by having to carry out mechanically an activity that he already fully understands.

The complete producer, therefore, must be both knowledgeable in his field in order to make the correct decisions and have the achievement need to carry those decisions out. He knows what needs to be done and how it should be done, and he then goes and gets it done.

In the rest of this book, whenever the effect of the producing role (P) is discussed, it is assumed that the person who performs it is both knowledgeable in his field and has the need to achieve. If a person is low on P this means that he either has low achievement needs or is not knowledgeable about his tasks.

THE LONE RANGER STYLE

Let us consider for a moment what happens when a manager performs only the role of producer. We will code him a P––– in the PAEI code. This indicates that he is not an administrator, nor an entrepreneur, nor an integrator—that he is only a producer, though he may be an excellent one.

What happens to a manager who is only a producer? He does not coordinate, administer, delegate, plan, follow up, control, and so on. He fails to come up with new directions or thrusts, and he does not relate well to people. He does not build a team or develop the capabilities of others around him—he is too busy producing. When a new problem is brought to his attention, he drops whatever he is doing and plunges indiscriminately into the new task. In fact, observations show that he is constantly rushing from task to task, from crisis to crisis. The more running around he does, the better he thinks he is working. This is why the unmitigated producer, **P----**, is usually called a Lone Ranger or a Fire Fighter.

The Lone Ranger's view of time is that it should be used to solve the immediate problems of an organization. He has no thought for long-range planning, new directions, or "ten years down the pike."

The Lone Ranger is easily recognized in any department of any organization. No matter what his sphere of responsibility—accounting, research, sales, operations—he is busy doing, doing, and doing. He has a compulsion to do everything himself. He is the first one to arrive in the morning, and the last one to leave at night. He is a workaholic, so if he has no work to do, he manifests anxiety. If he has nothing to worry about . . . he worries!

When I see a manager who views every task as his own responsibility, a manager who resists delegation of authority or responsibility to his subordinates, I know I am dealing with a Lone Ranger. And in an organization managed by a Lone Ranger, there is a significant imbalance in the work load. While the manager is overworked, the rest of the organization is underworked. In visiting such an organization, one notices a lack of tension in the atmosphere. People seem to have all the time in the world to spend with a visitor. But when one enters the office of the manager, the contrast is conspicuous. The atmosphere is tense; the manager speaks rapidly and disjointedly; the phone rings constantly; secretaries come and go in a hurry.

Such a manager's subordinates are hardly more than spectators at a performance. If the manager has a secretary, the secretary is usually burdened with a work load that cannot possibly get done. Yet despite the Lone Ranger's constant complaining that he is overburdened, he is happiest when he is busiest. This may stem from his perception of his role and his consequent self-evaluation.

The Lone Ranger measures his success and his contribution to the organization by how hard he works. When you ask him, "How are you doing?" his typical answer will be, "We sold [or produced, or whatever] . . . ," or "I've been working till midnight lately." And "lately" in his case might be his entire working life!

When it is suggested that the Lone Ranger reduce his work load, he has many excuses at hand to show that this would be impossible. As he accepts more and more tasks, he will begin to fail in some of them, since he will try to do everything himself.

When the Lone Ranger is asked why he does not delegate some of his tasks, his typical answer is, "They can't do it right." When he is asked, "Why don't you train them?" he will typically answer, "I have no time to train." So the Lone Ranger is caught in his own trap. He overworks himself, employing all of his time to produce results. This leaves him with no time to train others, which in turn means that he has no trained people to whom he can delegate—which in turn means that he *has* to be overworked. The result is that he is the hardest working individual in the organization.

The Lone Ranger's typical complaint is that the day is too short. He would like a week with at least two Sundays to catch up with work.

The Lone Ranger refuses to delegate because of his perception of himself. If he delegates, there will be less work for him to do, and thus he won't see himself as a good manager.

He wants to be indispensable, to have problems waiting in line for him. His desk is always loaded with paperwork, with incomplete assignments. He is always rushed, and he likes it that way. Delegation would take all the fun out of his job.

But since the Lone Ranger cannot do everything himself, he makes extensive use of "expediters"—that is, individuals who assist him with errands and short-term assignments, but have no permanent long-term responsibilities. These people spend most of their time waiting for their next assignment, which will come in the form of a crisis that should have been handled "yesterday." They have often had no previous training for the task they are given, and the manager usually presents it as a request to "Please help to deal with the crisis."

The Lone Ranger is a universal phenomenon. And the Lone Ranger's subordinates are the same everywhere, though their names may vary in different countries. In the United States they are called "go-fors." In Mexico, they are called *inginiero ibeme* which means "Go bring me something." In Israel they are called "errand boys."

These go-fors and errand boys are not just low-level executives. In many companies top vice presidents work in this capacity for a Lone Ranger. They are assistants to the president, but they do little except go for him. As a rule of thumb, when there are many "assistants to the president" in an organization chart, one can assume that there is a Lone Ranger at the top. He does not delegate; he just has assistants to help him with the latest crisis.

The Lone Ranger respects doers, producers, and achievers, but he considers anyone who tries to help him systematize his efforts or to aid him in administering and delegating as merely an "academician," as a person who "can't do." His typical response to administrative attempts to improve planning, communication, and so on, via staff meetings is, "We can't afford to spend too much time on the long run. There is too much to do right away. If we don't produce results today, there might not be a tomorrow!" Or he may say, "It is foolish to worry about the future so much. We have a railroad to run." And off he dashes to make a sale or another telephone call, or to put out one of the fires that he sees springing up constantly.

In his day-to-day running of the railroad, the Lone Ranger feels little or no concern about the direction in which it is going. He pays no heed to where the tracks are or where the equipment is coming from. What is important to him is how the railroad is operating *today.*

His planning is often limited to a week or a month. The Lone Ranger might therefore be running a very efficient railroad, but in the wrong direction, because he has no time to oversee the laying of the tracks so that the railroad can arrive at its proper destination.

The Peter Principle contains an interesting description of an exclusive **P** (that is, **P——**) type of manager. As an auto mechanic, this manager had been an excellent worker. He was able to diagnose engine faults and showed endless patience in eliminating them. When he was promoted, he could seldom be found at his desk. He was usually in the shop, working on an engine. The subordinate who was supposed to repair the car would stand by watching. Other workers sat around, waiting to be assigned new tasks. The shop was always crowded with work, and deadlines were often missed.[4]

The Lone Ranger likes to be on the firing line. He prefers doing the job himself to directing others. One can find many examples of this type in creative professional organizations. Many such organizations have suffered from overzealous artistic directors who would rather direct plays themselves than plan what plays others will direct. Visiting directors have been known to resign during rehearsals because of the constant interference of such artistic directors. The artistic director of one of the leading opera houses in America is very fond of conducting. It is said that his continuous "suggestions" caused one conductor to throw his baton on the floor and walk out.

Architects often lament the fact that as managers they no

longer design. Such architects will stop off at the design room repeatedly, and if anyone happens to ask them a question, they will use this as an excuse to take over, to start designing. Field sales managers and doctors who become administrators of hospitals have been known to behave in a similar manner.

The Lone Ranger's desire to do everything himself can be seen both in his disinclination to train others and in the training methods he uses. He sees no value in the systematic training of subordinates. He prefers the apprenticeship approach, in which subordinates have to learn by actually performing all of the duties in the organization and by imitating him. "Why don't they show motivation, take initiative, show me what they can do?" he usually complains. "Who trained me? Nobody! I learned by myself! Why don't they learn? In this business there aren't any secrets; just get the job done. If someone is willing to work hard, he should have no problem getting the job done."

Thus, for the **P———** the recipe for success is simple: hard work and blind dedication. If a person "fails," the explanation is also very simple: he did not try, or he did not want to work hard enough.

The Lone Ranger resents subordinates who do not produce results—he blames this on the subordinates and he will not listen to their complaints that they were given no systematic support (meaning that he gave them none).

I once encountered a classic example of the Lone Ranger. He was a vice president who worked longer hours than anyone else. His subordinates were underutilized and undertrained. He was always immersed in a crisis. While I was working on budgetary procedure with one of his people (since he had no time for that sort of thing), he stuck his head in the door and asked, "What are you doing?" "We're preparing a budgetary procedure. How about you?" "I was busy making sales to pay for all of this!" he replied sarcastically.

The organization that the Lone Ranger manages cannot grow, since he is not growing. He is inflexible and simple-minded. He can easily "burn out" and become obsolete, as we will see later. When he leaves a company, he leaves untrained people behind. Since he has had no time to train people, there is nobody to whom he can delegate his responsibilities.

The Lone Ranger performs one of the necessary roles of management, but that role alone is not sufficient.

SUMMARY OF THE LONE RANGER STYLE

The Person's Style

Exclusive role: Producer of results.

How he excels: Getting things done.

Predominant behavior: Compulsively busy.

Focus of attention: What is being done at the moment.

Most distinctive personality traits: Totally dedicated to the field; hard worker.

Appraises himself by: How hard he personally works.

Typical complaints: The day is too short; there is too much to do; I don't have enough time.

Decision making: Shoots from the hip; acts first, thinks and listens later.

If he has free time: He will find more work that he can do himself.

He prefers to hire: The ever-ready errand boy: go-fors; those who can get things done regardless of direction; people like himself.

Subordinates

Subordinates' style: Go-fors.

Subordinates are promoted: If they are always available and accept all errands supportively; if they get the job done, irrespective of how or why.

What subordinates get praised for: Results.

Subordinates do not inform him about: How much they could really do.

Dysfunctional behavior of subordinates: Horsing around while waiting to be given something to do.

Time Management, Staff Meetings, and Managerial Practice

He arrives at and leaves work: First in, last out.

Subordinates arrive and leave: Arrive after the manager and leave before he does.

Frequency and advance notice of staff meetings: Rarely has meetings, and when he does, he calls people in impromptu, sees them on a one-to-one basis, standing around; claims that he has no time for meetings.

Staff meeting attendance: Dictated by the problem; usually very small.

Staff meeting agenda: The latest crisis; reactive to a situation that already exists or is imminent.

Who talks at staff meetings: One-to-one; mostly top-down assignments.

Training practices: "Do as I do."

Attitude toward systematic management: Demeans it; says that it takes too much time away from "running the railroad."

Attitude toward conflict: Annoyed with it; feels that subordinates should just get the job done.

Attitude toward change: Resists it since he has no time to do more; will accept it if it produces results promptly.

Focus and type of information he cherishes: technical professional information; will not share it; has no time to acquire it.

Focus of creativity: Dispersed throughout the organization.

Attitude toward Other Managers

Exclusive producer (Lone Ranger, P---): People like himself; appreciates.

Exclusive administrator (Bureaucrat, -A--): Disrespects.

Exclusive entrepreneur (Arsonist, --E-): Avoids.

Exclusive integrators (Superfollower, ---I): Disrespects or ignores.

Deadwood (----, or no managerial roles): Despises.

NOTES

1. An individual is not necessarily **P** oriented at all times. One might be a **P** at work and something else in sports. A person's style of behavior in one environment does not necessarily repeat itself in another environment.

2. For additional discussion of the problems in role perceptions and the need for know-how in the arts, see I. Adizes, "Boards of Directors in the Performing Arts: A Managerial Analysis," in *California Management Review,* 15 (1972), no. 2, 109–17.

3. For the relationship between technology and the process of decision making, see Joan Woodward, *Industrial Organization: Theory and Practice* (New York: Oxford University Press, 1965) and the writings of people in social-technical analysis and organizational design such as Lou Davis and James Taylor.

4. Laurence J. Peter and Raymond Hull, *The Peter Principle* (New York: William Morrow, 1969), p. 23.

Chapter *3*

-A--: The Bureaucrat

THE ROLE OF ADMINISTERING
AN ORGANIZATION

The administrator is a person who keeps track of the details. He or she is well organized and concerned with follow-up and implementation. He has an excellent memory (or is fortified by systems, which means that he does not have to rely only on his memory), and he works to see that the system will operate as it was designed to operate. Because of his methodical approach and his constant effort to manage details, he supervises the system that keeps things in order within an organization.

It is important to any organization to have an effective administration. Good administration means routinization and systemization. If the Producer (P) role provides for effectiveness, the Administrator (A) role provides for efficiency. Administering entails seeing to it that people appointed in accordance with predetermined processes and allocated resources, operate in the desired manner.

A manager, then, should be more than a person who can

produce results himself. He should also be capable of administering others, of seeing to it that they also produce the desired results, systematically and efficiently.

Administering means "serving," whereas managing involves goal definition and includes the authority to define objectives. An administrator facilitates implementation; he monitors the work of the organization but is not engaged in producing the results for which the organization exists or even in defining what they are supposed to be in the first place.

The concept administration has a service connotation in health, educational, art, and governmental organizations. Those who serve in what could be recognized as managerial roles in such organizations are called administrators. Calling them managers would mean that they also define the goals of the organization, which is usually not so; in such organizations the goals are set by a constituency of members, for example, the medical or academic personnel.

The role of the administrators is to serve those goals, to enable their implementation. Thus, we have health or hospital administrators, education or arts administrators, and public administrators (i.e., public service officers). These administrators do not decide independently what the goals of the organization should be. They service those goals; they administer for the decision makers, for those who are actually engaged in producing results.

Unfortunately, most writers about management use the terms *management* and *administration* synonymously. I prefer to use the term *management* for the whole process and to restrict the term *administration* to that part of the managerial process which consists of implementation and organization.

The basic difference between administration and management is that in administration, especially public administration, whatever is not specifically permitted is prohibited. The administrator is *given* the rules by which he is to play the game.

In effective management the conditions are reversed: whatever is not specifically forbidden is permitted. The manager takes initiative, plans, and acts. He develops his own constraints within the realm of the possible and the legal.

An analysis of the complex facets of the chicanery that we call Watergate provides an interesting analogy. The very fine distinction between administration and management was crossed. The planners of that affair apparently took the approach of identifying the desired results and then acting to achieve them. The planners of Watergate were not *serving* the system, that is, the American political system; they were trying to *manage* it.

Similarly, the initiatives taken by a person who tried to manage a system that should be administered would quite probably violate prescribed procedures that an administrator would have no difficulty in living with.

The more centralized a system is, the more administrative, rather than managerial, is the job of middle management. When a centralized organization is decentralized, those who have only administered in the past have to begin taking risks and making decisions, rather than just implement "by the book."[1]

Thus, while the administrative role is a necessary component of the managerial process, it is not equivalent to the managerial process. What happens, however, when the administrative role is performed to the exclusion of the other managerial roles?

THE BUREAUCRATIC STYLE

A person who performs only the administrative role is not organizational results oriented. He does not produce results or even know *how* to produce results. In our model his behavior is coded –A––. Thus, in the code that designates his style there is a "–" in place of a **P**. Such a person is neither an entrepreneur nor an integrator of people. He acts exclusively by the book. He knows the standard operating procedures by heart, and he manages by means of directives, usually in writing. We call this kind of manager a Bureaucrat.

The Bureaucrat is easily recognized by his or her concern with the *how* of an activity rather than the *what* or the *why*. When you walk into a Bureaucrat's organization, you see everyone at his own desk, carefully avoiding any transgressions against "the system." The Bureaucrat and his staff arrive and leave with clockwise regularity. The Bureaucrat will have an organization chart on his wall, or at least readily accessible. He will have no trouble finding any of the rules or procedures of the organization at a moment's notice.

The Bureaucrat abhors ambiguity. He insists that everything be in writing and that all spheres of responsibility be clearly delineated. He is meticulously organized, and he usually has a fantastic memory for details. He is very loyal, and he does not change organizations easily.

The Bureaucrat avoids change as much as possible. His ingenuity in finding reasons to discourage new projects makes him an obstructionist. The organization has to achieve its goals in spite of him, and the individuals in the organization who are committed to getting things done learn to bypass him in trying to implement change.

Administration means a rejection of the idea of conflict as a desirable element of society. Administration wants extremes adjusted; it wants differences settled; it wants to find which way is best and use that way exclusively.

From Charles Reich, *The Greening of America* (New York: Random House, 1970), p. 50.

The Bureaucrat transfers his love of structure and detail to an organization or task that he is concerned with. He loves to get things organized. It is bureaucratic tendencies that impart much of the hierarchical nature to organizations.

"*I'm sorry. My responsibility doesn't go beyond this bubble.*"

Drawing by David Pascal; © 1976
The New Yorker Magazine, Inc.

In contrast to the Lone Ranger, a hyperbusy achiever and performer who is concerned with *what* is achieved rather than *how,* the Bureaucrat spends inordinate amounts of time worrying about administrative details. He is more concerned about *how* things are done than about *what* is being done. He prefers to do things right rather than to do the right things. He rebukes his subordinates if they do not follow standard operating procedures, even when such violations are needed to achieve results. He always has arguments—usually legalistic and unrelated to the objectives of the organization—to show why the system must be left intact. He considers himself the guardian of the system, viewing the mission of the system as secondary.

The Bureaucrat, or **–A––,** often subverts the goals of the organization, through his insistence on observing the letter of the law, even when departures from it are essential. His primary and often exclusive commitment is to the implementation of a plan, regardless of its wisdom or even its ethics.

Adolf Eichmann's line of defense at his trial for exterminating 6 million Jews is a morbid and extreme example of this type of behavior. Eichmann described his role in the Third Reich as having been that of an administrator of trains. At one end of the railway were the victims' home, and at the other end were the extermination camps. But he maintained that the outcome did not concern him. He felt that his responsibility was confined to ensuring the punctuality of train operations.

Administration is an essential component of good management, but a disproportionate emphasis on administration can be counterproductive.[2]

Unlike the Lone Ranger (**P———**), who comes to work before anyone else and leaves after everyone else, the Bureaucrat (**-A—**) arrives and leaves on time. The Bureaucrat's desk is kept meticulously clean.

The Lone Ranger will accept a subordinate's transgressions of procedures as long as good results are achieved. The Bureaucrat, however, is exclusively concerned with the methods used to achieve the results. To illustrate the difference, let us take the example of a salesman who has done extraordinarily well. If the salesman works for a Lone Ranger and tries to tell him about this, the Lone Ranger will say, "Great, great, but tell me about it later," and the salesman won't be able to get into the details. A Bureaucrat, on the other hand, will want full details of what the salesman did. He will look for some transgression, some violation of the rules. When he finds one, he plays a game from *Games People Play*. It is called, "I Got You, You S.O.B." From that point on, the Bureaucrat forgets the results achieved and focuses on the transgression: How dare the salesman violate a rule or a procedure?

People who work for Bureaucrats are typical yes-yes people. They do as they are told and do not take initiative. They do not ask questions, and they do not rock the boat. They come on time, leave on time, and in between they do very little.

In Herman Wouk's *The Caine Mutiny* we see an extreme example of the Bureaucrat (**-A—**) in Captain Queeg, who rose in the ranks of the Navy, not because he was able to run a ship or a crew, but because he followed rules. He says so himself: "I don't pretend to be the cleverest or the smoothest officer . . . but I'll tell you this, Sir, I'm one of the stubbornest. I've sweated through tougher assignments than this. I haven't won any popularity contests, but I have bitched and crabbed and hollered and bullied until I've gotten things done . . . *by the book*" (italics added).

During a typhoon it seemed that Captain Queeg would let his ship sink rather than change a predetermined course. Captain Queeg did not want the people around him to think either. He was a Bureaucrat on the point of becoming Deadwood (see Chapter 6).

While the Lone Ranger evaluates himself by how hard *he works* and by the results he achieves, the Bureaucrat evaluates himself by how well *he controls* the system and by his success in eliminating digressions from standard operating procedures and in minimizing uncertainty. Because of this, he tends to be a crowning example of Parkinson's law.[3] He gets increasing numbers of subordinates to perform the same job, without achieving any apparent increase in productivity. The only apparent changes are that more people are involved in more systems and that more procedures are designed to further control what already appears to be overcontrolled!

Over a period of time, the department managed by the Bureaucrat will perform the same duties, but with more and more complex procedures to assure maximum conformity and minimum uncertainty. This behavior hinders change, because the mushrooming bureaucracy makes change more and more expensive. Thus, both the Lone Ranger and the Bureaucrat inhibit the effective growth of the organization. The Lone Ranger cannot effectively perform additional tasks because he performs effectively only the amount of work that he can perform alone. The bureaucrat does not allow effective changes to be made if he perceives them as a threat to his ability to control.

By the time the Bureaucrat is eliminated from an organization, it may be so regimented that it will have difficulty in adapting to long overdue changes in its internal or external environment. Innovations in a bureaucratic system are not made easily, and "surgery" is often needed to make them. People are fired, and "new blood" is called in. It takes some organizations a long time to recuperate from such changes. A new manager may have a great deal of trouble in trying to alter the established procedures, and may even have to adapt himself to them.

Free time is abused by both the Lone Ranger and the Bureaucrat. When the Lone Ranger has free time (a rather rare occurrence), he goes back to the "firing line" or the drafting board, or he makes a sale or a call. The Bureaucrat's free time is spent uncovering some transgression that he hasn't discovered yet. Then he zealously designs a new form, a new report, or a new policy that will prevent the transgression from being repeated. The Bureaucrat manages "by the book," and he uses his free time to write it!

The Bureaucrat's subordinates behave different from the Lone Ranger's subordinates. The Lone Ranger's go-fors "horse around" while waiting for an errand or a task. But what the Bureaucrat's yes-yes clerks do is somewhat more dangerous. These subordinates frequently try to beat the system without being caught. They may go so far as to lie, misinform, and falsify reports in order to prove to themselves and to their manager that the system is not controllable.

The Lone Ranger has hardly any staff meetings. The few meetings he does call are informal and scantily attended. His typical procedure is to tell a person what needs to be done "right now."

The Bureaucrat's approach to meetings and instructions is very different. He holds regularly scheduled meetings that everybody must attend. The agendas are long; secretaries take minutes; and the last meeting's conclusions are discussed and voted on. There is order, and along with it there is boredom with the myriad details that the Bureaucrat insists on covering. Most of the people present see little significance in what is being discussed, but to the Bureaucrat everything is crucial. Nothing can be put aside without the risk of failure in some respect. Assignments are discussed, but instead of emphasizing their purpose and validity, the discussion centers on how they will be implemented.

The Bureaucrat likes training. He wishes that he could program everybody, make everything a routine. Strategic planning usually entails analysis of threats and opportunities. But under the Bureaucrat, strategic planning is at best an exercise in forecasting, and quite often it is centered on the past. The Bureaucrat sees hardly any opportunities, and he regards change as a threat. The Lone Ranger, on the other hand, is oblivious to both strategic threats and opportunities. He is completely absorbed in the crisis that has to be solved "right now."

The Bureaucrat abhors conflict and change. He feels that interpersonal conflict will "rock the boat" and endanger his control of the system and, therefore keeps aloof from it. But he is hardly aloof to the possibility of a change in processes or direction. Such change is a threat of major proportions, and the Bureaucrat will keep on hand a never-ending arsenal of reasons for fighting it.

A consultant once told me that when he worked for a computer manager and an accountant, a change in budget seemed to be the equivalent of giving birth. It took months to accomplish, and "delivery" was accompanied by great labor pains.

The Bureaucrat monopolizes all information of an administrative nature. This information is concerned mostly with "how to get things done right." Proposing a budget may require a hundred or so steps; dozens of steps and dozens of forms may be used in hiring or firing someone; and so on.

If there is any creativity in the organization, it is suffocated by the Bureaucrat. He hires people like himself—people who come on time, leave on time, and make no trouble.

> It is horrible to think that the world could one day be filled with nothing but those little cogs, little men clinking to little jobs and striving toward bigger ones—a state of affairs which is to be seen once more, as in the Egyptian records, playing an ever increasing part in the spirit of our present administrative system, and especially of its offspring, the students. This passion for Bureaucracy is enough to drive one to despair.
>
> *Max Weber*

Administration is another necessary facet of the managerial process—necessary, but not in itself sufficient for effective management. The reader may readily identify managers who are excellent administrators, who see that the people under them perform their tasks and that standard procedures are followed and goals achieved. But these may still be incompetent managers. They may implement the plans that are given to them, yet lack the initiative to define new goals and seek new horizons. For a type of management that initiates, the **E** role of entrepreneuring must be performed.[4]

SUMMARY OF THE BUREAUCRATIC STYLE

The Person's Style

Exclusive role: Implementer, administrator.
How he excels: Putting and keeping things in order.
Predominant behavior: Controlling implementation.
Focus of attention: How work is being done.
Most distinctive personality traits: Meticulously organized, slow and careful, thoughtful, conservative.
Appraises himself by: How placid and how well controlled the office is.
Typical complaint: Someone violated some rule or procedure.
Decision making: Follows existing decisions.

If he has free time: He will think of new forms, controls, etc.

He prefers to hire: The conforming yes-yes clerk or people like himself.

Subordinates

Subordinates' style: Yes-yes people.

Subordinates are promoted: If they appear organized and violate no rules.

What subordinates get praised for: The process, with little notice taken of the results.

Subordinates do not inform him about: Organizational transgressions.

Dysfunctional behavior of subordinates: Beating the system to prove that it can't be controlled.

Time Management, Staff Meetings, and Managerial Practice

He arrives at and leaves work: On the dot.

Subordinates arrive and leave: On the dot.

Frequency and advance notice of staff meetings: Frequent, regular, and scheduled.

Staff meeting attendance: Monitored, required, with roll call.

Staff meeting agenda: Long, detailed, fixed, minuscule.

Who talks at staff meetings: One-to-many, mostly top-down; some questions are asked about how to get the job done; details are discussed fully.

Training practices: Overdone, with excessive details.

Attitude toward systematic management: Elaborates on it and enjoys it as long as it means more control and procedures, but sees it mostly as forecasting; sees threats rather than opportunities.

Attitude toward conflict: Ignores it or fights it, depending on whether or not it threatens his control.

Attitude toward change: Resists it because he fears losing control.

Focus and type of information he cherishes: Administrative; will not share it.

Focus of creativity: Throughout the organization; suffocated when it appears.

Attitude toward Other Managers

Exclusive producer (Lone Ranger, **P–––**): Qualified criticism.
Exclusive administrator (Bureaucrat, **–A––**): Approves.
Exclusive entrepreneur (Arsonist, **––E–**): Abhors.
Exclusive integrator (Superfollower, **–––I**): Suspicious.
Deadwood (––––*):* Ignores.
*Textbook manager (***PAEI***):* Qualified approval.

NOTES

1. Yugoslavian developments provide empirical evidence of the difficulties and anxieties that arise when previously structured positions change and more latitude is provided for discretionary decision making. See I. Adizes, *Industrial Democracy: Yugoslav Style* (New York: Free Press, 1971; reprinted, Los Angeles: MDOR Institute, 1977).

2. The literature provides numerous examples of the ways in which bureaucratic management frustrates and inhibits productivity. For example, Soviet factory managers, according to Berliner, find it impossible to meet their official production quotes without continually violating state laws, industrial regulations, and the party line. See Joseph S. Berliner, *Factory and Manager in the USSR* (Cambridge, Mass.: Harvard University Press, 1957).

Francis and Stone point out that the same imbalance between **A** and **P** existed in an American bureaucracy, in which the work ethic conflicted with the tendency toward mindless overregulation. See Roy G. Francis and Robert C. Stone, *Service and Procedure in Bureaucracy: A Case Study* (Minneapolis: University of Minnesota Press, 1956).

As has been stated in the text, subordinates with a production orientation soon learn to bypass the Bureaucrat in order to get things done. Blau and Page have documented the presence of informal systems which coexist with the official organization, allowing subordinates to achieve their objectives and to avoid the stifling effects of the exclusive (A) management style. See Peter M. Blau, *The Dynamics of Bureaucracy* (Chicago: University of Chicago Press, 1956).

3. C. Northcote Parkinson, *Parkinson's Law* (Boston: Houghton Mifflin, 1960).

4. See the discussion of bureaucratic control in Dwight Waldo, ed., *Ideas and Issues in Public Administration* (New York: McGraw-Hill, 1963) especially part 1. On the role of the manager as administrator and entrepreneur, see Peter F. Drucker, *Management: Tasks, Responsibilities, Practices* (New York: Harper & Row, 1973), pp. 45–57.

Chapter 4

--E-: The Arsonist

THE ENTREPRENEURIAL ROLE

In a changing environment, organizations need new ideas in order to survive. Opportunities and threats arise, and organizations must be able to meet them.

In a changing environment a good manager must do more than produce results and see to it that others produce results. He or she must also be an entrepreneur, an initiator of action, a person who can initiate change so that the organization can adapt to environmental changes.[1]

An entrepreneur analyzes the forces of the environment as they affect the organization. He analyzes the strengths and weaknesses of the organization and then identifies the course of action which will best meet the changes in the external environment.

Entrepreneurship is not confined to the business world. There are, indeed, economically oriented entrepreneurs (business people) who try to exploit the monetary opportunities of the market. But in our postindustrial environment there are also other kinds of entrepreneurs, and their importance is in-

> Reasonable men adapt to their environment; unreasonable men try to adapt their environment to themselves. Thus all progress is the result of the efforts of unreasonable men.
>
> *George Bernard Shaw*

creasing. Among them are the social entrepreneurs who initiate change in the social and political sphere, and the educational and artistic entrepreneurs who initiate activities which satisfy existing aesthetic needs and generate new ones.

Whereas the administrator is given certain plans to carry out or certain decisions to implement, the entrepreneur has to generate his own plan of action. In a changing environment, an entrepreneur's failure to initiate and take risks will eventually cause his organization to lag behind more responsive competitors.

Thus, whereas no risks are involved in the administrative facet of managerial functioning, a manager who performs the entrepreneurial role should be willing to take risks and should be sufficiently creative to identify possible courses of action.

> You can't expect to hit the jackpot if you don't put a few nickels in the machine.
>
> *Flip Wilson*

If an entrepreneur is not creative, he may end up as an administrator who needs to be told what to initiate. If he is unable to take risks, he may end up as a staff man, a consultant, or a teacher-researcher who can identify possible courses of action but does not undertake them himself.

> No responsibility is taken where no hazard is to be met, and a hazard is a liability to failure.
>
> *M. Polanyi*

Since creativity and risk-taking are complementary attributes, we can conceive of creative persons who do not take risks and of risk-taking persons who are not creative. Consultants may be creative persons who are not risk-takers. They may provide ideas to other people that they do not dare to carry out themselves. On the other hand, risk-takers who are uncreative may function more like gamblers than like entrepreneurial planners. Success in the entrepreneurial role requires both creativity and the ability to take risks.

THE ARSONIST STYLE

> Full speed ahead—in neutral.

Entrepreneurship—creativity and a willingness to take risks—is the third role in the **PAEI** model. What happens, however, if the entrepreneurial role is performed to the exclusion of the other three roles—that is, if a manager has the --E- style? This management style is exhibited when a manager's efforts are devoted exclusively to innovating, to charging at any target that appears on his or her organizational horizon.

For the subordinates of such a manager, Monday morning is often the most hectic time of the week. Over the weekend the manager dreams up new ideas, and on Monday morning he changes priorities. He hands out new assignments (forgetting those he has already made), and he expects his subordinates to execute them instantaneously.

He attempts to exploit all opportunities whenever they arise, thus spreading himself and his organization thin. He comes into an organization with new ideas and new methods, and tries to change the "what" and "how" of tasks simultaneously.

If the **P---**, or Lone Ranger, may be described as a fire fighter, the **--E-** can be called an Arsonist. If the Lone Ranger gets ulcers, the Arsonist causes them.

The Arsonist likes to witness the furor which results from his initiatives. He likes an atmosphere of urgency and is delighted when his subordinates rush in and out, trying to cope with the crises he has created. He seeks maximum short-run impact, and he obtains it by generating crises.

Under such managers, rehearsals in artistic organizations start when it is almost too late. The creative process must then take place under pressure; the staff is forced to work second and third shifts; and crucial details remain in a state of flux right up to the time of the performance. People who like a highly structured environment will be highly frustrated by his behavior.

An Arsonist has little sense of what people can accomplish. He gets upset when objectives are not achieved "yesterday." He is so excited about his own creative capability that he is impatient with any limited accomplishments.

Subordinates soon learn not to ask the Arsonist for help in solving the problems that he assigned them. If they do, instead of trying to identify the barriers to a solution, he changes the assignment altogether, and in the process he overloads his subordinates with new problems.

Subordinates avoid both the Arsonist and the Bureaucrat, but for different reasons. The Bureaucrat's subordinates avoid him because he is constantly telling them what they *should not* do. The Arsonist's subordinates avoid him because he is always assigning new tasks, forgetting about the tasks that he assigned earlier and that already fully occupy the subordinates' time.

Even a well-meaning subordinate will find it very hard to follow the Arsonist's directives and instructions. The Arsonist is usually just plain vague in handing out assignments. He has an idea, but he refuses to figure out the details. He leaves that to his subordinates. A joke told by Will Rogers illustrates this well.

During World War I, the Allies were unable to cope with the German submarines. The Navy called in a consultant. The consultant studied the entire situation and recommended that the ocean be heated to a temperature of 180 degrees. He explained that this would force the Germans to surface their submarines, which could then be shot at will. The Navy thought this was a fine idea but did not know how to heat the ocean. When questioned on this matter, the consultant replied, "I'm a planner. These are details. I have done the planning. Now you worry about the details."

The Arsonist typically will develop fantastic ideas and then expect everyone else to determine how to implement them. If he is pressed for specifics he gets highly annoyed.

An organization managed by a Bureaucrat may achieve its goals in spite of its manager because people learn to bypass him. However, the harder the Arsonist tries to manage, the further behind his organization gets. While the Arsonist is busy making everyone else busy, the organization is going nowhere. The Arsonist changes direction too often, and his subordinates do not actually cooperate. The Arsonist fails because an organization cannot constantly change direction.

We can look at an organization as a series of meshing gears. The manager is a large gear with many cogs around its circumference. His subordinates and their subordinates are represented by smaller and smaller gears. Whenever the "big wheel" turns even a little, the smaller wheels are forced to turn a great deal.

If the "big wheel" is an Arsonist, it will frequently change direction while the smaller wheels are in motion. Eventually the gears of the smaller wheels are stripped and the big wheel spins alone. Hence, the Arsonist's typical complaint is: "Nothing ever gets done around here." Unfortunately he does not realize that he is responsible for the breakdown.

One can tell a great deal about a manager's style by looking at the behavior of his or her subordinates. At a meeting where an Arsonist is putting forth his latest bright ideas, subordinates will sit and look at one another with sly, knowing smiles on their faces. They really don't intend to do what the manager says. Why should they? The big wheel will soon change direction again.

The Arsonist's subordinates have learned that he is not to be taken too seriously. No task that he delegates is really intended to be accomplished; in a very short time, he will change his mind. But the Arsonist's subordinates have also learned not to reject his tasks outright, because the Arsonist identifies himself with his ideas to such an extent that he will view their rejection as a personal rejection. Thus, the subordinates see no use in trying to achieve the Arsonist's tasks, yet cannot refuse to accept them. Their way out is to accept the tasks but to do

Drawing by McCallister; © *1976*
The New Yorker Magazine, Inc.

very little about them and then to come up with creative excuses for not having accomplished them—that is, they try to appear cooperative without actually being so. The subordinates of an Arsonist always explain why a task *could* not be done rather than why it *should* not have been attempted.

An Arsonist's subordinates must be at work before he is, and they leave just after he does. Whenever the Arsonist is in sight, they pretend to be busy with his pet project. In companies managed by Arsonists, vice presidents have been known to sit in their offices "watching their nails grow" as they waited for the boss to go home so that they could leave too. If the Arsonist pokes his head into a subordinate's office and asks, "How are you doing?" the typical answer is "Busy, busy, busy." (If you fail to tell an Arsonist how busy you are, he will *make* you busy.)

The Arsonist's subordinates try to impress him with their high level of commitment to his projects, and they try to look busy whenever he is watching. But if he does not inquire about an assignment or he leaves the office, they drop it. The situation is reminiscent of another war story. During World War I, an Italian captain emerged from the trenches wearing a velvet uniform and a hat bedecked with feathers. He pulled out his saber with a flourish and brandished it in the air, shouting *"A-V-A-N-T-I"* at the top of his lungs. Meanwhile, the soldiers in the trenches clapped their hands softly and whispered "Bravooooooo." Obviously the captain was not taken seriously. Neither is the Arsonist.

The Lone Ranger's subordinates come to work after he does and often leave before he does. While at work, they are usually waiting to be given an errand. They learn that they can take long breaks if they are available on short notice "to help get things done." The Bureaucrat's subordinates learn that their jobs are secure as long as they arrive on time, leave on time, comply with all regulations, and don't ask too many questions.

The Arsonist's subordinates must look busy whenever he

is in sight. However, no one knows when an Arsonist will come to work or when he will leave. At seven o'clock in the evening he may just be arriving. So his subordinates try to predict when he will show up so that they can be there ahead of him—not because there is work to do but as a defensive strategy against the creation of *busy-busy* work.

The Arsonist keeps his subordinates busy, but he complains that they are inefficient. He refuses to see that his constant changes in goals are responsible for their ineffectiveness. However, as long as his subordinates seem to be trying to accomplish his plans, he is satisfied.

If the subordinates of the Lone Ranger (**P----**) are go-fors and the subordinates of the Bureaucrat (**-A--**) are "yes-yes" people, the typical subordinates of the Arsonist (**--E-**) are claques. (Claques are the hired hands in opera houses who start clapping when a singer is finished with an aria, to induce the rest of the audience to clap as well.)

The subordinates of the Arsonist must agree with his ideas, or at least they should never disagree with the Arsonist in public. An Arsonist views a public disagreement much as an opera singer might view a heckler who boos when the singer is at his high C. The Arsonist will hold a grudge against the dissident; he will not easily forget this threat to his ego.

One way a subordinate can handle an Arsonist (**--E-**) when he feels that the Arsonist's request is not prudent is to wait until the meeting (performance) is over and then go to the Arsonist's office. There the subordinate should quietly discuss the *repercussions* of the Arsonist's suggestions and the more detailed his questions are the better, since Arsonists by and large hate details. In order to accomplish the new assignment, the organization must set priorities. There is a price for doing anything. These are "opportunity costs,"—that is, if the ideas are to be carried out with resources that are already being used fully, something else must be given up. The subordinate can then ask the Arsonist to decide, which again the Arsonist does not like to do. He prefers to keep things "in the air."

Once the Arsonist is convinced that a subordinate is committed to the job, that the subordinate is "tending the fire," the Arsonist will usually suggest that the subordinate do whatever he thinks is best. The Arsonist's interest is not in whether the job is done, nor even in how it is done, but rather in whether everyone agrees that it *should* be done. He is interested in the process, the novelty, and not necessarily in the results. He is interested in the "whys," whereas the Lone Ranger is interested in the "whats," and the Administrator in the "hows."

Nothing is impossible for the man who doesn't have to do it himself.

From Thomas L. Martin, Jr., *Malice in Blunderland* (New York: McGraw-Hill, 1973), p. 103.

If a subordinate who has a problem works for a Lone Ranger and asks the boss for help, the boss will probably tell the subordinate to leave the problem with him. But the subordinate will not hear from the boss for a long time, and meanwhile the problem will become worse. Thus, the best course for the subordinate is to improvise some sort of solution all by himself.

If a Bureaucrat's subordinate has a problem, he must present it to his boss as a violation. Only that establishes it as a problem. Then the subordinate has to present a solution that cites half a dozen equivalent precedents. He must argue that the solution he recommends has been applied before, and that it can therefore be applied again. Then he has to write it all up formally. As long as the Bureaucrat is "covered," he will approve.

The Arsonist, however, will not sit still for long presentations. Before the subordinate has described the problem, the Arsonist will come up with a solution that might very well create greater difficulties than the one that originally needed attention.

One top executive uses this approach to handle his Arsonist boss. "First, tell him the problem. Make it very short and to the point so that he hears it to the end. Then give him a *possible* solution which you have designed. *Purposely* include one or two obvious mistakes in your solution. He will grab at the mistakes, correct them, add one or two ideas which you can ignore later, and off you go. He *has to* change your solution, so why not give him chance to do it your way?"

With a Lone Ranger (P———) or a Bureaucrat (–A——), the "deliberate error" approach would be disastrous for the subordinate. The P——— would say, "I knew you couldn't be trusted to do anything right. Leave it on my desk, and I'll correct it *tonight*." The subordinate would be given no further problems to solve. The –A—— would probably chew the subordinate to pieces for "the obvious mistakes of . . ."

The Arsonist is usually very likable, since he is stimulating, enterprising, and full of energy. Working for him can be exciting until one learns that no matter what one does, the Arsonist will be dissatisfied because he always comes up with new projects before the old ones have been accomplished.

The Arsonist is not himself a producer of results, although he is highly critical of the failures of his subordinates. Whereas the Lone Ranger appraises himself by how hard *he* works and by the results *he* produces, and the Bureaucrat appraises himself by the *control* that he feels he has, the Arsonist appraises himself by how hard his subordinates *appear* to be working. He gets his reinforcement from the appearance of productivity, the beehive atmosphere of activity which attests to the influence of his creative ideas.

If a Lone Ranger's subordinates all seemed to be working peacefully at their desks, the Lone Ranger wouldn't notice them; he would be too busy with his own work. In the same situation, a Bureaucrat would look for a small detail or problem which he could control—a cigarette butt on the floor or a burned-out light bulb. He would ask his subordinates, "Is everything OK?" and they would answer, "Yes, sir."

But, the Arsonist would be upset. The peacefulness would disturb him. In the absence of a crisis, he would act to create one.

An Arsonist is like an actor—he is constantly performing. He needs an audience desperately, and he usually hates to be alone. So he calls meetings all the time and without warning. When everyone is in the middle of some activity or getting ready to go home: "It's meeting time! And who does all the speaking at this meeting? Obviously the Arsonist. The agenda has only one item, the first, and the presentation proceeds by free association. The Arsonist keeps the ball rolling, while the subordinates sit quietly and signify approval.

The Arsonist demands undivided loyalty. There are no weekends or holidays for him, and he does not approve them for his subordinates either. For him a good subordinate is one who never takes a vacation. He expects his people to be available whenever he needs them.

For the Arsonist, planning does not mean committing the organization to a course of action. Planning is stating the desired. His approach to planning is quite different from that of the Bureaucrat, who interprets planning as "forecasting," and arrives at next year's budget by adding some low percentage to last year's budget. If the Arsonist has a budget, it is usually unrealistic. Frequently he does not know what happened last year, and yet he expects *quite a change* in the year to come. In addition, he find that stating very high goals is a good way to set fires under his subordinates' feet.

The Arsonist's approach to planning also differs from that of the Lone Ranger. The Lone Ranger will usually see neither opportunities nor threats because he is too busy doing whatever has to be done. He is so deeply involved in fighting fires that he does not realize what is actually happening around him. The Arsonist, on the other hand, is usually so preoccupied with opportunities that he sees few if any threats. He even creates threats for the organization by trying to exploit too many opportunities at once. As a Yugoslav proverb says, "What he builds during the day, he burns at night." That is, he is capable of wasting all of the organization's so painstakingly accumulated profits in a few ill-conceived plans.

> The longest journey starts with a single misstep.
>
> *Charles Christopher Mark*

Management should identify the threats and opportunities of the changing environment. Then it should plan to capitalize on the organization's strength and fortify its weak areas (that is, exploit the opportunities and provide protection against the threats). None of the management styles presented thus far does this. The Lone Ranger, the Bureaucrat, and the Arsonist all perform planning inadequately.

A subordinate described one Arsonist as follows (the account is abridged and paraphrased):

> I hate to see him go on vacation, and Monday mornings are just as bad. I know that as soon as he comes back we will have a new set of priorities. . . . We are always in a state of flux. My title, position, and responsibilities change too frequently for me to take hold. If you try to dispute any of his ideas, he will produce information, figures, quotes—you name it—to prove he is right. He is fantastic at juggling, throwing out his evidence like a magician to prove that his new pet project is absolutely the best, and that it's your fault if you don't understand how it is related to the previous project. Later on, after we fail, it becomes our fault that we didn't understand him, and before you know it he is presenting all the arguments against it that you presented to him when he first suggested the project. The worst thing that you can do is to remind him that that's what you said in the first place. . . .

If you suggest a project of your own, he will have a hundred reasons why it cannot be done. But a week later, he will be back with the same idea. This time he will present it as *his,* and as a top-priority project which should have been done yesterday; he will be angry that no one thought of it before. . . .

He likes to have people around him to listen sympathetically to his ideas, and if they leave, he gets hurt. He always has to have an audience, whether it's his secretary or his executive vice president. He will keep his audience long after the working day is over. This is the price we have to pay to show we take his ideas seriously. Many of his subordinates have gotten divorced or soon will be, because of the sort of unequivocal loyalty he demands from them. . . .

Every so often he comes up with five or six new ideas and starts making the rounds of the offices, presenting them to people. You have to decide which ones you're going to fight and how. After a while he's left with two ideas, which he pushes through. Then you get out a few memos to show that you have tried to do something about them, and you get ready for the next bag of ideas. Do not get overenthusiastic and excited though; when he shows up the next day with the next ideas he might be highly upset if he finds that you are too busy to get involved with the latest project. . . .

He is very charismatic. He often makes you feel at odds with yourself. If you fail in a task, he can show you how you misunderstood his genius. It is always you who were dumb . . . his idea was really so simple. . . .

You should always tell him about successes. If you tell him about a problem, he will listen, but by the time he is done helping you, you will probably have ten new projects ten times more problematic than the original one.

A person who worked for an Arsonist in Washington (in government, of all places) stated the following:

Never disagree with an idea of his. If you do, that is almost an assurance that he will come back and ask you how you are doing with it. He won't let go of that one idea. To make him forget an idea that you think is bad, do the opposite of disagreeing. Start working on it and bring him a detailed plan, so detailed that he cannot find his way through it. He will probably tell you to put it on the back burner. He hates details. That is how you exorcise the idea.

A friend of mine is a typical Arsonist. He changes jobs frequently, gets bored easily, and like challenges. One day I went to play tennis with him. His wife refused to join us. "He makes me awfully nervous," she said. "You can't win with him no matter what you do."

I soon realized what she meant. He was unbeatable at *his game*. He did not play to win; he did not even keep score. What was important was *how* he hit the ball. And each hit was different. After hitting the ball outside the court, he would stop with a grin and say: "Did you see that? Nice, huh?" He was innovating with each volley. I was just there to hit the balls back to him. His wife was right—we were playing different games.

On the other hand, a Lone Ranger sweats out each point. He usually shouts the score at the end of each rally. He curses when he misses and he curses well. A Bureaucrat plays by the book. He makes each move as he was taught to make it. "Is that how I *should* have done it?" he will ask.

The Arsonist is like the Lone Ranger in his individualism, but the Lone Ranger implements decisions *made for him*, whereas the Arsonist *makes decisions for others to implement*.

The Arsonist's individualism creates centralization in decision making, but it is decision making with an interesting managerial twist. The Arsonist's decisions are extremely vague, and yet he expects the details to be worked out in exact accordance with wishes that he never explained fully and was probably unaware of initially.

Since the Arsonist is constantly "dreaming," he is always changing his plans. Yet he expects his subordinates to be up-to-date on his latest ideas, even though he himself can't describe them very well (since he has never finalized them). This puts the subordinates in a difficult situation. They are held responsible for decisions whose full components they do not understand. That is equivalent to not having the authority to really implement those decisions. They cannot absolve themselves of this responsibility, however, because the Arsonist considers a lack of implementation to be a lack of loyalty equivalent to high treason.

Thus, the Arsonist's subordinate must exhibit guilt and remorse as manifestations of his responsibility. He must accept the responsibility for failing to complete tasks and demonstrate that uncontrollable reasons kept him from doing so. However, deep inside he knows that he was not responsible and that the tasks could easily have been completed if the boss had been reasonable, that is, had not started fires all the time, had not kept changing his mind, and had fully explained what he wanted.

All of this causes the Arsonist's subordinates to live in constant conflict. They express one set of feelings in public and a totally different set in private or on the psychiatrist's couch.

Although the Lone Ranger, like the Arsonist, makes all of the decisions by himself, his impact on the organization is different. His decisions are usually of a tactical nature, so that their impact is minimal. Furthermore, he delegates tasks *and* the authority to carry them out, though he does the latter by default—that is, he does not explain or care how they should be done. He wants them done, period. As a result, his subordinates improvise. They take authority into their own hands and get the job done.

The Arsonist resembles the Bureaucrat in caring about the "how." The difference is that the Arsonist wants to know about the "how" so that he can monopolize opportunities and change processes. He wants his ideas to be carried out by his latest method. On the other hand, the Bureaucrat's interest in the "how" stems from a desire to perpetuate processes and to see that tasks are carried out "by the book." He is there to guard the system, not to change it.

The Arsonist loves conflict. He often introduces it himself, using it to prod the organization into frantic activity. For the very same reason, he loves change.

One might expect to find creativity throughout an organization managed by an Arsonist, but the opposite is usually true. The Arsonist monopolizes the organization's creativity. He regards any other entrepreneurs as competitors who must be eliminated. An organization managed by an Arsonist is not a creative, flexible structure but a slave ship—a claque of applauders. The Arsonist sets the course, changes direction, delights in the suffering of his subordinates, and takes all the credit for successes.

The Arsonist approves somewhat of the Lone Ranger, since the **P---** works hard for the organization, but his approval is qualified because the Lone Ranger has no time to listen to the Arsonist, who of course needs an audience. The Arsonist gets along very well with the Superfollower, whom we will meet in the following chapter.

The Arsonist, like the Lone Ranger and the Bureaucrat, bequeaths a mismanaged organization to his successor. With the Lone Ranger (**P---**), there are no subordinates who have been trained to take over. With the Bureaucrat (**-A--**), the subordinates are not creative and afraid to take risks.

When the Arsonist leaves, the organization is a shambles and its people are exhausted. They think that anyone would be better than the Arsonist. They look for peace and quiet, for some stability. As a result, they usually get stuck with a Bureaucrat, and they get stuck because they ask for it.

SUMMARY OF THE ARSONIST STYLE

The Person's Style

Exclusive role: Innovator, entrepreneur.
How he excels: Getting ideas and new projects.
Predominant behavior: Creating new projects.

Focus of attention: What is *new* that is being done and how it might be done otherwise.

Most distinctive personality traits: Enthusiastic, stimulating, charismatic, creative, and exciting.

Appraises himself by: The existence of a beehive atmosphere; the appearance of productivity, usually manifested in crisis.

Typical complaints: "Things don't get done around here"; *"They carry out the wrong priorities";* "They don't understand what I want, said, or meant to say."

Decision making: Temporary, no permanent commitments; proactive decisions, but no follow-up.

If he has free time: He will create a new project or crisis for the organization.

He prefers to hire: Claques; people who listen to anything anytime, not people like himself; admirers who accept his latest ideas enthusiastically and appear to understand them promptly.

Subordinates

Subordinates' style: Claques.

Subordinates are promoted: If they seem to follow directions enthusiastically and if they seem to work very hard at his assignments.

What subordinates get praised for: The appearance of hard work.

Subordinates do not inform him about: Why projects should not be done.

Dysfunctional behavior of subordinates: Producing excuses for lack of performance.

Time Management, Staff Meetings, and Management Practice

He arrives at and leaves work: Randomly.

Subordinates arrive and leave: Arrive before him and leave after him; are expected to be available at all hours.

Frequency and advance notice of staff meetings: Frequent and impromptu.

Staff meeting attendance: Required.

Staff meeting agenda: His latest idea is the first item; the rest is stream of consciousness.

Who talks at staff meetings: One-to-many, top-down; no questions asked; no details analyzed.

Training practices: Acceptable if they don't take time away from his latest pet project.

Attitude toward systematic management: Avoids and abhors it; does not want to commit himself to anything.

Attitude toward conflict: Uses it to prod subordinates to frantic activity; frequently introduces it himself.

Attitude toward change: Thrives on it and loves it if he introduces it; resists change generated by others.

Focus and type of information he cherishes: Information on opportunities and threats; will not share it.

Focus of creativity: Monopolized by him.

Attitude toward Other Managers

Exclusive producer (Lone Ranger, P−−−): Qualified approval.

Exclusive administrator (Bureaucrat, −A−−): Abhors.

Exclusive entrepreneur (Arsonist, −−E−): Resents.

Exclusive integrator (Superfollower, −−−I): Likes.

Deadwood (−−−−): Ignores.

NOTES

1. For a definition of entrepreneurship, see Joseph Schumpeter, *Business Cycles* (New York: McGraw-Hill, 1939), pp. 102–9; and Peter F. Drucker, *Management: Tasks, Responsibilities, Practices* (New York: Harper & Row, 1973), chap. 10.

Chapter 5

---I: The Superfollower

THE ROLE OF INTEGRATING PEOPLE

We have seen the need for an ability to produce, to get the job done—**P**; for an ability to administer, organize, and schedule the job—**A**; and for an ability to recognize and exploit opportunities in the environment—**E**. I suggest that these are not all that is required for a complete managerial process.

Many organizations that have been managed by a **PAE**– have nose-dived when this manager died or left. Since an organization's life span is much longer than the life of any single individual, a good manager must build a *team of people* to ensure continuity.

Organizations are composed of people and managers must be sensitive to the needs of those people. It is important, therefore, that management have the ability to integrate people.[1] People must be brought together and allowed to express their feelings and ideas, and a facilitator for developing a consensus, or at least compromises, is needed. The integrator is the manager who is concerned with people, who is concerned with smoothing the workings of the system from a people point of view. He is able to listen to people and to integrate their ideas.

Integration means the ability of an individual to generate a decision supported by the people who are actually going to implement or be affected by that decision. Integration turns individual entrepreneurship into group entrepreneurship.

If a manager does not integrate, does not nourish group entrepreneurship, then in extreme cases the manager will be the only one who knows what should be done and how to go about doing it, and he will be the only one to initiate action.

> Getting together is a beginning.
> Staying together is progress.
> Working together is success.
>
> *Henry Ford I*

An organization that relies on any one individual for continuous success in its operations will experience a major crisis if that individual leaves or dies. Many companies face serious difficulties when some key individual who is an excellent producer, administrator, or entrepreneur leaves before a team feeling—an esprit de corps around an effective course of action—has been developed. Integration that creates group effort is necessary for the effective, long-range operation of any organization.

Not only does the integrator provide for future organizational stability, but more important he or she enables the organization to function smoothly in the present. Management is constantly faced with conflicting demands from outside the organization. In addition, friction arises within the organization because of differences in the personalities and perspectives of different managers. Intramanagement turbulence will be discussed in more detail in Chapter 10. Here it is important to recognize that the I role, or integration, is required to make such conflict useful and bearable.

Integration is accomplished by clarifying issues, by finding

the common threads of agreement in deep rather than superficial issues, and by analyzing contrasting values and conflicting and divergent assumptions and expectations.

What range of integration does an integrator (I) seek to
achieve? Is it one-to-one integration or one-to-few, or one-to-
many? This will depend on what other roles he or she wishes
to perform. An integrating manager who is also oriented to
an A role will often use a one-to-one mode in talking to
people and gathering data to influence them, but his primary
orientation will be one-to-few (small group dynamics). An exclusively one-to-one orientation is more characteristic of the
Producer-Integrator (P——I).

A person cannot integrate a society by integrating on a
personal basis. Ideas and ideologies unify a society. The entrepreneurial role (E) is indispensable for those who wish to
integrate people with whom they are not in personal contact.
Therefore, one finds that the one-to-many orientation is characteristic of the Entrepreneur-Integrator. Performing the E
role exclusively won't integrate a society, since the Arsonist
creates ideas that fit only his perception of reality and often
introduces division and conflict among his followers. It is the
EI combination that gives a person leadership on a larger
than small group scale. This combination of roles will be discussed in more detail in the appendix. Here we focus on the
empathy of the integrator, his capacity to identify his followers' aspirations, and his ability to find courses of action
that unite people.

A successful integrator makes himself dispensable. He will
have subordinates who are capable of replacing him. The
cohesion of the group will be such that almost any member
can initiate action, administer programs, and produce results.
To take a military example, if any soldier in a squad can take
the corporal's place when the corporal is killed, this shows
that the corporal was a good integrator. If the squad scatters
when the corporal is killed, this shows the corporal's integration of the unit was insufficient, though he may have been a
competent commander in other respects.

The integrating role has several components which make it function. The integrator is sensitive to others—(i.e., empathetic), and he is capable of deductive thinking—(i.e., able to infer what people want to say from what they do say). He has no ego problems of his own and is therefore able to deal with other people's expectations, problems, and needs.

The role of integration has two dimensions (passive and active) and three directions (upward, lateral, and downward).

A passive integrator can integrate himself into a group of people. An active integrator can integrate a group of people among themselves. In management, integration *must* be active. Since the **PAEI** model deals with management, it concerns itself only with active integration.

Upward integration is the ability to integrate (active) or be integrated (passive) with people who are higher in status, authority, rank, and so on. Lateral integration is the ability to integrate oneself with peers (passive) or to integrate peers into a cohesive group (active).

Downward integration is the ability to work with people whose rank is lower. In a passive mode, the downward integrator is capable of being accepted by his subordinates. In the active mode, he provides leadership by establishing cohesion among his subordinates.

The integrator's mode of operation varies according to the group with which he or she is working. Very effective lateral integrators may function poorly as downward integrators. With subordinates they might tend to be arrogant. It is unusual for a person to be an active integrator in all directions.[2]

Although the **I** role is necessary for the adequate functioning of the managerial process, it is not sufficient. What is the style of management of a person who is only capable of integrating?

THE SUPERFOLLOWER STYLE

The exclusive integrator is not an entrepreneur, a producer, or an administrator—he merely unifies people behind a cause.

I call this manager the Superfollower because he tries to find out what plan will be acceptable to the largest number of people and then tries to unite them behind that plan. That is, he does not really lead—he follows.

The exclusive integrator has no ideas of his own that he would like to implement (no **E**), no tangible results that he wants to achieve (no **P**). Like the Bureaucrat who does not care what he produces so long as it is implemented according to the rules, the Superfollower shows little concern about what or how he integrates so long as there is an appearance of consensus, a "united front." He is not committed to a particular system (he has no **A**); he will follow any system that will achieve an *appearance* of consensus.

An integrator deals exclusively with the interactions of others. As such, he is not bound by the limits of his own organizational unit. An integrator who is sincerely interested in others is likely to exhibit this interest both inside and outside the organization. On the other hand, an integrator who is a manipulator of others "gets things done with people," whether he cares for the people or not.

The ———**I** style of management falls in the low-task, high-social (0.9) range of Blake and Mouton's managerial grid.[3] This grid has two axes—task and orientation to people. Blake and Mouton use the grid to describe managerial behavior. According to their model, a person like the integrator is extremely responsive to what others think and wants to gain their approval. In order to avoid rejection, he avoids rejecting others. He accepts the opinions, attitudes, and ideas of others in preference to pushing his own. "As a result," say Blake

---

Sam Rayburn's Rule

If you want to get along, go along!

---

and Mouton, "when convictions are expressed, they are more likely to be reflections of what his boss, his peers, or his subordinates think and want, as opposed to his own convictions and desires. He is rarely in an initiating role in issues which call for exerting positive leadership."

One can easily identify a Superfollower at meetings. Consider a hypothetical meeting at which the four different types of managers—the Lone Ranger (**P----**), Bureaucrat (**-A--**), Arsonist (**--E-**), and Superfollower (**----I**)—are present. The **--E-** is doing most of the talking. Typically, the Bureaucrat (**-A--**) disagrees and shows why things cannot be done. The Lone Ranger (**P----**) is restless, and he either steps out every few minutes to make a call, or he takes care of some correspondence while giving partial attention to what he sees as a "waste of time." The Superfollower (**----I**) is listening attentively. Who says what? Where does the power lie? He is searching for the underlying arguments, trying to identify the motives of each participant and the bases of any contention. He rarely presents real new alternatives, and he does not mind changing his suggestions as long as an increasing number of people find them acceptable.

If a decision agreeable to all cannot be arrived at, the Superfollower, if he is the chairman of the meeting, is apt to have a subcommittee study the problem further. He will postpone the decision to another time, waiting for a consensus or compromise to emerge.

If the subordinates of the Lone Ranger are go-fors, those of the Bureaucrat yes-yes people, and those of the Arsonist claques, then the followers of the Superfollower are "informers" and "oilers." Their tasks are to keep the boss up-to-date and to help him "lubricate" the machinery. It is their duty to feed the boss the latest office "news." They must keep "on top" of everything and impart their knowledge about people, positions, attitudes, and opinions to him.

If the Superfollower has free time, he spends it socializing, listening to complaints, and trying to convince the complainers that the situation is not as bad as it seems to be.

Subordinates do not inform the Superfollower of real, deep conflicts. He is not capable of handling situations where he actually has to take a stand; he is, overall, too wishy-washy for that.

The Superfollower wishes to remove superficial conflict. He will certainly not initiate it. He feels that it threatens the appearance of unity which he regards as so important. He interprets the tensions that accompany conflict as a rejection of himself. He works to relieve tensions, to achieve unity even for a short time, no matter what the long-term costs may be. This quality was also observed by Blake and Mouton, who suggest that such a person rarely generates conflict but that when it does appear, either between himself and others or between others, he tries to soothe bad feelings. When tensions between people do arise, the Superfollower attempts to reduce them.[4]

A desire to resolve conflicts is not useful at all times. A course of action which resolves a short-term need adequately may not be beneficial to the organization in the long run. A consensus achieved among certain members of an organization at a particular time may satisfy their immediate interests at the expense of the interests of the total organization, which includes groups that are not always represented in its decision-making bodies. An important role of the manager is to represent future interests. The Superfollower is less interested in these than in the interests of his immediate constituency.

Bell called a person who manifested this style "The Pleaser."[5] The Pleaser works hard to make you like him. He has a strong need for acceptance and seeks relationships that are free of conflict. Therefore, he does not wish to make decisions alone. He is group-reliant rather than self-reliant.

The Pleaser is a nice person who performs well in social tasks. He uses humor and wit to release tensions. He is kind to others and sensitive to their feelings. Because of his desire to please, his mind can be changed quickly and easily; that is, he sways with popular opinions. Bell quotes a Pleaser as saying during a board meeting, "I really think we should seek new financing through a stock issue." As he spoke, other directors indicated disagreement. Almost without pausing, the speaker continued, "but I don't feel strongly about this point."[6]

The Pleaser has little concern for efficiency in an organization. Morale tends to be good under him, although he lacks purpose, direction, and courage. Typically, an organization managed by a Pleaser adapts selectively to its environment. Nonetheless, it produces below-average results because of its informality and its lack of concern for efficiency.

It has been said that a politician worries about the next election, whereas a statesman worries about the next generation. In his context, the Superfollower is definitely a politician. He will not take the risk or undertake the fighting necessary to upset short-term consensus for a long-term program. The statesman is a leader whose present course of action is not necessarily accepted in the short run. Achieving a consensus that will benefit future generations means undertaking projects whose outcome is uncertain. This involves risk, and the Superfollower (–––I) does not take risks.

Short-range interest groups flourish under the Superfollower because he does not identify corporate goals for them but rather considers a goal to be that which is desired at a particular time by a consensus of those participating in the decision-making process. The Superfollower does not attempt to lift himself above the temporary interests of the organization and decide the direction which the organization *should take.* He will not threaten an existing consensus. He does not like to confront subordinates. He will not absorb the aggression that is created when a course of action offends a particular group. He tries to identify himself *with* a direction that is already acceptable to the organization rather than to identify *for* the organization the direction that would be best in light of all the conditions that the organization faces. He is always asking, "What do we agree about?" Instead of making his own suggestions, he quotes others: "So and so said that . . . , and so and so agrees that . . ."

Each of the managerial styles treated earlier had its characteristic complaints. The Lone Ranger complains that he never has enough time. The Bureaucrat complains that rules are being violated. The Arsonist complains that his real priorities never get accomplished. If the Superfollower complains at all, it is usually to say that someone did not understand him correctly.

The reaction of subordinates to this type of management can range from enthusiasm to apathy or rebellion. Those who are getting all they want from the organization will accept the Superfollower. On the other hand, rebellion can be aroused when the company is following a direction that a minority knows to be disastrous.

In the event of a power struggle among members of the organization, the Superfollower will try to determine which side is likely to win. Then he will "jump on the bandwagon" while pretending to lead the parade. He will seek to achieve unity by extracting compromises from the various parties involved. He will not mobilize support for a controversial alternative—especially one which requires concessions from the dominant group.

Under the Superfollower, power struggles can be very dysfunctional. People turn against each other while he maneuvers around them all. Compare this to the other managerial styles: With the Lone Ranger, power struggles are minimal. If such struggles do exist, he is too busy to get involved with them. The Arsonist will manipulate power struggles, either by introducing them or by channeling them into his latest project. The Bureaucrat will ignore a power struggle unless it poses a threat to his control and if it does, he will fight it with all his might. The Superfollower will thrive on a power struggle which he can control. Since he does not present a long-term, uplifting, and unifying alternative, but rather advocates the dominant, short-term, acceptable alternative, when people turn against each other, it makes the unifying role he plays indispensable and his position in the organization a central one.

The Superfollower does not really unite. For unity, a deep recognition of common goals is necessary. He is more interested in the immediate appearance of unity, which is not a real unity. In the long run, the group never becomes united—thus, its dysfunctional behavior.

Management under a Superfollower has other long-term repercussions. Since the organization changes direction or becomes petrified, depending on the power structure shifts within it, it lacks a unified and consistent consciously made long-term policy. The organization finds itself either oscillating from one direction to another or staying on one course of action, regardless of its needs. Both outcomes are undesirable for a planned, effective adaptation of an organization to its environment.

The Superfollower likes to train, but most of his training is focused on interpersonal relations. He wants to know who thinks what about whom, and he wants everyone to agree on everything. He welcomes any training that either improves his ability to understand human nature or contributes to the appearance of unity.

The subordinates of the Superfollower see through his shallowness quite rapidly. Thus, in his presence they appear peaceful and accepting, remembering that the Superfollower likes people whom other people like. They realize that in order to be promoted they have to be accepted by others. Eventually, his subordinates conceal their true feelings from him, because they feel emotionally exploited or manipulated. Sometimes, to attract attention, Superfollower's subordinates will start rumors that unity is in danger. Such rumors are not only a means of getting the Superfollower's immediate attention; they are also used to "ease out" a colleague.

The goals of the Lone Ranger and the Bureaucrat are very short-term. The Lone Ranger wants to get the job done, and the Bureaucrat wants to keep the system tight and intact. The long-range goals are found in the activities of the Arsonist. However, these goals tend to be scattered. The Superfollower does not really *have* any goals for the organization. He is constantly seeking consensus, and his goal-type behavior could be compared to that of a school of fish that swims in the direction of the prevailing current. The "current" also determines the direction of the Superfollower. He is a leader because he finds himself at the head of the "school." When the whole school changes direction, he asks, "Where would you like me to lead you?"

> It is said that during the French Revolution Robespierre was sitting in a café one afternoon when a group of Jacobins went racing by. He hurriedly finished his wine, stating, "There go my people. I must follow them and see where they are going because I am their leader."

The decision-making behavior of an organization provides clues as to the management styles being employed. The decisions of the Lone Ranger are usually based on technical knowledge. He really does not wish to waste a lot of time making decisions, because he is anxious to get out and implement them. The Bureaucrat, again, is not a strong decision maker. He wants decisions to be *in writing* so that he can allocate the responsibility for any violations of rules. This is in direct contrast to the approach of the Arsonist, who would like his decision to be as loose as possible. That is, he does not want them in writing. He does not wish to be inhibited or confined by fixed decisions. The Superfollower, on the other hand, tends to avoid decisions as much as possible. When decisions exist, he seeks agreement on them. He rarely makes a decision by himself.

The management process requires a response to the opportunities and threats of the environment. The Lone Ranger is so busy working that he fails to see threats and opportunities. The Arsonist, on the other hand, is so preoccupied with potential opportunities that he fails to recognize immediate threats. The Lone Ranger's time horizon for planning is often next week. He is tending too many fires to worry about what creates them. The Arsonist, on the other hand, resents planning because it means that he has to commit himself to something. He wants to keep all his options open, to keep loose, to be able to change direction at will. For him, planning is mostly dreaming up ideas, exchanging views, and getting excited. It consists of discussing what is desired as opposed to what is possible.

The Bureaucrat sees planning as a mechanism for firmly establishing his book of rules. For him, planning is basically equivalent to scheduling, coordinating details, setting control points, and establishing report systems.

The Superfollower would like to use planning as an integrating vehicle. He uses it as a means for exchanging views, as a consciousness-raising experience in which people express their individual aspirations and expectations, as an occasion for identifying conflicts which he can subsequently resolve. He might say, "Dream up . . . What are your fantasies? What are your scenarios of the future?" When conflicting aspirations and expectations are clarified, he seeks to integrate them superficially, since he lacks the qualities that are needed to resolve deep-seated differences.

When a Superfollower leaves an organization, the superficial integration he established may crumble. Different middle-level managers are likely to start pulling in different directions, threatening to shake the organization apart. Often an administrator is brought in to resolve the problem. This, in effect, replaces the integration of people, the development of appropriate compromises, with a set of regulations to force order, irrespective of its value to the organization in a changing environment.

THE COMMON CHARACTERISTIC

For all their differences, the four managerial styles (**P‒‒‒,** **‒A‒‒, ‒‒E‒,** and **‒‒‒I**) have one characteristic in common.

They are all inflexible stereotypes. The persons who exhibit these styles are not well-rounded individuals in terms of their needs or their behavior. They have unidimensional, one-track minds. They have a limited perception of what they are and of what they are supposed to do in life.[7]

Inflexible, unidimensional behavior is dysfunctional for an organization since it causes mismanagement. But more important, inflexibility has negative effects on the person and on his ability to function in the organization. Anyone who exhibits an exclusive management style might, for this reason, become a Deadwood (----), a fanatic, or a martyr, if he is lucky. The Deadwood is described in the next chapter.

Several of the management roles discussed in this book parallel those described in Wilkerson's law, which states that the anatomy of any community or organization includes four kinds of bones:

Backbones who get behind the wheel and do the work (the Producer).

Knucklebones who knock everything everyone else does (the Entrepreneur).

Wishbones who will go along with an idea but want someone else to do the work (the Integrator).

Jawbones who do a lot of talking but little else (Deadwood, or the lack of any role).

From Thomas L. Martin, Jr., *Malice in Blunderland* (New York: McGraw-Hill, 1973), pp. 66–67.

SUMMARY OF THE SUPERFOLLOWER STYLE

The Person's Style

Exclusive role: Integrator of people.
How he excels: Getting agreement, compromising.
Predominant behavior: Compromising, integrating people's ideas.
Focus of attention: The acceptability of what is done

Most distinctive personality traits: Smooth, sensitive, people-oriented, understanding, thankful for being introduced into the secrets of the organization.

Appraises himself by: How central he is to the power play.

Typical complaint: We do not get along as well as we should.

Decision making: Only when there is a group consensus.

If he has free time: He will identify new conflicts (even imaginary ones) that only he can resolve; will spread rumors or collect information to the effect that such conflicts exist.

He prefers to hire: Submissive people; people who are not clique epicenters like himself.

Subordinates

Subordinates' style: "Sunshine spreaders."

Subordinates are promoted: If they get along.

What subordinates get praised for: Getting along.

Subordinates do not inform him about: Their true feelings if these might destroy a consensus.

Dysfunctional behavior of subordinates: Create rumors to get attention.

Time Management, Staff Meetings, and Managerial Practice

He arrives at and leaves work: Appropriately; as expected.

Subordinates arrive and leave: With him.

Frequency and advance notice of staff meetings: Regular; as expected.

Staff meeting attendance: Desired.

Staff meeting agenda: Freewheeling; whatever people want to talk about.

Who talks at staff meetings: Anyone and everyone with a human problem.

Training practices: Focused on interpersonal relations.

Attitude toward systematic management: Is suspicious of it; dislikes it if it resolves conflict institutionally; will fight it if he considers it a threat to the pseudo-unity he creates or if it will make him dispensable.

Attitude toward conflict: Likes it if he can be instrumental in resolving it.

Attitude toward change: Accepts it if it augments his role as a conflict resolver and does not impair unity.

Focus and type of information he cherishes: Information on who stands where on what issues; will not share it.

Focus of creativity: Integrated by him.

Attitude toward Other Managers

Exclusive producer (Lone Ranger, P———): Accepts.
Exclusive administrator (Bureaucrat, –A––): Dislikes.
Exclusive entrepreneur (Arsonist, ––E–): Plays up to.
Exclusive integrator (Superfollower, –––I): Suspicious.
Deadwood (––––): Likes.

NOTES

1. On the role of integration, see P. R. Lawrence and J. W. Lorsch, "New Managerial Job: The Integrator," *Harvard Business Review, 45* (November 1967), 142–51.

2. The **I** component, as has been pointed out, is essential to good management at all levels, because the manager must work through others to achieve organizational goals. Where management has succeeded in integrating the individual members of an organization into a group, we may expect greater identification with the organization, more job satisfaction, and better performance. The importance of interpersonal relationships for the successful operation of organizations has been repeatedly demonstrated in the literature. Argyris found that the worker's skill and his pride in his work were directly related to his on-the-job friendships. See Chris Argyris, "The Fusion of an Individual with the Organization," *American Sociological Review, 19* (1954), 145–67; and idem, "Personality vs. Organization," *Organizational Dynamics, 3* (1974) no. 2, 2–17.

A similar association between level of competence and degree of integration with the organization was reported by Blau in a study of law enforcement agents. See Peter M. Blau, "Patterns of Interaction among a Group of Officials in a Government Agency," *Human Relations*, 7 (1954), 337–48.

3. Robert Blake and Jane Mouton, *The Managerial Grid* (Houston: Gulf Publishing 1964), p. 75.

4. Ibid.

5. Gerald Bell, *The Achievers* (Chapel Hill, N.C.: Preston Hill, 1973), chap 7.

6. Ibid., p. 77.

7. I am grateful to Bob Tannenbaum of UCLA for having directed my attention to this common characteristic.

Chapter 6

----: The Deadwood

THE DEADWOOD STYLE

What happens when a manager does not perform any of the four roles well? He is not an integrator because he does not have the social sensitivity or the capacity for communication. He is not an entrepreneur because he is neither creative nor capable of taking risks. He is not an administrator because he cannot organize, delegate, coordinate, motivate, or whatever else is necessary to carry out a predetermined task. He fails even as a producer because he is not technically competent or results-oriented.

A person who is in a managerial position but does not perform any of the managerial roles is a Deadwood (----). How can a Deadwood be a manager? Nepotism is one explanation— people get positions due to family connections. But such cases are less common than the organizationally created Deadwood. However, before we analyze how an organization creates a Deadwood, let us describe his behavior.

Behavior

Deadwood is apathetic. He waits to be told what to do. He does not produce; he does not administer; he does not provide sparks, as does the Arsonist; and he does not get involved with power intrigues, as does the Superfollower. If he has any good ideas or opinions about others, he keeps them to himself.

Deadwood is mostly worried about how to survive until retirement. His goal is to keep intact the little world he has created. In his free time he looks for successes that he can take credit for. Change is a serious threat to him. He knows that any change threatens his position. To maximize his chances for survival, he resists change, attributes successes to himself, and avoids starting anything new (jobs, projects, etc.).

Deadwood's hiring practices reflect this strategy for survival. He favors not-so-bright subordinates, even to the point of advancing those who will produce less than he does. Thus, the major danger of Deadwood is that more Deadwoods accumulate under him. Any subordinates who wish to grow and develop are completely frustrated by a Deadwood manager. They leave, and the ones who remain behind become Deadwoods. In this way, one Deadwood manager can create a cancerous disequilibrium in the organization.

Deadwood has no complaints. He thinks that a complaint would reflect on him, so he always says, "Everything is going well; we are making excellent progress." Meanwhile, the company may be going bankrupt.

Deadwood trains, but his heart is not in it. Why should he train his own replacement? What's the hurry? Hence, he will only go through the motions of training.

Deadwood is afraid of conflicts, which may mean change. So he tries to cover up conflicts and explain them away as mere misunderstandings.

Planning, organizing, and controlling are only words to Deadwood. They mean more work. Since he is not a producer, an implementer, an entrepreneur, or an integrator, the process of management is a mere ritual to him. He acts it out religiously, but only for the sake of his personal survival.

At one time Deadwood might have been any one of the other mismanagers, and he still evinces what were once his dominant personality traits. One can still see in him from time to time traces of the enthusiastic Arsonist or the meticulous Bureaucrat that he once was. But by the time he has become Deadwood, his main characteristic is a low metabolism. He smokes or drinks a lot. He coughs, hums, and nods his head in agreement, he confides to you how well he is doing, or how well he did in the past, or how well he will do, but you sense that not much is to be expected from him.

He is, however, very agreeable, friendly, and nonthreatening. He is liked, much as a friendly old uncle is liked, but he is not respected. So people endure him and do not want to hurt him. In the meantime, the organization suffers.

Deadwood is usually out of the information network. If

Boren's Laws

First law: When in charge, ponder.
Second law: When in trouble, delegate.
Third law: When in doubt, mumble.

From Thomas L. Martin, Jr., *Malice in Blunderland* (New York: McGraw-Hill, 1973), p. 74.

he does get access to any information, he cherishes it and uses it whenever possible. It may be irrelevant to the situation, but its possession proves to the rest of the organization that he is still plugged in and kicking.

Bell identifies and describes a personality style that he calls "The Avoider."[1] The Avoider is similar to our Deadwood. He refrains from making decisions and gets others to select the jobs and goals to be accomplished. If possible, he will select jobs where the goals are set and relatively easy to accomplish. Bell's Avoider has a low capacity for criticism or humiliation. Therefore, he spends a great deal of energy seeking to avoid trouble.

Rangnekar's Rules for Decision Avoidance

Rule 1: If you can avoid a decision, do so.
Rule 2: If you can avoid a decision, don't delay it.
Rule 3: If you can get somebody else to avoid a decision, don't avoid it yourself.
Rule 4: If you cannot get one person to avoid the decision, appoint a committee.

From Thomas L. Martin, Jr., *Malice in Blunderland* (New York: McGraw-Hill, 1973), pp. 77 and 78.

An organization managed by an Avoider tends to shrink. Instead of adapting to situational demands, he ignores them, thus losing touch with the outside world. According to Bell, "Left under his direction, his department will slowly become

invisible." The worst thing that can happen is to have Deadwood at the top of an organization. This means that the whole
organization is dying. Although such management sometimes
tries to disguise itself as conservative, it is moribund. One may
have an old executive who is tired and does not want to work
or produce. He no longer wants to change; he is happy with
what he has done in the past.

Origins

How does a person develop into a Deadwood? A person who
embodies any of the "pure" styles can become a Deadwood
because of inflexibility and one-sidedness. The unidimensional personality "burns up" either himself or the organization.

Take the Lone Ranger (P————), for instance. Most people
who work produce an average return for their effort, but some
seem to be superproducers. Real estate brokers describe their
"star salesmen" as follows: "The guy is a terrific self-starter.
He goes and goes and goes. He is never in the office, but rather
out showing houses to new prospects or finding homes to sell.
Within three months to a year of coming to this office, he is
the number one salesman. He is making tremendous amounts
of money!" But after a couple of years such a salesman burns
out. His star descends, and he becomes an average salesman,
or worse, a Deadwood.

One can lose one's P for several reasons. The usual reason
is psychic exhaustion (ennui), but a sudden change in the
technology of producing results can also change a Lone
Ranger (P————) into a Deadwood (————).

Moreover, the P——— is, in effect, already three-fourths
Deadwood. When he loses his P, he becomes a full-fledged
Deadwood.

A P——— is so busy making the sale that he has no time to see
the general picture. He does not sense changes in the market;
he does not appreciate trends in the industry; he is not par-

ticularly concerned about cultivating customers who will return to him in future years. Eventually, his professional advantage, the ability to make sales, dissipates. It becomes increasingly difficult for him to produce the results that he is accustomed to producing, so he works even harder, sees even less of his working environment. The process continues until he is exhausted. This phenomenon is so widespread that many real estate brokers have said that they would rather have good, albeit limited, salespersons in their offices than the spectacular ones.

Since the Lone Ranger is almost exclusively short-term results oriented, he has no time to train others. Worse, he has no time to train himself. Over time he becomes an obsolete Deadwood. Often, a person who is said to have had 20 years of experience has merely repeated the same experiences for 20 successive years. When all that a person does is repeat the same practices year after year, in time he becomes obsolete.

There is a tragic quality in the fate of the Lone Ranger who becomes Deadwood. The Lone Ranger, you will remember, is a very hardworking individual. He dedicates his life to the company and usually neglects his family. Because of his short-term orientation, he is so busy "doing" that he has no time to learn new things, to develop himself. Years later, he is still working hard, but the results are not what they used to be. He has become obsolete. When the time comes to fire the nonperformers, the Lone Ranger may be the first to go. And he usually does not understand why the organization is thankless.

Similar problems are encountered with the –A––. Instead of being oriented toward producing results, the exclusive A fixes his attention primarily on establishing controls. He too loses sight of the big picture. His efforts to control the present system make him so rigid that a major systemic upheaval will crack him. An unexpected shift in the internal or external business environment will reduce the –A–– to a ––––. The burning out of the A has more widespread effects than that of the P. The big A's department suffers a seizure, much the way a poorly timed engine might freeze. Suddenly it cannot move; it goes nowhere; it does nothing.

Such a situation often arises when a new computer is introduced into a Bureaucrat's department. When the old book by which the Bureaucrat manages is thrown out, he cannot adapt; he becomes Deadwood or obsolete. The A capability may also be lost when "they change the books." Companies merge or are acquired. In most such cases, old accountants or the administrators who can't learn new tricks are eliminated.

The typical Arsonist (——E–) is prone to become Deadwood because he overextends himself. Before you know it, he is all over the place and nowhere. Eventually he will run out of cash or working capital. Then his organization will go bankrupt or be purchased by another company. If the Arsonist is bought out, the buyer will "kick him upstairs." He will become an adviser or a consultant for a period of years. However, he will be deprived of any ability to start anything.

The Arsonist may also become Deadwood when "the wheels break down" because of his incessant changes of direction. In that case, the Arsonist might become paranoid. On the one hand, his subordinates all tell him how hard they work, and they all seem to be working hard. On the other hand, his projects and instructions do not get carried out. He comes to believe that there are two realities—the one he observes and another whose existence he suspects. When that happens, he loses his self-confidence and begins to fade away.

The Superfollower (———I) diminishes in importance as people stop listening to him. He either fails to live up to what they seek, or they get tired of the same old approach, or the conflict becomes too big for him to master it by his customary superficial measures. Also, in time new people fail to become members of "the group" and the Superfollower fails to integrate.

A Superfollower (———I) may also become a Deadwood (————) if a more charismatic leader appears in the organization. People no longer follow the Superfollower, and he becomes a plain follower.

The **P---**, **-A--**, **--E-**, and **---I**, are all, then, three-fourths Deadwood. The capabilities of these individuals are neither wide-ranging nor flexible enough to allow adaptation to new situations. They become unable to produce, administer, be an entrepreneur, or integrate as necessary. They burn out.

Although the phenomenon of burning out occurs in many guises, it is neatly described in its most general form by Ralph Ablon.

> Inevitably, when you do have that very fortunate circumstance of the man and the moment meeting, the situation begins to deteriorate because the moment changes; and the man is very reluctant to change. Sooner or later, the man becomes an anachronism because he no longer suits the situation. He cannot change that much, so he will not accept the fact that the moment has changed. He will denounce the world because it wouldn't freeze itself in his moment.

Thus, change can produce Deadwood, and over time Deadwood will spread. Since Deadwood does not complain, the "spreading cancer" might not be noticed until it is too late. If organizations do not invest in training and development to remove dashes, at a rate at least commensurate to the rate of change that the organizations are experiencing, they will tend to develop cancerous elements (nonfunctional spreading substances) that will eventually cause them to die.

When a Deadwood is eliminated from an organization (he usually does not leave on his own, but dies on the job, is fired, or retires), he is not missed, but by the time he goes the organization is usually dead as well. No purposeful activity, no creativity, no integration of people is evident.

P---, **-A--**, **--E-** and **---I** can become Deadwood (**----**). But the real danger of such managers lies elsewhere. Three-fourths Deadwoods create full-fledged Deadwoods. The go-fors who work for the Lone Ranger and the yes-yes clerks who work for the Bureaucrat become Deadwood. The claques who work for the Arsonist eventually learn to suppress their own aspirations and to live in his shadow. They learn to "do little but make a lot of noise"—they become Deadwood. The subordinates of the Superfollower become Deadwood, too. They do not know what *really* needs to be done. They become sick and tired of the political game, so they give up and plainly follow. Where? Nowhere, since the Superfollower gives no direction.

SUMMARY OF THE DEADWOOD STYLE

The Person's Style

Exclusive role: Does nothing well.

How he excels: Keeping out of trouble.

Predominant behavior: Waiting to be told what to do next.

Focus of attention: No distinct emphasis, except for his own survival.

Most distinctive personality traits: Submissive, friendly, non-threatening, yielding, agreeing.

Appraises himself by: How successful he is personally in surviving in the organization; how well he is accepted.

Typical complaints: None.

Decision making: Avoided.

If he has free time: He will look for any successes he can take credit for; he will document achievements he can attribute to himself.

He prefers to hire: The not-so-bright individual who will pose no threat; other Deadwood; does not promote; hires people like himself.

Subordinates

Subordinates' style: Deadwood or transients.

Subordinates are promoted: If they do not do anything; if they don't make waves or are not rate-busters; usually they don't get promoted—he blocks advancement channels.

What subordinates get praised for: Anything that can add to his glory.

Subordinates do not inform him about: Anything; he is usually ignored.

Dysfunctional behavior of subordinates: Don't do much of anything; minor motions; no results; high turnover; get out while they still can.

Time Management, Staff Meetings, and Managerial Practice

He arrives at and leaves work: As needed for survival.

Subordinates arrive and leave: As they wish.

Frequency and advance notice of staff meetings: Regular, but rare.

Staff meeting attendance: High absence rate.

Staff meeting agenda: Past irrelevant successes.

Who talks at staff meetings: Someone does the talking; few if any do the listening.

Training practices: The motions, without the substance.

Attitude toward systematic management: The rituals, without the reality.

Attitude toward conflict: Fears it for the same reason that he fears change; masks it as a mere misunderstanding.

Focus and type of information he cherishes: Any information he can get; he will not share it.

Focus of creativity: None.

Attitude toward Other Managers

Exclusive producer (Lone Ranger, P----): Uses, exploits.

Exclusive administrator (Bureaucrat, -A--): Adapts to.

Exclusive entrepreneur (Arsonist, --E-): Scared stiff of.

Exclusive integrator (Superfollower, ---I): Likes.

Deadwood (----): Comfortable with.

NOTES

1. Gerald Bell, *The Achievers* (Chapel Hill, N.C.: Preston Hill, 1973), chap. 4.

Chapter 7

PAEI: The Textbook Manager

THE TEXTBOOK MANAGER (PAEI)

How does a perfect manager behave? The Textbook Manager (**PAEI**) is a producer of results, an excellent administrator, an entrepreneur, and an integrator. He or she initiates action systematically, integrating human resources to that end. He delegates, and he develops the organization's markets, production facilities, finances, and human resources continuously and systematically. Unlike the Lone Ranger, he appraises himself by how well *the group* that he manages performs; by how well, together and individually, its members achieve their respective goals, and by how instrumental and supportive he was in *facilitating* their goal achievement.

He listens carefully, whenever time allows, to what is being said and to what is *not* being said. He is aware of the need to change. He cautiously, selectively, and systematically introduces change in a planned fashion. He is not afraid to hire bright and challenging subordinates; he looks for potential and is able to identify it. He is sufficiently self-confident and self-realized to respect people who act like himself. He does not manifest anxiety by complaining. He offers constructive criticism instead. He trains systematically. He resolves conflicts in a statesmanlike manner, seeking consensus by elevating people's aspirations and expectations and by appealing to their social consciences. He is at once analytic and action-oriented; sensitive, yet not overly emotional. He seeks results, but not at the expense of the process. He seeks maximal integrity in the process, but not at the expense of the necessary short-term results. He does not monopolize information and use it as a source of power. His subordinates are not afraid to report failures; they know that he will be reasonable and supportive. He promotes those with managerial potential and encourages constructive creativity. His organization is a well-integrated, goal-seeking structure whose members cooperate and fully accept one another and the judgment of their managers. No dysfunctional behavior on the part of his subordinates is easily observable.

Have you ever known a manager who fits the above description? Have you ever been capable of performing as a **PAEI**?

I call the **PAEI** the Textbook Manager because one finds him only in textbooks.[1] At this point, what should be clear is that no one person behaves like a **PAEI**. The textbooks that describe management assume a perfect person who does not exist.

Most of us believe the rest of us are incompetent.

A sign in Robert B. Andrews office—
Professor, UCLA.

McClelland theorizes that there are three basic personality needs: the need for achievement (n/Ach), the need for power (n/Pwr), and the need for affiliation (n/Aff).[2]

According to McClelland, people with a high need for achievement and an intense desire for success have an equally intense fear of failure and want to be challenged. They set difficult goals for themselves, take a realistic approach to risks, prefer to assume personal responsibility to get a job done, like specific and prompt feedback, tend to be restless, like to work long hours, do not worry unduly about failure, and like to run their own shows.[3]

The need for power is correlated with concern for exercising influence and control. People with a high need for power seek positions of leadership. They are good conversationalists, often argumentative, forceful, outspoken, hardheaded, and demanding, and they enjoy teaching and public speaking.[4]

The need for affiliation is found in people who derive pleasure from being loved and tend to avoid being rejected. They are likely to be concerned with maintaining pleasant social relationships, and they enjoy a sense of intimacy and understanding. They are ready to console and help others in trouble, and they enjoy friendly interaction with others.[5]

It could be postulated that people with strong n/Ach behave like the **P----**, that is, the need to produce results could be equated to the need to achieve. Similarly, the need for power (n/Pwr) is correlated to the administrative role, and the need for affiliation (n/Aff) to the integrating role.

In the past McClelland expressed the view that the achievement need was the most powerful predictor of management success and performance.[6] However, in a recent article co-authored with David Burnham, he came to somewhat different conclusions:

> While it sounds as if everyone ought to have the need to achieve, in fact, as psychologists define and measure achievement motivation, it leads people to behave in very special ways that do not necessarily lead to good management.
>
> For one thing, because they focus on personal improvement, on doing things better by themselves, achievement-motivated people want to do things themselves. For another, they want concrete short-term feedback on their performance so that they can tell how well they are doing. Yet the manager, particularly one in a large complex organization, cannot

perform all the tasks necessary for success by himself or herself. He must manage others so that they will do things for the organization. Also, feedback on his subordinates' performance may be vaguer and more delayed than it would be if he were doing everything himself.

The manager's job seems to call more for someone who can influence people than for someone who does things better on his own. In motivational terms, then, we might expect the successful manager to have a greater "need for power" than a need to achieve.[7]

It all sounds quite familiar, does it not? In this article McClelland reversed his earlier exclusive reliance on the need for achievement as a means of identifying good managers. The person with exclusive n/Ach turns out to be a Lone Ranger.

McClelland now suggests that a person with n/Pwr who is institutionally oriented will be a better manager than an n/Ach. In our code such a person is a **PA?I**, someone who enforces rules for the benefit of the organization rather than for his own aggrandizement.

In reading various textbook descriptions of the manager, one has to stop and wonder: How many real-life managers match the descriptions? The textbooks say that a good manager is supposed to have a desirable personality, which is rare to say the least. He is also supposed to be knowledgeable, creative, and logical; achievement-oriented, people-oriented, and organizationally oriented; intuitive, yet rational; capable of abstraction, yet attentive to detail; sensitive to people's needs, yet concerned about organizational needs; and so on, and so on.

Such descriptions seem to be drawn, not from life, but from a search for perfection which tells us what we should be rather than what we can be.

But in actuality the **PAEI** does not seem to exist. If the task orientation in Blake and Mouton's model[8] is the **PE,** and the people process orientation is the **AI,** how many people come up with a 9.9 rating?

Hersey and Blanchard state the qualities of a good manager, and they also state that people who possess those qualities are rare.[9] The psychologists and the business schools try to create **PAEIs**, but this seems to be an exercise in futility. All that education can do is to remove the dashes from the **PAEI** code.

> I think it is very dangerous to believe in genius. I think it exists very, very seldom. When it does exist, it exists in terms of a man's personal or individual output, whether it be painting or music or whatever. It certainly does not exist in a corporation. Any corporation will be extraordinarily limited if it depends upon what any individual can do, even if you assume he is an outstandingly competent individual.
>
> *Ralph Ablon*

No one individual can have all the qualities that are needed for effective management. The effective manager, the manager without faults, the **PAEI**, does not exist. *The search for individuals who possess all the qualities, traits, needs, and behavioral styles that are required for effective management is bound to fail.* It is bound to fail because too many personality traits are required to perform all of the managerial roles equally well and because some of the traits required are incompatible.

Peter Drucker has recognized this. He states:

> A peculiar characteristic of top management is that it requires a diversity of capabilities and, above all, temperaments. It requires the capacity to analyze, to think, to weigh alternatives, and to harmonize dissent. But it also requires the capacity for quick and decisive action, for boldness and for intuitive courage. It requires being at home with abstract ideas, concepts, calculations and figures. It also requires perception of people, human awareness, empathy, and an altogether lively interest and respect for people. Some tasks demand that a man work by himself, and alone. Others are tasks of representation and ceremonial outside tasks, that re-

quire enjoyment of crowds and protocol (such as the task of a politician).

"The top management tasks" according to Drucker, "require at least four different kinds of human beings." Drucker identifies these as "the thought man," "the action man," "the people man," and "the front man." These are obviously analogous to the styles of the **PAEI** model. Drucker recognizes the incompatibility among the characteristics required by these four kinds of people, for he says that "those four temperaments are almost never found in the same person."[10]

Although Drucker is only talking about the temperamental requirements of top management, we feel that the same requirements apply to all management positions within an organization. For example, the foreperson needs to be knowledgeable (**P**); to have administrative capabilities (**A**); to be flexible, adaptive, and innovative (**E**); and to relate well to people (**I**). Few if any forepersons possess all of these qualifications. Management at any level must relate to internal and external environments, technology, and people simultaneously and with the same degree of perfection. This makes the textbook manager a necessity at all managerial levels.

Lord Acton's Law

Power tends to corrupt, and absolute power corrupts absolutely.

From Thomas L. Martin, Jr., *Malice in Blunderland* (New York: McGraw-Hill, 1973), p. 104.

Leadership by one person whose style is dysfunctional can easily head an organization in the wrong direction. Joel Ross and Michael Kami suggest that what causes big corporations to fail is one-man rule.[11] The initial success of many conglomerates was due to one-man rule, to the boss who believed he knew it all. The collapse of the conglomerates was swift and dramatic. Ross and Kami pin their failure on the very factor which explained their initial success. No evolution to a longer term style had occurred, and no one person can be everything.

A person cannot excel in performing all of the **PAEI** roles since, as has been noted, the roles require internally conflicting personality traits. **A** and **E** are in conflict because **A** is conservative and wants control, whereas **E** wants change. **P** and **E** are also in conflict because **P** has a short horizon which requires short-term feedback, whereas **E** takes time to develop and looks to the long term for feedback. **E** and **I** are in conflict because **E** must talk, whereas **I** must listen. Very few people can both talk *and* listen effectively—that is, communicate well.

The four roles are not mutually exclusive, but they are mutually inhibitive. The capacity for functioning effectively in one of the four management styles is likely to inhibit the performance of another.

Thus the individual producer who likes functional involvement resents the time he spends in administration. For example, many artistic directors would rather direct themselves than hire others to do so. Senior architects may express anguish at having to administer, solicit new projects, and motivate others to do the designing that they would love to do themselves. Similarly, becoming chairperson of a university department is personally costly to those who love research.

On the other hand, those who love administration have "reentry blues" when their mandate expires. They have a difficult time getting back into research after having experienced the gratification that administering others gives them.

The administrator who feels rewarded by protecting the system feels threatened by change and does not function well as an entrepreneur. The creative entrepreneur does not like to be harnessed into a system. And the integrator with his concern for people feels uncomfortable about inaugurating changes because his followers might not be willing to accept them.

So it is highly improbable that any one individual will have all of the qualities that make for excellence in all four roles.

Since the perfectly effective manager does not exist, studies focused on the traits that will enable *individual leaders* to manage an organization are barking up the wrong tree. In studying the traits of the leader, they ignore the complementary traits of the followers.

What we should be looking at is *managerial teams.* Since no one person can be a **PAEI**, it must be a combination of persons, a "managerial mix," that creates it. This mix is composed of people who are neither mismanagers nor **PAEIs**—they are human.

The fact that a person is not a **PAEI** does not mean that he must be a mismanager. The difference between a manager and a mismanager is one of degree. A person with no dashes in his code—that is, a person who is capable of performing all four managerial roles even if he cannot excel in all of them—is a potentially good and useful manager without being a **PAEI.** What is needed, then, is persons who can perform all of the roles, albeit with different degrees of excellence, and also work well with others as part of a managerial team (see Chapter 9).

What roles a person will have to perform will depend on the organization, the task that is being managed, and the prevailing conditions. It will also depend on what the other members of the managerial mix are capable of doing. One would also expect different demands to exist at different stages of an organization's development. How the organization's behavior changes over time is presented in Chapter 8.

SUMMARY OF THE TEXTBOOK MANAGER STYLE

The Person's Style

Exclusive role: All roles—producer, administrator, entrepreneur, and integrator.

How he excels: Facilitating individual and organizational growth.

Predominant behavior: Initiating, innovating, integrating, systematically delegating, developing himself and organization, predicting and adapting.

Focus of attention: Organizational survival in the long run.

Most distinctive personality traits: Mature, assertive, self-actualized, self-confident, flexible, analytical, action-oriented, communicative, sensitive to other people's needs and capable of integrating those needs with the needs of the organization.

Appraises himself by: How well the company will succeed in the long run and how well the team works together.

Typical complaints: He discourages complaining, encourages constructive suggestions.

Decision making: Participative, strategic, shared, proactive.

If he has free time: He will listen and think before acting, plan for the future.

He prefers to hire: Those who will produce, advance the organization, cooperate, be team members; people like himself.

Subordinates

Subordinates' style: Varies, but all are team members.

Subordinates are promoted: If they are of managerial quality, create results by planning and organizing their work, are creative and constructively critical, are good team members.

What subordinates get praised for: Process and results contribution to the organization.

Subordinates do not inform him about: No fear of reporting anything, including failures.

Dysfunctional behavior of subordinates: Easily observable and constructively treated.

Time Management, Staff Meetings, and Managerial Practice

He arrives at and leaves work: Regularly and as needed to contribute any necessary inputs for decision making.

Subordinates arrive and leave: As needed by the job to be done.

Frequency and advance notice of staff meetings: Regular and/or impromptu, as needed.

Staff meeting attendance: By those who have something to contribute to the solution or can benefit from learning about the solution.

Staff meeting agenda: Strategic, proactive planning.

Who talks at staff meetings: Anyone with a significant, relevant contribution; the others listen.

Training practices: Learn from one another.

Attitude toward systematic management: Fully acknowledges its value and practices it.

Attitude toward conflict: Makes a statesmanlike attempt to resolve it constructively.

Attitude toward change: Introduces it cautiously, selectively, and systematically.

Focus and type of information he cherishes: Information located where it is needed; shares information whenever possible.

Focus of creativity: Constructive, action-oriented; creative activity encouraged.

Attitude toward Other Managers

Attitude toward all types of mismanagers (**P---, -A--, --E-, ---I, ----, PA--, P-E-, P--I, PAE-, P-EI, -AE-, -A-I, -AEI, --EI**): Will develop or change.

Attitude toward all types of managers (**Paei, pAei, paEi, paeI, paei, PAei, PaEi, PaeI, PAEi, PAeI, PAEI, pAeI, paEI,** etc.): Will nourish and integrate.

NOTES

1. Other authors who oppose one-rule man include: Harold J. Leavitt, *Managerial Psychology* (Chicago: University of Chicago

Press, 1964), pp. 297–99: Joel E. Ross and Michael J. Kami, *Corporate Management in Crisis: Why the Mighty Fall* (Englewood Cliffs, N.J.: Prentice-Hall, 1973); and Peter F. Drucker, *The Effective Executive*, 1st ed. (New York: Harper & Row, 1967).

2. David McClelland, *The Achieving Society* (Princeton, N.J.: Van Nostrand, 1961).

3. On the need for achievement, see also John W. Atkinson, *An Introduction to Motivation* (Princeton, N.J.: Van Nostrand, 1964), pp. 240–68; and Heinz Heckhausen, *The Anatomy of Achievement Motivation* (New York: Academic Press, 1967), pp. 64–65.

4. On the need for power, see also David C. McClelland, "The Two Faces of Power"; McClelland and Robert Watson, "Power Motivation and Risk Taking Behavior"; and David G. Winter, "The Need for Power"; all in *Human Motivation*, ed. McClelland and Robert S. Steele (Princeton, N.J.: General Learning Press, 1973).

5. On the need for affiliation, see also: Richard E. Boyatzis, "Affiliation Motivation," in McClelland and Steele, *Human Motivation*.

6. David C. McClelland and David H. Burnham, "Power Is a Great Motivator," *Harvard Business Review* 54, no. 2 (March–April 1976), pp. 100–110.

7. Ibid., pp. 100–101.

8. Robert Blake and Jane Mouton, *The Managerial Grid* (Houston: Gulf Publishing, 1964).

9. Paul Hersey and K. H. Blanchard, *Management of Organizations* (Englewood Cliffs, N.J.: Prentice-Hall, 1972).

10. Peter F. Drucker, *Management: Tasks, Responsibilities, Practices* (New York: Harper & Row, 1973), p. 616.

11. Joel Ross and Michael Kami, *Corporate Management in Crisis: Why the Mighty Fall* (Englewood Cliffs, N.J.: Prentice-Hall, 1973).

Chapter 8

Organizational Styles

THE ORGANIZATIONAL LIFE CYCLE

paEi	Courtship	Courting the idea of an organization
Paei	Birth	The Infant organization
PaEi	Childhood	The Go-go organization
pAEi	Teenage years	The Adolescent organization
PAEi	Maturity	The Prime organization
PAeI	Middle age	The Stable organization
pAeI	Twilight years	The Aristocratic organization
–A–i	Retirement	Early Bureaucracy
–A––	Senility	Bureaucracy
––––	Death	Bankruptcy

ORGANIZATIONAL PASSAGES[1]

Thus far, I have described managerial styles and their effects on subordinates and on organizations. In this chapter, I discuss *organizational styles*. An organization that can be expected to act in the same way under the same conditions has a style. An example is a "bureaucracy." Clients of a bureaucracy know that they cannot expect a decision for a long time and that the red tape will be endless.

People, products, markets, and even societies have life cycles. They are born, grow, mature, arrive at old age, and die. At every stage, phase, or passage of their lives they have a typical pattern of behavior, or style. The behavior of organizations will be described using the **PAEI** code (see Figure 1).

The Courtship Stage (paEi)

At the Courtship stage there is no organization yet. The founders are basically dreaming about what they might do. There is excitement; promises are made which later might appear to have been made irresponsibly, without sufficient regard for the facts. The excitement is accompanied by frantic activity. One gets a sense that the founders are falling into a trance. They seem to be looking for an audience to listen to

FIGURE 1
PAEI Organizational Life Cycle

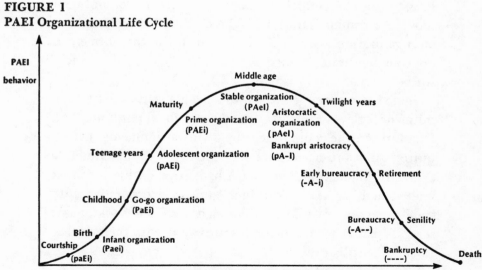

how great it's going to be. They appear to be in love with their idea—hypnotizing themselves.

It appears as if this process of "selling the idea" to others is actually reinforcing the founders' own commitment to it. The accumulation of energy, love, and commitment to the idea is an indispensable ingredient if the founders are to build an organization from scratch. It is analogous to the way a pilot revs the engines before taking off; he builds up a tremendous forward thrust while standing still.

When people present ideas for establishing a new organization, their "noise level" should be tested: How honest-to-goodness committed are they? Is their commitment based on rational cost-benefit thinking? Or is it an emotional, value-loaded commitment and thus somewhat fanatical? The bigger the task, the more zealous should be the commitment. The difficulty of establishing an organization can be evaluated by the complexity of putting it together, by the promptness of positive feedback (How long will it take before positive results will come in?), and by the degree of innovation necessary (How many existing "sacred cows" must be slaughtered?). What causes an organization to be born is not just the initial idea, but also the commitment behind it, and the commitment should be commensurate with the difficulty of making such an organization work in the long run. If the commitment is not commensurate, it is expended on the "labor pains" and a stillborn organization is delivered.

Some ideas never give birth to an organization. The commitment fizzles out the first time there is a real test under fire. One can test the commitment by giving assignments that require significant sacrifice. One of the deans of the Graduate School of Management at UCLA had a sign on his door that read something like: "Warning: I might incorporate *you* to implement your own ideas." The sign itself, I was told, made several creative faculty members turn away with their suggestions while still at the door.

Infant Organization (Paei)

There are several signs that indicate when the organization is "born." There is a payroll to be met, a place is rented, or the founder resigns his or her previous job.

Birth does not come without pain. The commitment is tested and *real* sacrifices have to be made. When it finally happens there is a definite change in the style of behavior. The frenzy of creating ideas and the excitement about what will be accomplished are discouraged. The entrepreneur role (**E**) declines rapidly and is replaced by the producer role (**P**, produce results). At this stage of the organization's life, what counts is not what one thinks but what one *does*. The question the founder is asked or the question he asks his employees is "What have you *done?* Did you sell, produce, or get anything *done?*" The dreamers of yesterday are shunned and discouraged. "I have no time to think," will be the typical complaint of the manager of the Infant organization. "There is just too much I have to *do*."

The Infant organization has few policies, systems, procedures, or even budgets. The whole administrative system might be written on the back of an old envelope in the founder's vest pocket. Most people in this organization, including the president, are out selling—doing. There are few staff meetings. The organization is highly centralized and best described as a one-person show.

The Infant organization rushes ahead at full speed, but without knowledge of its strengths and weaknesses. It is like a baby who hits instead of touches because he still does not know how much pressure to exert. Similarly, the Infant organization makes excessive commitments in the mistaken belief that it can keep them. Later its members realize that the schedule is already full and that they have to postpone delivery dates. If a product does arrive on time, parts may be missing or the service manual may be unavailable. However, the organization is responsive to client complaints. Its members try to do something abut them, usually by working on weekends and holidays.

The Infant organization is very personal. Everybody is on a first-name basis and there are hardly any ranks. The organization has no system for hiring or for evaluating performance. People are hired when needed because they impress those who hire them. They are usually asked to start working right away, because the Infant organization is late in hiring the help it needs: It wants tomorrow the people it needed yesterday. People get promoted if they produce results or if they know how to exert pressure on their boss.

This organization is like an infant: it requires its "milk" (operating capital) every so often. It is also very vulnerable. It usually has no managerial depth, that is, no one else capable of leading if the founder dies. It has no track record or experience, so a mistake in product design, sales, service, or financial planning can have fatal repercussions. Such mistakes have a high probability of occurring since the organization is usually a "shoestring operation" with no capital to afford the complementary team that is necessary to make well-balanced business decisions. The complementary staff does not have to be made up of managers. For an Infant organization a "team" of only the president (PaEi) and a secretary (pAeI) might be effective.

The organization cannot remain an infant forever, however. The time and emotions necessary to keep an Infant organization alive are often far beyond the economic returns. Eventually the "pride of ownership" wilts in the harsh light of reality. The founder/owner is exhausted and gives up. In this case the death of the organization is not imminent and sudden, as in previous cases; it is a prolonged process with an ever-decreasing level of emotional commitment to the enterprise manifested by constantly increasing complaints about how bad it is.

The Infant organization is so busy doing that managers have little chance to think and analyze the horizons—to identify opportunities for growth and expansion. They have a tendency to miss long-range opportunities because of short-term tactical pressures. If an organization does not move to the next stage—that is, if the dreams do not catch on and move the organization ahead—it simply burns itself out. Many small enterprises that never see the large picture go bankrupt, or remain small and hardworking but never get anywhere. Those that survive are probably subsidized by the owner, who takes less money home than he would take if he were an employee—that is, he may be paying for the pride of ownership.

What keeps Infant organizations alive is the total dedication of the founder; his "hovering hen" behavior often enables the Infant organization to overcome threats to its existence. This dedication, however, may later become a barrier to organizational growth. The founder may resent the fact that the organization has grown beyond his capability to control it. His efforts to maintain control may then either destroy the organization or limit its ability to grow further.

The emergence of the entrepreneurial spirit (E) is crucial for the growth of the Infant organization. If E emerges, the organization may move on to the next stage of development. Entrepreneurial horizons will emerge in Infant organizations if managers can pull themselves out of their day-to-day activities and "dream" again: Where are we going? What can be done with our product? What are our goals? How do we compare with our competitors? How far can we expect to go?

The emergence of E requires risk-taking and vision. Some organizations never realize their potential, since the opportunity to do so does not present itself in a manner that managers can easily recognize. They may be so busy producing the mousetrap in the basement that they are unaware of the opportunities that exist on the street. Someone who is not trapped in doing and who has vision must actually push the decision makers to realize those oportunities. This process of developing a vision is painful because the Infant organization is extremely oriented to the short run.

On the other hand, an organization that succeeds in developing an entrepreneurial vision and is willing to follow up on it will become a **PaEi**, a Go-go organization.

The Go-Go Stage (PaEi)

This stage is analogous to the baby who can finally see and focus. The whole world opens before its eyes, and everything looks like an opportunity. Only in retrospect do managers realize that some opportunities are threats that should have been avoided.

A Go-go organization has the same producer (**P**) orientation as an Infant organization, but it also has a vision. It moves fast and makes decisions often intuitively and without experience. It can lose virtually overnight what it painstakingly earned in a whole year. It tends to get into a Vietnam-type of endeavor—"easy in, but very hard out."

Almost every opportunity seems to become a priority. At one meeting of a Go-go organization's managers, they were asked to list individually the organizational priorities as they perceived them. When the suggestions were put together there turned out to be 173 different priorities!

In the Go-go organization, space is tight because the organization is growing so fast. The Go-go organization may have a whole array of people with different capabilities and incentive systems. Since it has no systems or established policies, its people are hired at different times under different agreements. Some are highly qualified and some might be hangers-on, but the Go-go organization doesn't have the time or the attention span to weed out the incompetents. There is hardly any training.

In the Go-go organization, people share responsibilities. They work together, and there is very little specialization. In one such organization, the president was also the chief buyer, the top salesperson, and the designer. The salespersons also did some buying, and the accountant was a part-time office manager.

In the Go-go organization, marketing is equated with selling. Basically, there is no marketing strategy. The organization frequently plunges into new opportunities and tries them out. However, the Go-go organization's interest span is short. Managers jump from task to task, trying to cover all bases. If the organization has no focus, it may go bankrupt. Unless it develops some policies about what *not* to do rather than what *else* to do, and unless it develops a cohesive sense of direction that is independent of its founder's, it can suffer another fate: the founder's trap.

The Founder's Trap. While the motherlike commitment of the founder is necessary for the survival of the Infant organization, it becomes dysfunctional after the Go-go stages. The loving embrace becomes a stranglehold. The founder refuses to depersonalize policies and institutionalize his leadership, that is, to establish some workable systems, procedures, and policies that do not require his personal judgment. To avoid the founder's trap, the administrator role (**A**) has to grow in importance in the organization. (See Figure 2.)

FIGURE 2
Premature Mortality

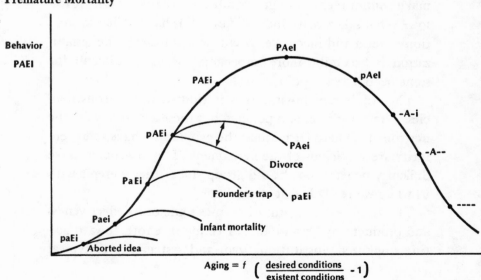

The Adolescent Organization (pAEi)

When the administrative role (**A**) increases in importance, more time is spent on planning and coordinating meetings. A computer is installed, a consultant or salaried administrator is brought in, training programs are developed, and labor policies are established. All these cost money and take time away from producing results (**P**) in the short run. Top management might refuse to allow the decline in **P**. In that case, the organizational climate changes and adversely affects the entrepreneurial spirit (**E**); people's growth aspirations are depressed. They spend the time required for planning the "how" at the expense of analyzing the "why."

When the growth in **A** is at the expense of **E**, I call it "premature aging." The organization loses its vision. In a "healthy" adolescence the growth in **A** is at the expense of **P**. In other words, management consciously decides to spend a year or so "entrenching," or getting organized. The result could be that the time that was spent on selling is now spent on getting organized. But at the same time, the long-range goals are not lost.

The Adolescent organization is full of conflicts. It must make commitments and get stabilized. What style will it follow? What salary scale and policies will it have? What promotion criteria and incentive systems will it foster? The organization is becoming more impersonal, which is difficult for some people to accept.

The Adolescent organization is riddled with inconsistencies. There are rules and policies, but these are mostly for the newcomers. There are cliques; the people who have some seniority are suspicious of the newcomers. The newcomers have difficulty penetrating the old group since "they weren't with us when we really had it rough."

The Adolescent organization loses some of its effectiveness and productivity because it is directing its efforts toward getting organized, institutionalized, and systemized. A typical complaint is that instead of selling, people are having meetings all day.

However, an organization needs to structure and institutionalize itself (depersonalize itself) in order to grow further. If an organization cannot create a system for itself, or if confusion causes it to lose too many people, it will not grow. It will probably revert to the Go-go stage and may regress even further to become a stabilized, small Infant organization (if it doesn't fold).

It is difficult to decide to "cool off" the growth rate for a while so that a new plateau can be achieved in the long run. If the organization is a partnership, cliques often develop and the conflict becomes evident. One P-oriented group would like to stop those "endless meetings," stop spending money on all those consultants, and get back to work. "What really counts in our business," they say, "is selling, and not which computer you have or the quality of your policy manuals." Another group disagrees vehemently and claims that the investment in organizational systems and overhead is necessary for the long-term growth of the company.

If the Adolescent organization is a partnership, this is the time when the partners might get "divorced." The original commitment built during Courtship was consumed by day-to-day fighting for survival and by now might be depleted to zero. A period of retrospective analysis is in order. They re-evaluate: Do our present and future activities reflect what we want in life, from each other and from the organization?

The partners are experienced from being on the firing line, and have strong feelings about which frontiers they would like to fight on. If there is a split in the partnership, one group continues in the PAei mode—the conservative, less ambitious route—and the other becomes the "unfulfilled entrepreneurs" (paEi), who look for another opportunity to start all over again.

If the organization sails safely through Adolescence without losing its high aspirations (E), it may enter the Prime stage of the organizational life cycle. (A later section of this chapter describes how to maintain a healthy growth.)

The Prime Organization (PAEi)

The Prime organization knows its annual goals, and it has a results orientation (P). Furthermore, it has plans and procedures to achieve efficiency and to repeat its successful operations (A). At the same time, it has not lost its awareness of what is happening "out there"; it knows the opportunities and threats. It has long-term goals and strategies, too. While in the Go-go organization the rate of growth in sales and profits is helter-skelter, these rates are stable and predictable in the Prime organization. One knows that the quarterly predictions will be met, and their performance sets the standards for the industry.

The Aging Process. Staying in the Prime stage is not assured, however. It depends on the aspirations of top management. The aspirations of the managerial group in charge of strategic decision making affects the style (i.e., aging) of the organization. If management aspires to more than what it has achieved, growth is still possible. If this managerial group is satisfied with existing conditions, however, aspirations are not a source of energy for change, because.

$$\text{Aspiration rate} = \frac{\text{Desired conditions}}{\text{Expected conditions}} - 1$$

The level of aspirations is affected mainly by three factors: (1) the mental age of people in strategic power positions, (2) the relative market share, and (3) the functionality of the organizational structure. (See Figure 3.)

Age. At a certain age, which is different for different persons, people start looking at the time left in their lives and wish to enjoy rather than further build up their accomplishments. This state of mind is often correlated with age. It is assumed that a young person is willing to invest time and

FIGURE 3
Organizational Passages

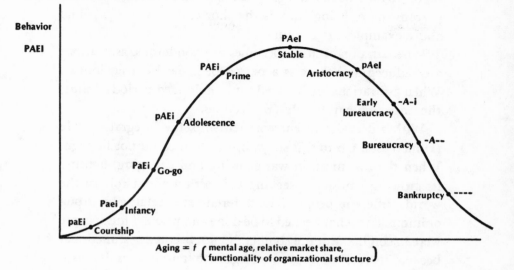

$$\text{Aging} = f \left(\begin{array}{l} \text{mental age, relative market share,} \\ \text{functionality of organizational structure} \end{array} \right)$$

energy in building something up because his desired condition is different from the existing situation. The older person learns to live with the present, accepting it as the desired.

Market Share.   When a company arrives at a stage where further growth is not economically, politically, or legally viable, the existing state of affairs is accepted as the desired.

Functionality of the Organizational Structure.   As the organization grows from Infant to Prime, new people, products, markets, and departments are added. Often this is done under pressure, considering tactical rather than strategic factors. The end result can be a ponderous and confusing organizational structure with ambiguity about authority and the hierarchy. (People wear several "hats" at the same time, some of which have built-in conflicts.) The organization does not reflect the needs of the market or of the technology. One organization (with $200 million in sales) divides Canada to report to two different U.S. regions, one headquartered in Boston and the other in Buffalo, thus ignoring the sociopolitical and language differences. ("That was how they penetrated the Canadian market 30 years ago.") In another company, Mexican divisions report to the Louisiana region headquartered in New Orleans. ("From there, flying time is the shortest," I was told.) The above examples are not unique.

When an organization becomes too ponderous, aspirations are reduced and there is a period of inward entrenchment. When aspirations are lowered for a prolonged period of time, the entrepreneurial role (E) declines.

With a decrease in entrepreneurship, the integrating role (I) increases. Up to this stage, integration could not be high. When the organization was growing and changing, fighting its growing pains, and seeking a direction and a role in the world, different people had different and relatively strong opinions as to what needed to be done and when. Thus, people were in conflict. But the conflict did not become dysfunctional because its resolution produced growth, and the results justified the emotional investment. When E declines and the sense of urgency and desire to grow and change decline, when the organization can start enjoying the fruits of yesterday's efforts, then it can afford inward orientation to improve interpersonal relations. That is when the organization becomes mature.

Middle Age: The Stable Organization (PAeI)

As the entrepreneurial role (E) declines, the organization mellows. It is still results-oriented and well organized. Also, there is less conflict than in the previous stages: the decline in E permits the growth of I. There is less to fight about and less threat from aggressive colleagues. In such an organization, there is increasing adherence to precedence and reliance on what has worked before. By this time, the organization has usually achieved a stable position in the marketplace. It develops a sense of security which may be unfounded in the long run. Creativity and a sense of urgency can still be noticed from time to time, but they are short-lived. Orderliness prevails and conservative approaches are adopted in order not to endanger what has been so painstakingly put together.

In the stable organization, people spend more time in the office with each other than with the clients or the salesmen, as they used to. Disagreements that before were quite vocal are now expressed with a sheepish grin, as if to say, "It's not really that important." The sense of urgency is no longer there. People are willing to prolong a meeting for another hour. When a new meeting is announced, the protests that were loud and clear before ("Where the hell do I find the time for another meeting?") are few and rare. The climate also becomes more formal. New ideas are listened to, but the excitement is not there.

At the Stable stage several changes take place. One is a change in budgets. Resources for research are reduced in favor of development spending. Similarly, budgets for marketing research are reduced to boost the profitability of the company. Management development is substituted with management training.

Short-range profitability considerations take over. Thus, the second change is a power shift within the organization. The finance people become more important than the marketing or the engineering (research and development) people. Return on investment becomes a sacred cow. Measurements replace the conceptual "soft" thinking. The organization takes fewer risks and has fewer incentives to maintain its vision.

The organization is still growing, but the underlying causes of decline are already present—its entrepreneurial spirit (E) has dwindled.

When things stop growing, they begin to die.

Charles Gow

The Twilight Years: The Aristocratic Organization (pAeI)

The decline in entrepreneurial spirit (**E**) has a long-range effect: eventually the **P** role, the orientation to achieve and produce results, declines. As people dream less about the long run, their achievement drive for the short run inevitably suffers too. They produce results, but the "stretching" is not there. The short-term, relatively assured results take over, and the seeds of mediocrity are planted.

The decline in result orientation (**P**) creates a new style of organizational behavior The climate in the Aristocratic organization is relatively stale. What counts in this organization is "not what you did and why you did it, but *how* you did it. As long as you lie low long enough and make no waves, you can survive and even get promoted regardless of what you have produced."

The Aristocratic organization can be distinguished from other organizations by the clothes managers wear, by the mode of their speech and what they talk about, how they address one another, and where they meet.

Managerial Uniforms. In the Infant organization dress has no meaning. "As long as you can produce results you can wear your shirt inside out—who cares?" said one executive. In the Go-go organization ties and jackets appear but are not required. By the time the organization is Aristocratic, managers dress as for a funeral or wedding. They seem to be trying to outdo each other in the amount they spend on suits. Three-piece suits are *de rigueur,* the darker the better.

Mode of Addressing Each Other. In the Infant organization nicknames are frequently used. In the Adolescent stage the way they refer to each other is unprintable. In the Aristocratic organization, however, last names are used exclusively. During meetings "Mr. Such-and-Such" will be used even though the people have known each other for years and address each other by first names outside the meeting room.

In Aristocratic organizations, form counts very much.

There are unspoken, unwritten rules about how and when to address anyone. There are rituals: who can go to which washroom or coffee room or eat at which table. There are different elevators for the coolies and the brass.

Mode of Speech. In the Courtship stage people speak vaguely about what they think and feel. They repeat and contradict themselves, are easily annoyed, and show their sensitivities. In the Infant organization the mode of speech is short and direct, even somewhat offensive in its honesty. It is a sharp departure from the romantic era of Courtship. In the Adolescent stage conversation is a mixture of the two— direct and emotional, full of contradictions, but very opinionated.

In the Prime organization people measure what they say and they speak slowly as if verifying the weight and the impact of what they say. They use visual aids selectively. By the time the organization is Aristocratic, the mode of delivery is the essence—the medium is the message. Managers over-

"Senior Vice-President Buffington reporting, sir. Requests permission to advance and be recognized."

Drawing by Lorenz; © 1976
The New Yorker Magazine, Inc.

use visual aids, and in meetings people hedge when they talk. They use endless double negatives and qualifiers. Listening to such a meeting, one wonders what they *really* said. The transcript of an Aristocratic organization's meeting is often a mumbo jumbo of hints, insinuations, and veiled suggestions.

It is a mutual admiration society, too, where people do not make waves although "the enemy is at the gates." In an Aristocratic organization, clouds on the horizon and the first drops of rain do not engender a sense of urgency. On the contrary, such an organization behaves as if the problems are only temporary. "It will all go away sooner or later." This phenomenon might be termed the "Finzi-Contini syndrome."

The Garden of the Finzi-Continis is a motion picture in which an aristocratic Italian-Jewish family is depicted just prior to World War II. When the Fascists were starting to persecute Jews, the Finzi-Continis refused to believe that anything serious was going to happen. "We have been here too long," they said. "They need us. We are one of the most distinguished families of Italy." They continued to play tennis behind the high walls of their retreat and eat in chandeliered dining rooms (i.e., business as usual). While each person in the family was deeply worried individually, as a group they would not express their worries. They were paralyzed by the admiration for their past and the determination not to upset the present.

The Aristocratic business organization behaves in a similar fashion. First of all, they usually have beautiful and expensive buildings, with space wasted as if it cost nothing. They are individually worried about the company and its future, but in a formal meeting they do not express any of these doubts.

When one faces managers collectively and points to the threats from competition, they are prone to reply: "Don't worry. We have been here long enough. They need us. We have a name, a tradition, a know-how. . . ." But individually they agree with the consultant: the situation is bad and "someone" (usually someone other than the complainer) should do something. In one organization managers even said explicitly, "We don't like to compete. We would rather serve." This means to repeat tomorrow what they did yesterday.

Where to Meet. While the Infant organization operates out of a small room somewhere, and in the Go-go organization there is not enough space for all the employees to sit down, in the Aristocratic organization space is plentiful. The president's office is large, with a conference table, sofa, and small chairs. The entrance to the building is spacious and there are wide corridors, deep carpeting, and many meeting rooms.

The board of directors' room is characteristic of Aristocracy, too. In the Infant organization the board meets anywhere, anytime, sometimes on the train on the way to work or during breakfast. In the Go-go organization, the meeting is in the president's office around his table. In the Adolescent organization the meetings take place in various rooms, corridors, or locations, depending on which clique is involved. In the Prime organization, however, there is a specially designated room for meetings. The lights are bright, and the tables are in a U-shape. Flip charts from the last meeting are still taped to the wall. It is somewhat messy but alive. By the time the organization is Aristocratic, the board room has heavy drapes. The lights are low, and there is a long table with very soft chairs around it. Life-size paintings of the founders look down on the participants. The whole setup is formal and tends to make one complaint: "Don't make waves!" While outside the room people may be concerned about the market situation, inside the room the tone changes. Reports are given, and no threatening questions are asked. Business as usual continues.

The Aristocratic organization is usually the founder of the industry association and often the only one that truly respects the industry agreements. The new, aggressive competitor is despised as being unethical, although it is making progress legitimately in taking away markets.

Not being (**P**) result-oriented (what) or (**E**) entrepreneurial-oriented (why), the organization starts losing revenues and markets. In its budgets instead of allocating for the **P** and **E** roles like marketing research and research and development, money is allocated to **A** and **I** roles—more control systems, bigger and better computers, and more training programs rather than developmental programs.

To improve its looks (revenue), the Aristocratic organization goes through a "face lift." It increases the prices of its product. In the short run its revenues go up, but in the long run the quantity sold decreases. At that time, in order to continue to maintain a respectable revenue, prices are raised again. "They feed the dog with its own tail," said a disgusted executive.

Mergers and Acquisitions. The Aristocratic organization is cash-heavy. There are few demands for investments from its internal sources. The organizational climate of accepting the present as the desired is stronger than the aspirations of any individual within the organization. Thus, few, if any, risk-taking endeavors are proposed. With its cash, the Aristocratic organization seeks avenues for growth other than internal ones. It may buy growth companies—most frequently the Go-go ones. "They have a future and they are not expensive yet."

The reverse can happen, too. The Aristocratic organization, being cash-heavy, is a prime object for takeover, most probably by a Go-go organization, which in its eagerness to grow has no limits to its appetite.

In both cases the "marriage" is not easily consummated. When the Aristocratic organization buys the Go-go, the latter might feel suffocated. What made it exciting and vigorous was its flexibility, its speed of decision making. Many decisions were made intuitively; it had little place or respect for ritual. The Aristocratic organization is just the opposite. It requires budgets in a certain form by a certain time with certain details—all of which the Go-go group finds stifling.

When the Go-go acquires the Aristocratic organization, it is like the small fish that swallowed the whale. Digestion takes a very long time. The Go-go finds itself over its head with the problems of the Aristocratic organization. Milking the cash out of the Aristocratic organization does not make it a Prime organization; it only accentuates its decline. The Go-go group introduces sudden and forceful waves of change. It sometimes paralyzes the Aristocrats with fear, making a workable merger even more difficult. The Go-go might lose its growth momentum and orientation for several years while it is trying to digest its latest prey. If the Aristocracy is very old and the Go-go cannot easily solve the inherent problems of old age, the Aristocratic organization consumes all the time of the Go-go executives and both might go under.

Those who seek to reform an Aristocratic organization from within often do so at the price of their careers. The organization will eventually force them out, even though it benefited from their efforts. Thus, the creative employees that the organization needs most for its survival either leave or become useless and discouraged.

The Bankrupt Aristocracy (pA–I)

The stable organization's loss of entrepreneurship (E) is reflected in the declining production (P) of the Aristocratic organization. If the Aristocratic organization does not do anything significant about this situation, its E will disappear altogether and its P will be hardly noticeable. It will arrive at the stage of Bankrupt Aristocracy (pA–I).

At that stage, products are out of date. The clients know it, the salespeople know it, and even the president knows it, but nobody does anything about it. Complaints are filed. Meetings are not held, or they are short and useless. Everyone is waiting for the first shoe to fall. Many people leave the organization in an effort to save their necks. Those who cannot leave because they do not have attractive opportunities accuse the deserters of disloyalty.

There is a sense of doom, but at the same time the company spends money as if it were going out of style. What's even worse, the money is spent on economically useless purposes—gold medals for obscure achievements or poorly attended seminars in plush hotels. The company might even build an expensive and unnecessary new building. Managers spend on form as if it affects the content.

The Early Bureaucracy (–A–i)

If entrepreneurship (**E**) and production (**P**) are low for long enough—which means that for a prolonged period of time there is neither a desire for change nor a results orientation—the artificial "face lifts" of raising prices eventually have a negative effect. Finally, the day of reckoning arrives: the demand becomes inelastic and the increase in prices reduces the total revenues; the revenues and market share are steadily falling. At that time the mutual admiration society is dissolved and the knives are unceremoniously exposed. The fight for *personal* survival begins.

There is one main variable that distinguishes the Aristocratic organization from the Early Bureaucratic organization: managerial paranoia. In the Aristocratic group there is a silence before the storm. People smile, are friendly, and handle each other with kid gloves. When in the Early Bureaucracy the bad results are finally evident, instead of, fighting competition as they should, managers start fighting each other—and there are no gloves anymore, just bare knuckles. A ritual of human sacrifice starts: *someone* has to take the blame and be the sacrificial lamb. So every year or every few quarters someone is blamed for the adverse conditions of the company and gets fired. The paranoia stems from the fact that no one really knows who will be selected to assume the blame next. So they watch each other with suspicion. To survive, people circulate far-fetched explanations as to what is happening. For instance, if the sales manager decides to give a discount, the other executives do not explain it in rational terms by referring to competitive conditions; they attribute it to a Machiavellian strategy on the part of the sales manager to discredit the marketing department, and to expose the incompetence of the marketing vice president, and so on, and so on.

This behavior accentuates the decline. Managers fight each other, spending most of the time turned inward, building cliques and coalitions which are constantly changing, depending on how different people interpret the power bases. Their creative abilities are not directed to creating better products or developing a better marketing strategy, but to insuring personal survival by eliminating and discrediting each other. Thus, their performance declines further, making them even more paranoid. Since the better people are feared, they either are fired or leave. This process continues as a vicious cycle and the end result is full Bureaucracy.

Senility: Bureaucracy (–A––)

In Early Bureaucracy one could get something done if one knew the "right person"; thus the small i. In full-blown Bureaucracy very little that is meaningful gets done. The organization acts like a broken record, repeating the same phrase over and over again. The typical response to any question is "Wait" or "Someone will inform you soon," but there is no real answer. These managers are among the nicest to meet. They agree a lot, but nothing ever happens. There is no result orientation, no inclination to change, and no teamwork—only systems, forms, procedures, rules.

One of the most distinctive characteristics of a Bureaucracy is the worship of the written word. When a client or another executive asks for or suggests anything, the typical answer is: "Write to me about it."

Writing a letter to a Bureaucratic organization is, however, often a waste of time, paper, and stamps. It usually gets filed. In the files of one such organization was a letter threatening to sue unless the writer's complaint was handled soon. The letter had been stamped "Received on . . ." and filed. Asked why it had not been answered, the file clerk said that some needed information was missing.

A Bureaucratic organization is disorganized. Each of the client's efforts to obtain a decision is met with a request for another document. The Bureaucratic organization does not ask in advance for everything that is needed so that the client can prepare it all. Instead of showing its entire hand, the Bureaucratic organization shows one card at a time.

This behavior arises because no one in the Bureaucratic organization knows what should be done. Everyone has only a piece of the necessary information, and *the client* is expected to put all the pieces together. Employees do not know the salary policies; salespeople do not know the marketing strategy; marketing people do not know the company plans; finance does not know what sales are expected; production does not know how well the product is being received; customers do not know where to get effective attention. The customer service department often consists of a switchboard operator whose job is to listen, record complaints, and answer them with a letter: "We will do our best to. . . ."

This organization attempts to isolate itself from the environment. It is connected to the external world through only a very narrow channel. There are many examples of narrow channels, such as only one telephone line. To get through, a person has to spend hours or days trying. If one goes in person to the organization, there is a request that all people go first to one window which is open for only a few hours a day. A person might spend a day just waiting in line to find out where to go. If one writes to this organization it might take months to get an answer, and then it will be a form letter that frequently does not address the main issues. Often even this does not happen; the correspondence or file may simply be lost.

To get things done in such an organization, a client has to do the leg work himself. He has to go from office to office to find out what, where, and when. It seems as if the "nervous system" of the organization has broken down. The left hand does not know what the right hand is doing. One department rejects what another one requests. "They show you one card at a time, never the whole hand." The client is lost, puzzled, and frustrated.

How does an old person function when some organs are not operational? Usually he is put in a protective environment (hospital) and on different machines that bypass the nonworking organs, such as an artificial kidney. The same analogy seems to apply to the Bureaucratic organization.

Business organizations that *have* to work with a Bureaucracy usually have a special department whose full-time task is to provide the bypass system. They have different names for these departments. In some organizations they are called forthrightly "government relations." In others they are disguised as "public relations." These departments get to know the inner workings of the government agency and then split their responsibilities. Mr. A will work with undersecretary Y; Ms. B with bureau director Z; etc. Since Y and Z might not agree or know what to do together, A and B decide what they want and get Y and Z organized to function. Business organizations spend millions of dollars annually just to find out what government agencies want and when and how they want it.

Bureaucracies are kept alive by the monopoly they have on certain activities, the captive audience that is forced by law to "buy" their services, and the external bypass systems that the clients create. "Pulling the plug" would put many of these Bureaucracies out of business, and the taxpayers re-

volt of 1978 is one way to do that. (Note: I am not predicting
that cutting taxes will enhance the administrative "health"
of government agencies; it would rather speed up the death
of some of them.)

The health of a full-fledged Bureaucracy is very delicate.
What appears to be a dangerous monster may actually be relatively easy to destroy. Bureaucracies that seem to be a hard to
change monstrosity may actually be "rotten to the core" and
on the brink of bankruptcy. Any sudden change will do them
in. Bureaucracies that have to reorganize overnight often do
not survive the effort. A new computer, for example, may
throw a Bureaucratic system into a spin. The old system keeps
running as if nothing had happened, and next to it is the new
computer system to which people pay little attention.

Bureaucratic organizations may survive a protracted coma.
This happens when they can operate in isolation from the
external environment. Examples of such organizations include monopolies and government agencies. Unions or political pressures may keep them alive since no one dares to eliminate an agency that provides employment. This results in a
very expensive artificial prolongation of life. Death may take
years.

Death: Bankruptcy (————)

The most outstanding characteristic of organizational death
is the omnipresent agony of defeat. Those who were strong
enough to leave the organization left it a long time ago. Those
who remain are the weak, the uninformed, and the newcomers. Above all, they are the persons who had no choice.

Some members of the organization may recall "the good
old days" and try to analyze the reasons for the company's
failure; others just attribute it to hostile external forces, such
as government, labor, or an unscrupulous competitor. But
deep inside, most people realize that the organization has been
dying for a long time.

ANALYSIS AND PRESCRIPTION[2]

Up to maturity the organization operates on momentum (Area A in Figure 4). In its decline (Area B), it works on inertia.

Prior to maturation, an internal agent of change can facilitate organizational development. From maturity on (Area B) an external agent is necessary. I present this recommendation because it is easier to direct momentum than to change inertia. Up to maturity the organization is growing, and attempts to create change are not necessarily perceived as threats. Communication is usually open, and a person can be accepted and still do the necessary internal work of facilitating change. Furthermore, up to maturity (Area A) it is necessary to facilitate convergent thinking, which a trained person can do without making too many waves or threatening anyone's position. From maturity on, the need is to facilitate divergent thinking ("What else can be done?"). The facilitator has to build aspirations by increasing the perceived disparity between the desired and the expected (stimulate overt dissatis-

FIGURE 4
Momentum Versus Inertia

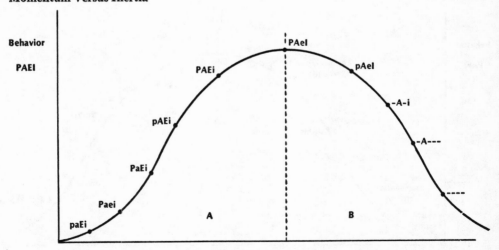

118

faction). He or she has to do it by changing the collective consciousness of the organization or, at least in the beginning, of the top managerial group. That means making waves. In such an organization the consultant must be an "insultant." If it is an internal person he is easily "calmed down" by being either fired or coopted by the peers or superiors.

Up to maturity (Area A), relatively speaking, everything is permitted unless specifically forbidden. From maturity on (Area B), relatively speaking, everything is forbidden unless specifically permitted. Furtherance of the organizational life cycle at Area B requires an independent, long-term, trusted external agent of change.

TREATMENT

Courtship

At this stage the best treatment is reality testing (Figure 5): confronting the idea person with some hard facts of life and checking his degree of dedication. There is nothing impossible

FIGURE 5
Treatment

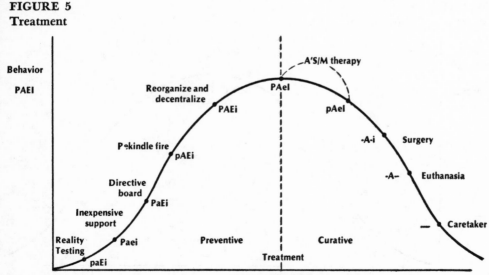

if one wants it badly enough. That, however, must be tested behaviorally.

Infancy

The Infant organization has no resources to pay any boards or hire external help. Thus, an advisory board composed of the lawyer, accountant, friends, and even employees can provide some of the know-how necessary. This should not be a board of directors because it might dampen the founder's commitment, which is necessary for the survival of the Infant organization. This commitment appears to me to be closely linked to the degree of freedom a person has.

Go-Go

The Go-go organization needs a strong, active, directive, and *external* board of directors to converge the Go-go group's thinking and deal with the typically sloppy planning of such an organization. This is a good and necessary beginning for the depersonalization of leadership and the institutionalization of some policies and plans in the organization. (Often the Go-go founder resents strong *external* boards. That might be the first sign that he is falling into the founder's trap.)

Adolescence

The recommended treatment at this stage, as opposed to the traditional approach of dealing with conflict, is to steer the organization away from interpersonal therapy (no sensitivity training, for instance) and to focus on the *task* at hand. So while a consultant might be invited because the partners cannot stand each other anymore, he should tend to ignore their demands and not judge the merits of their mutual accusations. He should rather facilitate planning sessions where the *future* is analyzed, threats and opportunities are identified, and goals and strategies designed. A new level of commitment *to the organization* needs to be built, trying to repeat the Courtship stage in a different form. The clearer the future plan and its components, the faster an administrative system will be established and the interpersonal relations stabilized. This does not mean that the partners will operate together as well as they did in the past, but the situation will be bearable. In the short run there is no love, but there are no hostilities either. When the future is clear, intervention with interpersonal dynamics and personal growth can increase the interpersonal commitment.

Prime

The Prime organization usually does not ask for external treatment. In their collective consciousness managers do not sense a need. They feel they are doing fine. This, however, is a trap because the Prime stage is the beginning of the end. The goal is not only to get to the Prime but to *remain* in Prime, and that requires measures to prevent aging. To do that, measures to maintain a high entrepreneurial orientation (E) need to be taken.

THE PROCESS OF REJUVENATION:
THE ADVISABILITY OF DECENTRALIZATION

In order to prevent organizational aging, an organization should decentralize itself while it is still in the Prime stage. During Early Bureaucracy, decentralization is often too strenuous for an organization that is not accustomed to creativity and change. Thus, a *new* life cycle must begin before an organization starts to decline (at the Prime stage). This process should continually repeat itself. A diagram of the pattern might look like that in Figure 6.

When an organization is decentralized, lower levels of the hierarchy are expected to show leadership, which involves the

FIGURE 6
Reorganization and Decentralization

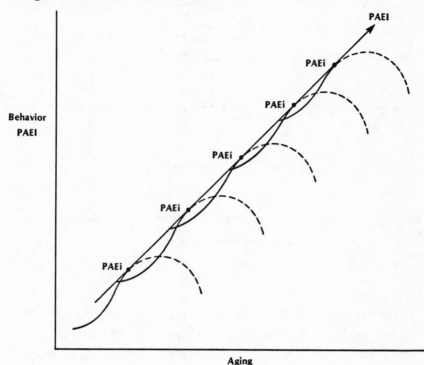

capability to take initiative (**E**) and to independently motivate and activate subordinates to follow those initiatives (**I**). Decentralization thus experientially develops **E** and **I**. The treatment of a Prime organization is, then, to reorganize for further decentralization. New entities (markets, products, profit centers) are positioned on the organization chart where they can get the necessary attention.

A healthy organization chart should show an "extended family," with the Aristocratic, Prime, and Infant organizations clearly identifiable. The **PAEI** model ties in well with the Boston Consulting Group model, in which the Aristocratic organization is the cash cow, and so on (see Figure 7).

The recommendation, then, is to periodically review the organizational chart, the market, and technological activities

FIGURE 7
Organizational Chart

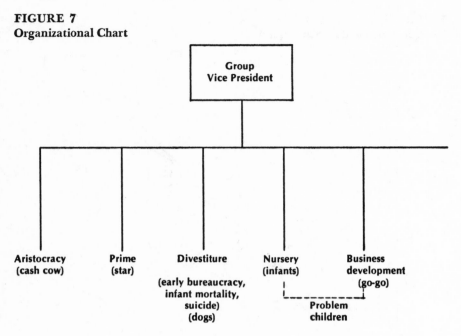

of the organization: Was anything "born" recently that needs to be "pulled out" and put into the nursery of business development? Has any Infant organization grown big enough to stand on its own as a profit center?

As a rule, one has to watch carefully that an Infant organization does not report to a Go-go or a Go-go report to an Aristocratic organization—a phenomenon I call "organizational incest." What is functional behavior for one could be suffocating for the other. The measures of success are different for each organizational unit depending on where it is in the life cycle.

With long-range planning, as suggested in Figure 6, one can plan the growth an organization might have and its future endeavors (markets, technologies, etc.), and future organizational charts can be derived from it. In that case, **PAEI** (all roles in capital letters) can be achieved (see Figure 6). The **E** and **I** roles are incompatible when the planning range is short.

Entrepreneurship and teamwork are at odds since entrepreneurs by nature are individualistic. Thus even in the Prime stage, I is a lowercase letter. With long-range planning, individual entrepreneurs can be integrated into the scheme of things and teamwork with individual creativity can be achieved.

An organization that wants to grow without decentralizing must do so via mergers and acquisitions. These are the usual techniques of the Aristocratic organization. It does not generate its own ideas or develop its own products and markets, so it buys other organizations. However, if such mergers and acquisitions do not lead to decentralization, the organization will choke itself to death by becoming too diverse technologically (being in too many markets at the same time).

Acquisitions that are not accompanied by some decentralization may result in further centralization since they need to be controlled. This means further organizational bureaucracy. To avoid decline in results the organization will need more acquisitions that will create further bureaucracy in the centralized organization, and so on. A vicious cycle is created.

The decentralization should be a periodic and repetitive process. If a company is to remain successful in the long run, it must decentralize whenever it reaches the Prime stage. Here, then, is a dilemma. An organization needs a managerial mix in order to be well managed. To establish this mix, managers with diverse styles are needed. However, at any stage, an organization may develop a style of its own that discourages certain managerial styles from operating within it.

Treating Mature and Aristocratic Organizations

Aristocratic organizations require external organizational intervention. I call it therapy in order to distinguish it from surgery, where management is fired and sudden changes in responsibilities are announced. Surgery is not necessary since the Aristocratic organization is still cash-heavy, and it has *time* to rejuvenate without taking drastic measures that are necessary only when time and economic pressures exist.[2]

To rejuvenate Aristocratic organizations, a method called A'S/M has been applied with varying degrees of success to over 50 organizations worldwide. The A'S/M therapeutic method basically attempts to change the consciousness of the organization by changing aspirations. It widens the horizons while at the same time providing tools of teamwork that make management feel able to successfully bring about change. It reverses the sense of helplessness that is characteristic of organizations in decline.

As a process, the Finzi-Contini syndrome must be overcome. During a diagnostic meeting, managers face the facts in a constructive manner. They end with a plan of action to solve problems that no one alone can solve but which they can solve together because they perceive them as critically important.

By opening the gates for constructive criticism and teamwork, the organization moves from a reactive to a proactive mode of behavior, which takes it into the Prime phase of the organizational life cycle. (For more details, see Chapter 12 and other publications of the MDOR Institute in Los Angeles.)[3]

Treating Early Bureaucracy

The "backbiting" that characterizes this stage requires prompt surgical treatment. Several people whose attitudes are negative, who poison the climate, or who are totally ineffective have to be replaced. This surgery should be done only once and very sparingly. If several surgical interventions are done in succession, it might paralyze the organization. Management's suspicions and paranoia, which are strong in this stage of the life cycle, might run rampant; in other words, the treatment might reinforce rather than treat the neurosis.

After the surgery, the same therapeutic treatment given to an Aristocracy is applied, except that the rate of intervention (the doses of treatment) is much higher. Intervention on one day a month for Aristocratic organizations is significant, whereas an Early Bureaucracy usually requires intervention three days a month.

Bureaucracy and Bankruptcy

I have had no experience with treating organizations at these stages.

POSSIBLE PITFALLS

A good model should have counterintuitive prescriptions. I suggest some below.

Delegation Treatment

One hears repeatedly that the founder's main problem is that he does not delegate. In the Go-go organization if the founder does not delegate, he will fall into the founder's trap. But the treatment is not easy to apply. If the organization is in its Infancy (where the founder works even harder than he does in the Go-go stage), delegation is not only unpalatable to the founder, it is also dangerous to the organization's "health."

Delegation is not a palatable treatment because unlimited dedication to the creation of his labors keeps the founder going. At this stage of the organization's life, asking the founder to delegate responsibility might threaten and alienate him from the organization, thus reducing his commitment. Futhermore, it is difficult to delegate nonprogrammed decisions. Decisions that will serve as precedents are just being created. Delegating these decisions is equivalent to decentralizing, which for an Infant organization means passing control from the founder to someone else. This is almost impossible because the organization has no managerial depth. Typically, a founder will question the consultant who recommends delegation by asking in an irritated voice: "Delegate? Fine! But to whom?"

Delegation of the founder's functions should start at the advanced stages of the Go-go organization when there is too much for everyone to do. The founder should not feel that by delegating he is giving all the fun (control) away. Furthermore, when approaching the Adolescent stage, administrative systems are being planned and programming is underway. The healthy Go-go organization needs policymaking—what *not* to do—which is also tantamount to decision programming. The more programmed the decisions, the easier it will be to delegate without losing control.

Thus, the validity of the recommendation to delegate, often given to small, busy managers, should be analyzed in light of where the organization is in its life cycle. The timing is crucial if the treatment is to succeed.

Ill-Timed and Unnecessary Surgery

Surgery—changing top management—is the fastest way to produce change, but it is also the most painful and dangerous treatment. It is often used because it can be done in a short time and is highly lucrative (to the consultant). Unfortunately, few "organizational surgeons" stay long enough to see the results of their surgery or accept the responsibility for the postsurgical complications.

What makes a successful surgeon is not how fast he cuts but how well he monitors the postsurgical complications that might occur when the body is weak and vulnerable. Many consultants who suggest a new organization chart, help in locating the people to fill the boxes, collect the fee, and consider their task done, have not completed their job. When the new structure is put into effect, the *real* "pain" of adaptation starts. The pain can be acute but managers refuse to complain about any problems. They fear that if they point to some problems, another surgical treatment might follow. They would rather suffer quietly than subject themselves to another surgery.

While organizational change is indispensable for long-run success (see Figure 6), if it is induced as a cure at the wrong time, it may produce an almost permanent relapse; the organization may refuse to submit to it. If surgery has been painful and ineffective and exclusively applied as a cure, the organization may refuse to be operated on for preventive purposes, especially when a problem is not even evident. Often we produce a reorganization only when there is a crisis (for example, in an Early Bureaucracy). At this stage surgery is inevitable. The treatment, however, should have been used when its effect would not have been so painful—at the Prime stage of the organization's life cycle. At that time the organizational climate is conducive to change. Due to growth and positive expectations for the future, the perceived threats from a change are much smaller and can be minimized even further. In an Early Bureaucracy, when the economic results are bad and the atmosphere is already ridden with suspicion, change reinforces fears rather than removing them.

If the organization is an Aristocracy, a *no firing* policy is recommended. Then for six months a change in the organizational climate to reflect expected opportunities for external growth is necessary to gain acceptance for internal change. Reorganization (no firing, just a reallocation of resources) and retraining are carried out. Overall such treatment has been successful.

SUMMARY

A model for codifying (**PAEI**) organizational behavior has been presented. A life cycle with distinct patterns of behavior permits us to predict the roles that need to be developed if an organization is to remain healthy. Possible treatments have been suggested. The model can also be used to clarify what possible mistakes consultants make in facilitating organizational change.

In the next part of this book, we will discuss how to train and develop good managers, how to compose complementary managerial teams, and how to change organizational climates using the **PAEI** model.

NOTES

1. The word "passages" was suggested by the title of Gail Sheehy's book, *Passages* (New York: Bantam, 1977) on the predictable phases in adult life.

2. Chapter 12 deals in depth with the specifics of therapy. Here we present some of the main analytical points derived from analyzing an organizational life cycle.

3. To study the method, see publications 1–13 published by the MDOR Institute, Los Angeles, California.

Part III

WHAT
TO DO
ABOUT IT?

Chapter **9**

What, Then,
Is a Good Manager?

OVERVIEW

We have described such mismanagers as the Lone Ranger, the Bureaucrat, the Arsonist, the Superfollower, and Deadwood (the worst of a bad lot!). All of these mismanagers lack one or more managerial roles in their **PAEI** code. At the same time, we have said that the integrating, being an entrepreneur, administering, and producing roles are necessary for effective management.

We have argued that each of the four managerial roles is a necessary but not a sufficient part of a good managerial style, that managers should excel in one or more roles but not to the exclusion of the others. Thus the producing manager should be a **Paei** rather than a **P---**, the administrating manager should be a **pAei** rather than a **-A--**, and so on. **-A--** style is dysfunctional not because it highlights one role but because the other roles are absent.

MANAGEMENT VERSUS MISMANAGEMENT STYLES

The difference between managers and mismanagers is that mismanagers lack the ability to perform certain roles. Thus we have the contrasting managerial types listed in the accompanying box. Under all conditions the role or roles in which both the manager and the mismanager excel are of the same "size." What differentiates the mismanager from the manager is that the mismanager lacks the ability to perform the roles while the manager just does not excel in them but can achieve a threshold level of performance.

THE MYTH OF THE TEXTBOOK MANAGER

Management theory focuses on **the manager.** It makes the same type of assumption that economic theory makes. Eco-

Mismanagement Styles		*Management Styles*
P--- = The Lone Ranger,	but	Paei = The Producer
-A-- = The Bureaucrat,	but	pAei = The Administrator
--E- = The Arsonist,	but	paEi = The Entrepreneur
---I = The Superfollower,	but	paeI = The Integrator
---- = Deadwood,	but	PAEI = The Textbook Manager
PA-- = The Slave Driver,	but	PAei = The Governor
PA-I = The Benevolent, Benign Prince,	but	PAeI = The Shepherd
-A-I = The Paternalistic Bureaucrat,	but	pAeI = The Participative Administrator
P--I = The Small-Time Coach,	but	PaeI = The Guide
P-E- = The Sprouting Founder,	but	PaEi = The Founder
PAE- = The Solo Developer,	but	PAEi = The Developer
--EI = The Demagogue,	but	paEI = The Teacher
-AEI = The False Leader,	but	pAEI = The Zealous Newcomer
-AE- = The Pain in the Neck,	but	pAEi = The Devil's Advocate
P-EI = The Charismatic Guru,	but	PaEI = The Statesman

nomic theory provides tools for predicting how a firm will behave. Under one set of conditions, the firm will raise prices; under another, it will reduce prices. It explains *why* decisions were made but neglects to explain *how* they were made. It personifies the group process of making a decision in an abstract entity called "the firm."

The same type of perceptual limitation prevails in management theory: the manager plans, controls, motivates, disciplines, and so on. But these are parts of a process in which no one person can possibly excel. While one person may excel in planning (pAEi), another may excel in organizing (PAei), a third in motivating (PaEI), and so on. We all know managers who are excellent in conceptualizing plans and ideas but are not good at carrying them out or who are sensitive, empathetic, and good at integration but cannot be expected to make hard decisions.

Although no manager is excellent in all of the managerial roles (PAEI), we continue to look for the textbook manager. Studies of leadership (for example, Fiedler) invariably focus on the individual. Few, if any, produce unequivocally verifiable findings. Their models have low predictability because the wrong subject is being studied—the individual leader rather than the leadership group. The capabilities of the other people in the group that the "leader" leads are ignored.

Most traditional management theory that assumes a prototypical manager is not a contingency theory because it assumes that all managers manage all tasks under all conditions in all organizations in the same way. It does not describe the circumstances under which managers plan, organize, and motivate differently.

Traditional business school education could therefore be detrimental to good management education. By and large, if such education tries to develop PAEIs, when the "graduate" begins to manage, he cannot live up to the expectations placed upon him and becomes defensive. Because he has been trained to believe that he should be a PAEI, admitting that he cannot do what he is being asked to do means accepting failure. By not accepting their own weaknesses or those of others, business school graduates could become a problem for their organizations.

The tools of accounting, marketing, and finance are all very valuable, but together with these tools business schools could inject an unhealthy attitude. They could program students to believe that they must be **PAEI**s and that their subordinates must be **PAEI**s. Consequently, they continue to be dissatisfied with themselves and with others with whom they work.

In the next chapter we will discuss in detail how to train managers. At this point, however, let us return to our initial question: If the **PAEI** is nonexistent, how should an individual avoid becoming a mismanager?

WHAT IS A GOOD MANAGER?

A good manager cannot possibly be an accumulation of all the virtues ever ascribed to management. However, a manager requires nine characteristics if he or she is going to be a team member.

1. He is capable of performing all four managerial roles, although he cannot excel in all of them. He excels in at least one role and meets the threshold demands of the others— that is, he has no dashes in his **PAEI** code.
2. He knows his own strengths and weaknesses.
3. He is in touch with his social environment. He accepts feedback from others in order to determine who he is. He realizes that he is what he does.
4. He has a balanced view of himself. He realizes both his strengths and weaknesses.
5. He *accepts* both his weaknesses and his strengths. He does not try to be something he isn't, at least in the short run.
6. He can identify excellence in others, even in roles he does not perform well himself.
7. He accepts the opinions of others in areas where their judgment is likely to be better than his own.

8. He can resolve the conflicts that necessarily arise when people with different needs and styles have to work together to create an effective managerial mix.
9. He creates a learning environment.

> The role of a competent manager is to create an environment in which the most desirable things are most likely to happen.
>
> *Ralph Ablon*

Now let us look at these characteristics in detail.

A Well-Rounded Person

The common denominator of the 15 styles of mismanagement that were listed in the box on page 132 is inflexibility. Each type of mismanager is "blind" to one or more of the managerial roles and thus would probably have difficulty in working with persons who excelled in those roles. The extreme cases were unidimensional managers—the Lone Ranger, the Bureaucrat, the Arsonist, and the Superfollower.

Good managers are neither **PAEI**s nor are they incapable of performing any managerial role. They have strengths and weaknesses—one may have a strong **P**, another a strong **E**, and so on—but their strengths do not preclude their performance of the other managerial roles.

An interesting counterpart of this point of view may be found in H. Storm's account of how the American Indians used the medicine wheel to classify personalities and plan the growth of individuals[1] The medicine wheel was a circle constructed from small stones or pebbles that indicated the directions north, south, east, and west. A particular personality characteristic, a totem or animal symbol, and a color were associated with each direction. For example, wisdom, the buffalo, and the color white were associated with the north (see Figure 8). "At birth," says Storm, " each of us is given a particu-

FIGURE 8
The Medicine Wheel

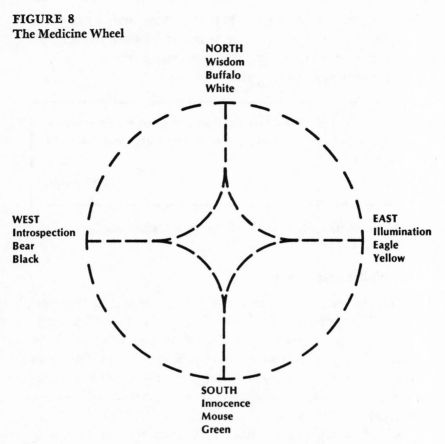

lar beginning place within the four great directions on the medicine wheel. This starting place gives us our first way of perceiving things, which will then be our easiest and most natural way throughout our lives."

A person who perceives from only one direction is incomplete. Persons who are identified exclusively with the north are called buffalo men. Such persons are wise, but cold and without feelings. Eagles, whose sign is the east, can see far and wide but are not close to things. They have no conception of the earthly repercussions of their sky-high movements. A man or woman who perceives from the west will go over the same thought again and again and will always be undecided. A person who perceives from the south will see everything with the eyes of the mouse. He will be too close to the ground and too nearsighted to see anything except what is right in front of him.

This description of personalities bears several obvious similarities to mismanagement styles. The eagle is very similar to the exclusive entrepreneur (--E-). He flies all over the place —expecting those on the ground to follow suit—without any understanding of the details that it takes to get things done. The mouse resembles the unadulterated producer (P---). He works hard, but has no long-term view. He sees only the short run, the nearby. Storm describes the mouse person as "one who saw everything close up, and his vision would be limited to the immediate world around him. He would be a gatherer of things. He might gather facts, information, material objects, or even ideas. But because he cannot see far enough to connect his world with that of the Great Prairie of the world around him, he would never be able to understand all that he saw and gathered." The powerful and slow bear who goes over every decision over and over again is similar to the exclusive administrator. (The medicine wheel has no analogue for the exclusive integrator.)

The American Indians, according to Storm, believed that people were born with some dominant inclination. The role of the tribal religious leader, the shaman, was to expose each person to experiences other than those he was used to until the person became well rounded. A person who was born an eagle had to watch the lives of mice and understand them well enough to know how they live.

In other words, the impossibility of becoming a **PAEI** does not signify a fatalistic acceptance of what we are. It means that we should aim at improving our performance of the necessary roles, removing the blank from our codes, and continuing to grow in the long run, while at the same time accepting the fact that we cannot be perfect. To be able to accomplish this growth, we must first know who and what we are.

Unfortunately, the practice of many corporations is not as enlightened as that of the American Indian shaman. If one is a good **P**, he might be left in that position, or might grow vertically in that position, until the person exhausts himself, i.e., becomes a Deadwood.

Knows Himself

To be good managers, we must know ourselves. We must know what facets of our **PAEI** model we can count on as strengths in ourselves and what facets we must circumvent as weaknesses.

> Make it thy business to know thyself, which is the most difficult lesson in the world.
>
> *Miguel de Cervantes*

Most people do not know themselves. All of us tend to be a bit hypnotized about ourselves, thinking that we are excellent producers, fine administrators, very creative, and good at relating to others. We do not know who we are, and this may be because we are favorably or unfavorably biased toward ourselves.

I suggest that we are what we do to others. In other words, we are how we behave. This means that one learns what a person is not from what he says he is, but by watching him and by learning what he has done and how he has done it.

This existentialist, behavioral approach implies that in order to know ourselves, we must be in touch with our surroundings. We must realize what effects we have on others. We can do this best if we are open enough to hear and to accept what people have to say about us even if what they say is not congruent with our own ideas or beliefs about ourselves. Otherwise, we will live with too many illusions about who we are.

> Oh wad some power the giftie gie us, to see oursels as others see us.
>
> *Robert Burns*

In my work in Mexico, I came across a fascinating example of what I am trying to communicate on these pages. The Spanish that I learned to speak was the old Castilian Spanish. In one of my lectures, trying to speak modern Spanish, I said something that left the audience puzzled. I asked someone who knew English to tell me in English what I had said, so that I could see what the source of the confusion was.

"You asked us if we *feel* you," he answered. What I wanted to ask, however, was "Do you *hear* me?" Then I realized something quite fascinating. Five hundred years ago the Spanish verb *sentir* meant to hear, to listen, and to feel. In modern Spanish, *oir* means "to hear," *escuchar* means "to listen," and *sentir* means "to feel." Today a person can hear and not listen, listen and not feel. However, in order to know himself a manager must get in touch with a surrounding world that is less censored, less controllable and more direct. He must feel what he hears and listens to. For a manager to be in touch with himself, he must be in touch with others.

> It takes two to know one.
>
> *S. Culbert*

Accepts Himself

A good manager does not try to be someone else. He accepts himself. He does not have an unbalanced view of himself. He knows his weaknesses and his strengths, and he accepts them.

Accepting oneself does not mean that a person does not want to improve. And the desire to improve can be realistic

if it is not based on a New-Year's-resolution-like commitment
to change one's personality completely.

> Nothing is a greater impediment to being on good terms
> with others than being ill at ease with yourself.
>
> *Honoré de Balzac*

Many managers are given psychological tests which may
show, for example, that a manager is too task-oriented. If so,
he is told, "You must become more people-oriented." This
type of limited feedback does not change the manager at all.
It cannot. If he could have been more people-oriented, he
probably would have been so already. Such an approach only
gives the manager cause to be less satisfied with what he is.
Thus his level of frustration rises without any significant
change in his behavior.

Accepting oneself is not a result of tests. It is part of becoming mature. An adolescent may act out his dreams, but
adults accept reality. As adults, we know our limitations and
like ourselves in spite of them.

We can know ourselves only by being in communication
with others, by being open to the assessments which others
make of us. We must actively seek an understanding of our
capabilities and limitations. In these ways we can help determine our place as managers on the **PAEI** map. In the next
chapters we will discuss techniques that have been used to
obtain information from others that will help us to understand how we function in the different managerial roles.

What has been stated above is really not new. Humanistic
psychologists have said for years that a manager should be a
mature, self-actualized person.

The Self-Actualized Personality. According to Maslow,
self-actualized people can accept themselves and others as they
are.[2] They do not shun those who have not become what they
"ought" to be. Nevertheless, self-actualized people are action-

oriented, and they are neither self-satisfied nor satisfied with the status quo.

Because self-actualized people are secure, they are not afraid to reveal their feelings to others. Their interpersonal relations are very deep. However, these relations are confined to fewer people than the interpersonal relations of the general population.

Self-actualized people tend to judge people and situations correctly and efficiently. In general, they are readily able to detect the spurious, the fake, and the dishonest.

Self-actualized people react to day-to-day occurrences with fresh, happy outlooks. They are filled with awe, pleasure, wonder, and even ecstasy. They respond to problems in a natural, logical manner.

Self-actualized people march to a different drummer. They are self-reliant and make their own judgments. They are autonomous and independent in thought and action. Their decisions are guided by internal standards and values rather than by what others are doing.

Self-actualized people are willing to learn from anyone. Maslow found that they enter into fruitful exchanges with anyone they meet. They are also willing to ask questions that others hesitate to ask. They do not fear blunders.

Other psychologists, such as Bell, have described effective managers as achievers—as self-actualizers. Bell characterizes achievers as people with high self-confidence. He suggests that achievers are spontaneous, natural, self-reliant, and goal-oriented and that they tend to center their energies on the problem rather than on themselves.

According to Bell, "Achievers are psychologically healthy. They have a genuine, positive feeling about themselves. They like themselves, feel contented with their place in life, accept their strengths and weaknesses. They are quite self-contained for they rely on their own values for deciding their lives, follow their feelings, and trust their judgment."[3]

An organization managed by an achiever produces above-average results. Achievers attain orderliness with out requiring the degree of systematization that slave drivers impose. Morale is typically high, and subordinates are encouraged to develop their capabilities. Achievers aim toward significant goals and foster genuine motivation in their subordinates. The management style of achievers is creative.

The Mature Personality Style. Argyris has developed a model of the mature/immature personality. Table 1 describes the differences. According to Argyris' model, a mature manager should take an active posture, be independent, behave in many ways, have deep, strong interests and a long time perspective, be in a superordinate position, be aware of himself, and have control over himself.

TABLE 1
Argyris' Immaturity/Maturity Continuum

Immaturity	Maturity
Passive	Active
Dependence	Independence
Behaving in a few ways	Behaving in many ways
Shallow interests	Deep, strong interests
Short time perspective	Long time perspective
Subordinate position	Superordinate position
Lack of self-awareness	Awareness and control over self

Identifies Excellence in Others

Once you know who you are, your next problem is to be able to identify the necessary qualities in others that you do not have yourself. To do this, you should know what qualities are required for effective management.

In order to understand what this involves, consider the differences between our description of snow and that of the Eskimo. Our description would probably seem very incomplete to an Eskimo. The Eskimo have five words for what we refer to as snow. They identify it as wet snow, powdered snow, big-flake snow, and so on. For their purposes, they must know all the different types and characteristics of snow.

Similarly, in order to understand management adequately, we need to know all of the different roles that must interweave for effective management. Since no one person can be a **PAEI**, a manager must be able to identify qualities in others which compensate for his own weaknesses.

However, unidimensional people who are "blind" to other roles have difficulty in identifying, accepting, and appreciating those roles.

The Lone Ranger hires go-fors and associates with other Lone Rangers. He suspects and despises the Bureaucrat, fears the Arsonist, and ignores the Superfollower. So how can he realistically be expected to identify or hire them? The Bureaucrat, on the other hand, tries to avoid the Arsonist and does his best to organize the Lone Ranger.

So knowing oneself as a manager is not enough. We must know all of the things that are required for effective management, and we must recognize characteristics in others that complement those at which we excel. Moreover, we must be able to respect those complementary characteristics.

Accepts Differences of Opinion

To form a **PAEI**, one needs a managerial mix—two or more people with complementary styles. But most managers are not self-confident enough to work with people whose styles differ from their own. They do not want complementarity; they want similarity.

If complementarity is forced upon a manager who does not know or accept himself, his lack of confidence will show in his treatment of his subordinates. If it is forced upon a manager who thinks he is a **PAEI**, that manager will become an obstruction to any teamwork, a petty dictator who will reject those who try to be more creative, to lead the organization informally, or even to make practical decisions.

Can you, as a manager, live with others whose strengths are not identical with your own? Can you accept your weaknesses? Can you accept having a subordinate who is strong in the areas in which you are weakest? Are you aware that since you cannot be superior in all of the four management roles, your subordinates must be superior to you in some respects?

> I have never met a person who was not my superior in some particular.
>
> *Ralph Waldo Emerson*

For the above reasons, it is a mistake to characterize people as subordinates and superiors. The superior-subordinate differentiation assumes that the manager is a **PAEI**, that he is superior to his subordinates in everything. Only if one believes in the cult of personality, as the Russians did during Stalin's era, is the superior-subordinate distinction appropriate. If we want complementary staffing and a managerial mix, however, we must avoid this approach. A manager is good if he is complemented by better people on his team.

> Everybody is ignorant, only on different subjects.
>
> *Will Rogers*

Can Manage Conflict

Since good management (**PAEI**) requires a mix of people with different managerial styles, conflict is inevitable. A good manager must be able to manage conflict: accept and respect differences of opinion and search for unifying strategies. Let us study several different alternatives of managerial teams:

P---	Paei	----
-A--	pAei	----
--E-	paEi	----
---I	paeI	----
Team 1	Team 2	Team 3

Team 1 forms a **PAEI**, but the conflict among the different styles of its members is probably not manageable. The people represented by the codes do not respect one another. Each of the people in team 1 is inflexible in some way, and will not accept the inflexibility of the others. This team will disintegrate in a short time.

Team 2 is infinitely better. Its members may well disagree, but the disagreement will be healthy, for each person on the team is flexible enough to respect the styles of the others.

There will be total silence, and therefore no conflict, on team 3, all of whose members are Deadwood (and therefore complain about nothing).

For good management, however, *conflict is inevitable—* and a certain degree of conflict is even desirable. Mary Parker Follett argued a generation ago that conflict can be functional, that friction keeps the wheels turning as long as there is not too much of it.[4]

But not all people can or like to take the "heat" that accompanies conflict. They shun friction and avoid situations in which nerves get raw. They are unable to take a stand for principles in spite of the fact that others may despise them, ridicule them, or simply ignore them (the worst punishment of all) for having failed to do so.

> Stand for something, lest you fall for anything.

Therefore, even a person who knows himself, accepts himself, and allows others to complement him can fail as a manager. If he withdraws from the first battle of the styles, or requests instant and permanent peace, he will not succeed as a manager.

Creates a Learning Environment

If conflict is inevitable, and moreover a sign of good management, how can it be controlled, harnessed, made functional? A good manager can do this by creating a supportive learning environment, one where conflict is perceived not as a threat but as an opportunity to learn and develop.

A learning environment is one in which people learn from one another. In such an environment, differences of opinion are viewed as educational opportunities by the parties involved.

Being a good manager is extremely difficult. It requires being a complete, mature, and well-balanced human being. And as will be shown in subsequent chapters, the design and intent of organizations minimize people's ability to be good managers.

KEEPING IT IN ORDER

The conditions required for being a good manager must be met in sequence. Whenever one of the conditions is not met, inadequate management will result.

First, we must know whether we know ourselves. Second, we must know how to know ourselves. We must get in touch with our surroundings; we must feel what we hear; we must be open to new ideas. We must be open to evaluations of ourselves which are not necessarily congruent with what we wish to be or how we wish to be seen. We must be willing to recognize our faults, and at the same time we must *accept* ourselves.

People who refuse to admit their faults will ultimately be shut off from reality. Such people will develop a dash or dashes in their **PAEI** codes and thus manifest a style of mismanagement.

Since a good manager knows his strengths but accepts his limits, and gives credit to what others do better than he could do, he uses the word *we* rather than *I* in referring to decisions made. It is not the royal *we*, however, because it truly reflects the work of a team.

Successful organizations are those which recognize that they are managed by deficient humans. Ray Kroc, the president of the McDonald's chain, has described himself as a "country boy." He does not pretend to know finance or in-depth management techniques. He views his role as that of finding the right people to work together.

This in itself is no revelation. Many managers claim that the whole managerial job is finding good people and getting them to work together. Unfortunately, this simple guideline for management is ignored in practice. Many managers who have no self-respect or are unable to accept people different from themselves fear excellence in others. They do not have the best people working for them. They are like the racehorse owner who keeps ponies in his stable but expects to win the triple crown.

After we know who we are and accept ourselves, we must identify and respect complementary qualities in others. Usually it is difficult for us to recognize qualities in others that we do not possess ourselves. When we reach the stage at which we recognize the qualities of others, our next step is to find out how to live with them. This means recognizing others as superior to us in some respects.

The superior-subordinate-superior type of relationship is accepted in research and development (R&D) departments. An R&D manager may have "under" him Ph.D.s who are geniuses in certain areas. These "subordinates" may be fantastic entrepreneurs (Es), whereas the R&D manager may be just an administrator (A). But the manager should not feel threatened by this. A problem would arise only if an administrator was hired who wanted to be both the best researcher *and* the best research director, who wanted to compete rather than support.

The same holds true for all types of organizations. For superior team performance, subordinates should be superior to the manager in some respects.

The good manager should be able to work with such subordinates, to live with an organization which includes a variety of managers with different strengths, and to harness conflict among these managers into a learning environment.

NOTES

1. H. Storm, *Seven Arrows* (New York: Harper & Row, 1972).

2. Abraham H. Maslow, ed., *Motivation and Personality* (New York: Harper & Row, 1954).

3. Gerald Bell, *The Achievers* (Chapel Hill, N.C.: Preston Hill, 1973), p. 123.

4. Mary Parker Follett, "Dynamic Administration," in *The Collected Papers of Mary Parker Follett,* ed. Henry C. Metcalf and L. Urwick (New York: Harper & Row, 1941).

Chapter **10**

Developing and Training a Good Manager

CHANGING THE MANAGERIAL STYLE BY CHANGING THE INDIVIDUAL: TRAINING AND DEVELOPMENT

The development of management into a profession and a "science" is a 20th-century phenomenon that has resulted in the growth of management education. Business schools and management training courses attempt to equip the newcomer with the knowledge and skills necessary for good management and to assist the veteran in improving his or her performance as a manager. These efforts are documented in the literature, which discusses training and various training approaches.[1]

The effort is all too often misguided, especially when the objective is to turn out a manager who excels in all of the functions or roles that have been defined as elements of "good management." Education based on this objective is a mistake, because the textbook manager is an abstraction, a more-than-human being. Though many descriptive studies of management have attempted to correct the abstract quality of the classic definitions of management by basing their work on the observation of real managers functioning in real situations, the results of these descriptive studies are equally liable to be misapplied.[2] Mintzberg's ten roles may be more specific than Fayol's four roles, but the individual who tries to master all ten roles is still attempting the impossible.[3]

The attention given to training or development in particular roles of the **PAEI** model varies greatly. With respect to the Producer (**P**) and the Administrator (**A**) training, the most common, it is sufficient to note that this is usually associated with a particular field or organization and is acquired from engineering schools, on-the-job training, and organizational regulations. With the advent of management information systems, a new area of training has opened, but it is still dealing with the Producer (**P**) and the Administrator (**A**) learning.

The qualities of the Entrepreneur (**E**) and the Integrator (**I**) which are most vital at the upper levels of management cannot be taught. They must be developed experientially. In recent years there has been a substantial effort to help management develop the **I** function. Typically, training for the increase of **I** is based on methods developed by the behavioral sciences—sensitivity training, the T-group, and so on.[4] Research has shown that the impact of these programs may be limited by the climate of the organization—that is, the degree to which it favors using the attitudes promoted in training.[5]

There have been some attempts to develop managers who are capable of more imaginative and innovative decision making, synectics for one. The Federal Executive Institute, for example, offered an eight-week session in which the participants spent much of their time "just thinking."[6]

An important facet of the A'S/M approach is modification of the environment to permit the development of **I** and **E**— that is, to create an atmosphere in which new integrative approaches will be fostered and collective creativity will surge.

However, even if training and development are applied correctly to an organizational situation, obstacles inherent in the nature of the organization may obstruct effective results. We will now explore some of these obstacles in order to aid in their identification and elimination.

OBSTACLES TO TRAINING AND DEVELOPMENT

The Deficiencies of Hierarchical Organizations

Potentially people have all of the qualities necessary to manage, although these qualities may be dormant as a result of neglect. We are all, latently at least, paeis. The environment in which we operate makes our latent capabilities either grow or disappear. Unless inhibited, people rise to meet challenges and to exercise any of the four management roles which may be called for.

However, the structure of the modern organization is usually more conducive to the elimination of managerial talents than to their development. Instead of fostering the growth of well-roundedness, it inhibits such growth. Consider the modern hierarchical system. It capitalizes on the strengths of individuals. A person who is a strong administrator will be promoted as an **A** and will climb the corporate ladder as an **A**. In the short run, an organization may be getting the maximum out of such a person, but in the long run, his lack of opportunities to develop **pei** can only be harmful to the organization.

Examples of such biases in promotion can be seen in the army. A person who is an excellent sergeant or staff sergeant may not be recommended for a commission because his commanding officer is afraid of losing a good adjutant. Thus, some people remain "sergeants major" throughout their lives because they are too good at what they are doing.

For such reasons, a person who may be a **paei** at the outset will rise in the corporation as a **pAei** if his **A** function develops more strongly. This reinforces **A**, but it develops nothing else.

Moreover, the rigid boundaries that have been set between workers and management breed mismanagement. When an organization draws its managers from a pool of workers, it will often have difficulty in developing **A, E,** and **I** and in relaxing their **P** to **p**. Those who climb up the organizational ladder from apprenticeships may therefore turn out to be Lone Rangers. While they were working on the line, they had no opportunity or experience that would equip them for the A, E, and I roles.

In the bottom ranks of most organizations, P is expected almost exclusively. Workers are not expected to be administers, entrepreneurs, or integrators. Management regards integration from the lowest levels as a potential threat, as unionization or the emergence of informal leadership.

At a slightly higher level, A is expected, but until an employee rises to the vice presidential level, neither E nor I is generally expected. At this level, however, he or she is *instantly* asked to be creative and to aid smooth organizational interactions. It is difficult for such an employee to find the emotional resources required to perform these new functions if he or she has been harnessed, suffocated, and divested of his creative impulses for 20 years or so.

Our educational system creates similar difficulties. For years we treat children as dependent adolescents, but when they graduate they are expected to become adults overnight. They must instantly cope with a reality that they have neither known nor been trained for. As a result, most people move from family dependence to organizational dependence, and they never really become free and responsible.

Management schools prolong such dependence and nourish the A in people. And there are reasons why it is dangerous to rely exclusively upon school-trained managers. If management is "school-trained," managers may never see the firing line. Thus they may become PA——s (Slave Drivers) who might be insensitive to the needs of their subordinates. Or worse, they may be programmed to believe that they have to be PAEIs. This may be why Robert Townsend recommends that one never hire an MBA from Harvard. According to him, they are taught to be presidents, not co-workers.[7]

Experiential learning can be more productive than classroom lectures on how and why managers should be responsible to labor. The Chinese require people in leadership positions to go back to the line occasionally, so that they will never

An old joke tells about a newly "minted" MBA from a leading school who became the president of a small firm. On his first day he was shown the factory and the office, and was introduced to his subordinates. He then sat down at his desk, hit it for reinforcement, and shouted, "OK, let's get to work! Where is the case?"

forget the experiences of those whom they are leading. Similarly, in Israel headquarters officers are periodically sent back to the front line to be reminded of where they are sending their subordinates. The reverse practice of putting workers in positions of management could be equally beneficial. In Yugoslavia, Peru, West Germany, Norway, Sweden, and elsewhere, putting workers on the board of directors often makes the workers more responsive to the realities that management faces.

People in organizations should be given the opportunity to develop as many roles as possible. This not only develops them as individuals but gives them insight into the problems of their co-workers. Since marketing is generally unaware of the realities of production, and production might not appreciate the pressures to which marketing must respond, exposing the marketing and production heads to each other's experiences is precisely what organizations should try to do. People can become effective managers only if they are given opportunities to develop roles other than their normal ones. And though many profit-oriented organizations would consider such a practice a luxury whose short-run costs are quite real, the long-run benefits will eventually outweigh them.

In the Israeli military lateral promotion is a matter of policy. An officer cannot be promoted beyond a certain rank unless he has held several lateral positions first. He must see the organization from many different angles—as a staff person from headquarters and as a line commander in the field.

In the Adizes Synergetic Method (A'S/M), a supportive

network of facilitators is built. People from production facilitate the problem solving of the people in marketing; people from marketing help the people in finance; and so on. The idea is that people can be most helpful if they are somewhat divorced from a problem, which is why most doctors do not treat their own families. In addition, such mutual support enables people to learn one another's jobs and to develop parts of their personalities that they cannot ordinarily express in their usual activities.[8]

Mismanagement Breeds Mismanagement

In addition to fostering exclusive orientations, organizations breed mismanagement in other ways.

Organizational roles are internally in conflict. Thus, if one role dominates—that is, if one style of mismanagement prevails—it will rule out the opportunity for other roles to develop. For instance, corporations founded by **P–E**–s grow rapidly (assuming that they are successful). While they are growing, they tend to lack the cohesion that good administration provides. In fact, efforts to create controls may well be met by antagonism from the founder. If the organization is to continue to grow, however, the administrative function has to be developed. As a result, the organization has to grow away from the founder—his control over it has to be reduced.

Generally a typical **pAei** is called in to establish some order. But with a **P–E–** at the top, the **pAei**'s chances of surviving are slim at best. The **P–E–** will change accountants and administrative managers more often than is prudent for organizational stability. The organization may have to get rid of the **P–E–** before a **pAei** can do an effective job.

If the by now large corporation grows too rapidly, the founder will become less able to control it personally. This may lead to a takeover by an outside firm. Then the founder either leaves or is shunted off to some innocuous position.

But if an **–A––** takes hold of an organization, bureaucracy develops. Any E who joins the organization has two choices—adapt and give up, or go elsewhere. Creative, aggressive people cannot survive intact in a bureaucracy.

In other words, a particular organizational climate or style may encourage or discourage specific roles from being performed. Thus, mismanagement breeds more mismanagement.

The most endangered role is the E. The P sees an E as a person who diverts him from his job. The A considers the E to be a source of turbulence and thus a prime target for domestication and control. The I feels much the same as the A—an E could become a source of turbulence which threatens the appearance of unity that he wishes to maintain. And Es do not like people like themselves since they compete for attention.

Thus, there is an open hunting season on Es. An E learns quickly not to make waves, not to stand out. But at the same time it is said that we have a leadership crisis. Miner has noted that there is an increasing scarcity in managerial talent. I suggest that he is referring to Es and Is.[9]

The bigger bureaucracies become and the more educated we become, the less capable we may be of emerging with our Es and Is intact. We are programmed to be organization persons and become less and less capable of producing leadership.

Throughout its history the United States has benefitted from a large immigration of Es. The vast size of the American continent gave them ample opportunity to grow. With an expanding population, space shrank. With high technology, big organizations emerged. The green pastures in which normal Es could develop began to shrink.

Therefore, Es are an endangered species. The technological society is becoming a bureaucratic society, and leadership is becoming extinct. We are becoming well-trained, establishment people, risk-averse and security-oriented. With increasing affluence, P declines in importance. Thus, at least in developed countries, there is a tendency toward a pAei orientation in training and in practice.

The organization breeds mismanagers, and at the same time it requires good management. The hierarchical organization inhibits the development of the human resources needed to solve the problems that hierarchy creates. The result is mismanagement that breeds further mismanagement. It is not strange, therefore, that the organizational environment is obviously becoming less and less tolerable.

How can this increasing **A** petrification be reversed? At least two things are needed. One is to train future managers as team members rather than in the individualistic "you better be a **PAEI**" tradition, and the other is to change the nature of our organizations. Both conditions must be met. Training managers will not suffice—organizations are powerful behavioral modifiers (manipulators). Changing organizations will not suffice—new organizational styles require managers who can make them work. The needed management training will be discussed in the following pages. How to change the nature of organizations will be discussed in Chapters 12 and 14.

THE NATURE OF MANAGEMENT TRAINING

Before we can discuss the training of individual managers, we must clarify the concept of decision programmability and the personality requirements of the **PAEI** model.

Decision-Making Programmability

The process of management is based upon the making of decisions. One cannot manage without deciding things. However, decisions may be programmed or nonprogrammed.

In computer terminology, a program is a ready-made decision that structures the computer's tasks. For instance, an inventory system is a programmed decision. A certain level of minimum desired inventory is predetermined. When the inventory reaches the minimum level, the computer will "decide" to print out an order. When a predetermined situation triggers a predetermined response, we can say that a decision is programmed.

Here is a concrete example of a *human* programmed decision. You leave your office to drive home, and the next thing you know you are in front of your garage. Your last vivid memory is that of leaving the office. What happened in the meantime? What streets did you cross? Which light were red or green? If you cannot remember, how did you drive? The answer is: in a programmed way. We can equate learning to drive with getting programmed. We are taught to stop at red lights by making certain motions. We are taught to accelerate at green lights by making certain other motions. Sooner or later, driving becomes an activity that we can perform without conscious thought.

Nonprogrammed decisions are decisions that one has to make from scratch, with conscious effort. To make a nonprogrammed decision, one must search for information, identify the problem, evaluate possible alternatives, and act. Let's use the same example. Imagine a car running a red light in front of you as you drive home. As this is not supposed to happen, you do not have a "programmed" decision right at your fingertips. You have to search for information: At what speed is the other car moving, and in what direction? You have to identify possible courses of action (stop, accelerate, turn right, turn left, etc.). You have to choose among the alternatives. And then you have to act. None of the important information had previously been given (predetermined).

Nonprogrammed decisions require creativity and a willingness to accept risk. If an individual is uncreative, he is incapable of identifying new possible courses of action or even of recognizing that a given situation is not customary and therefore requires a nonprogrammed decision. He will continue to act out of habit in situations in which his habitual behavior is inappropriate. Many business executives have made the mistake of reacting in a programmed way to altered situations which call for a new approach.

In a research study of automobile accidents, it was found that a large majority of such accidents occur within a ten-mile radius of the person's home. Why? Why don't we get into accidents more often on distant, unknown streets? Perhaps this phenomenon can be explained in part by the fact that when people hit familiar streets they turn on their programmed decision-making switches. That is, they tune out their immediate environment.[10] Unless we can remain defensive drivers—that is, drive in a nonprogrammed way—we may end up in an accident.

Why is programmed driving easier than nonprogrammed driving? Those of us who have driven in a foreign country know the answer to this question. A few hours of driving in a strange place can be as tiring as several days of driving at home. This is because when we drive in a strange place we have to make nonprogrammed decisions, which demand creativity (generating and evaluating alternatives) and risk-taking (judging which alternative to choose). The uncertainty and the risk that nonprogrammed decisions involve give rise to anxiety.

Given a choice between anxiety and security, an individual can be expected to choose security. That is, he or she would rather make decisions in a programmed way. However, an individual will be bored stiff if all of his decisions are programmed. It is a balance of programmed and nonprogrammed decisions that makes us feel capable or incapable of coping with a situation. People who cannot cope with a situation that requires nonprogrammed decisions are highly inflexible. They are able to act only in accordance with rules. By the same token, people who have to make every decision in a nonprogrammed way (even when the routine is self-evident) are also inflexible. They are constantly "reinventing the wheel." We might even say that their behavior is programmed to be nonprogrammed. They get exhausted fast, and they exhaust those around them.

The four management roles involve different kinds of

decision-making. Producing results and administering programs involve programmed decisions. Producing is a matter of applying a technology or a particular sequence to a task, whether it is manufacturing shoes, making sales, or raising funds. Occasionally nonprogrammed decisions will be needed in performing these tasks, but management tries to minimize such decisions in order to obtain maximum predictability of outcome.

We all know of door-to-door salespersons who have to start their pitch from the beginning if they are stopped in the middle; their sales presentation was too programmed. The same may hold true for production workers—industrial engineers, production managers, lathe operators. Their training can be considered as programming. Administrative decisions are also predominantly programmed, usually by a book of rules, policies, or guidelines.

WHAT IS TRAINING?

Many courses and training programs are nothing more than programming. That is, they provide the individual with a set of functions which he or she calls upon to perform some particular task.

The English were famous for their training of public servants, especially those who served overseas. The strength of the British Empire was attributed to the organizational skill of its administrators. Before being sent to posts, these officers were given in-depth training that amounted to programming. They could be expected to act in a certain way under certain conditions. The routinization and standardization of procedures enabled a few Englishmen to rule a great many colonials without running into organizational snafus. An officer in the foreign service could use the same procedures in both India and Africa.

In Ghana, every ministry of the government has an administrative head of professional administrators—a principal sec-

retary and those reporting to him. The professional administrators switch ministries every few years, a procedure which
stems from the era of English rule. They can work for any
ministry on very short notice. Regardless of the task, the administrative process is the same. The system is obviously designed for control, although managerially it could be a disaster, because different organizations need different structures
and processes.

In comparsion to **P** and **A**, **E** and **I** do not involve programmed decisions. There is no program that tells an integrator or an entrepreneur what to initiate, or when, or how. An
individual can be taught skills that are useful in dealing with
people, but whether he can *use* those skills depends on him.
Entrepreneuring and integrating are self-starting, discretionary processes which entail creativity and require a willingness
to take risks.

It is not at all strange, then, that the **E**'s work hours and
staff meetings are unpredictable. He gets an idea, and even
he may be unable to say what stimulated it.

The **I** is also nonprogrammed, because each assembly of
people is a new "happening"—even if the same group of
people meet repeatedly, they have different moods and deal
with different sets of circumstances.

Thus, the four management styles can be arranged in a
hierarchy, with the least programmable type of decision making at the top and the most programmable at the bottom.

1. Integrating   Least decision programmability
2. Entrepreneuring
3. Producing
4. Administering   Most decision programmability

The higher one ascends on this hierarchy, the more creativity
is required, since decisions have to be made from a more
diffused and less structured data base. Integrating is less programmable than entrepreneuring because entrepreneuring
does not necessarily deal with people, whereas integrating in-

volves uniting individuals behind a group decision. In fact, if one is trying to integrate or unite a group of entrepreneurs, a great deal more creativity is required than if one merely has to make an entrepreneurial contribution. In integrating entrepreneurs, one has to integrate their individual creativities into a cohesive unity—to forge group risk-taking from individual risk-taking, to fuse an individual sense of responsibility into a group sense of responsibility.

In the typical corporate hierarchy, the higher one ascends, the more nonprogrammed decision making is required. The Peter principle (that a person ascends to his level of incompetence) might be analyzed in terms of programmed decision making requirements.[11] At higher levels the individual must be more and more creative and must take greater and greater risks. Consequently, promoted managers frequently fail because they lack the necessary creativity and because they are afraid to take large risks.

P and A are programmed decisions. Thus they call for training. E and I are nonprogrammed decisions. Thus they call for development.

THE CONTENT OF TRAINING AND DEVELOPMENT PROGRAMS

Simple interventions do not change people's styles. An i cannot be changed into an I just by giving him a test which makes him aware of his deficiency.

Changing a style, increasing the effectiveness of a role, is a prolonged and complicated process. The change agent could be an educational institution.

The purpose of managerial education, whether at programs for top executives or at schools that grant MBAs, *should not* be to create a PAEI, but to remove the blanks that a person has in his code and to make him aware of the roles he has to perform. The classical type of business schools, however, actually promotes "personalitis." They train future presidents of corporations to be all-knowing individuals. These institutions may be brainwashing young students and programming them to believe that they can perform godlike functions. When the graduates fail, they can't understand why and usually look for scapegoats. They accuse others of inadequacy: their subordinates, their peers, their bosses.

The traditional executive training programs also make the mistake of focusing on the individual. Yet even if the president or the chairman of the board were to enroll in such a program, it is unlikely that this would bring about any changes in his or her organization. Most graduates of executive training programs will say, "I really can't tell you what I applied. . . . It must be here. . . . How I got my thoughts organized was the greatest benefit." The program may have been beneficial to the individual, but it was probably of little value to his or her organization.

Traditional programs for top executives train individuals because they mistakenly assume that a manager should be a **PAEI**, that a person who is well trained could make the necessary changes in his or her organization.

Executive training in organizations must be in clusters, teams of people from the same company developing both their cognitive know-how (**P**) and (**A**) (programmed decisions) and their interpersonal processes of working together, (**E**) and (**I**). Clusters of five or more persons from the same organization must work together as members of a team during the whole program.

Assuming that one trains a cluster of managers and that sufficient time is available, what should be taught? The program must be well rounded: no one discipline should be taught exclusively. Marketing people should not keep attending marketing programs, and accountants should not keep attending tax seminars. Cross-fertilization is necessary if one is to become a member of a team rather than a Lone Ranger, a Bureaucrat, an Arsonist, or a Superfollower.

Management education has gone through stages. For a long

time, training in accounting or engineering provided an entrée to a managerial job. A similar approach still prevails in professional organizations. The person who manages a hospital or the chief of medical services in a ministry of health is expected to be an M.D. The singer who has lost his voice, the dancer who has broken a leg, or the musician who can't makes the grade becomes an administrator—with little or no additional training.[12]

At universities, department chairmen show no interest in courses on management for administrators. They seem to consider a knowledge of, say, chemistry or physics to be sufficient for running their multimillion-dollar research departments.

Obviously, the know-how needed to produce results, the knowledge of a professional discipline is important for effective management. That knowledge is part of the **P** role of the **PAEI** model, but it is not enough. Thus, marketing managers should know accounting as well as marketing. Accounting executives should, of course, know accounting principles, but training for **A, E,** and **I** is also necessary in order to get the adequate all-around manager.

One of the mistakes made in management training has been to train managers exclusively in administration. This has been especially true in training for public administration, because the traditional focus has been on the institutional approach to organizations—understanding the administrative subsystems and the technology of decision implementation. The main difference between public administration and business administration seems to be that public administration raises fewer questions about the purpose of what is being administered. Business administration teaches how to go about identifying goals, how to scan the environment, and how to design strategies. So courses that are *exclusively* administrative can no more generate adequate management than can courses that are exclusively disciplinary. They train primarily for the administrative facet of the managerial process.

The same deficiency exists in management textbooks which

focus almost solely on the formal organizational structure. These may pay lip service to informal structure, to the human aspects of organizations, but they contain little material on how to manage conflict in organizations from a behavioral point of view.

In some universities, business schools are part of the school of economics because management is considered to be applied entrepreneurship. Such business schools believe that a good manager has to know finance and to estimate risk well. Managers who are educated only in economic theory may be trained to be entrepreneurs, to identify opportunities in the market, and to estimate their value in present terms. However, as was discussed above, the highly trained entrepreneur is not necessarily a good manager. If he or she does not bring in individuals who can establish a system of administration and lead the organization, skilled entrepreneurship can lead to economic disaster. For example, *Fortune* magazine has reported that Meshulam Riklis, an outstanding entrepreneur, failed in his business endeavors until he acquired deputies who developed a system of implementation and control that enable him to carry out his entrepreneurial activities fruitfully.

The latest kick in management training is behavioral science. Some psychologists who teach in management schools claim that human motivation and group dynamics are sufficient for the understanding of management. In their courses, endless hours are spent on analyzing interpersonal relations and listening to lectures about how to motivate followers. At best, a successful Superfollower could come out of this training. Such a person has no full familiarity of decisions that need to be made. He is unfamiliar with marketing, production, finance, or administration. At best, he or she can get along well with other people.

Thus, it is not sufficient to be trained *exclusively* in any one aspect of management. *All* aspects are necessary. To remove the blanks in one's code, one has to learn disciplinary material (P); administrative methods (A); how to identify goals, work under uncertainty, and be able to take risk (E); and how to work with others and manage the conflict that inevitably arises (I).

However, formal education should not be overdone. Some of the best and most successful present-day entrepreneurs had no formal education, and perhaps their success can be partially attributed to this fact. They have not yet had their E and I trained out of them. They know how to adapt, how to be creative in new environments. They do not turn to the rule book for solutions. They make their own solutions. A senior vice president of one of the largest banks in Mexico is a high school dropout, but his Ph.D. subordinates consider him a leader of stature. One of them said, "Unhindered by education, he can think."

Educated people can be programmed. They learn models which are particular answers to particular questions. The danger is that when a nonprogrammed question is asked, they might force an already available solution to fit it, even if it does not really fit. We spend more time teaching people the "right" answers than we spend teaching them to ask the "right" questions. Thus, Ivan Illich has argued that the education we provide is not educating people to learn for themselves, but rather programming them to live up to the expectations of the establishment.[13]

To sum up: A good manager is not necessarily a graduate of a leading school. Overschooling can be dangerous to his or her "managerial health."

TRAINING METHODS

Training for P and A

Training for P and A is quite straightforward. A P has to learn the discipline of his profession—selling, engineering, accounting, marketing, or whatever. Job-related courses fit

the bill here. Some experiential learning is necessary for reinforcement and behavioral absorption of the material, but
straight, traditional teaching makes sense.

For training in **A**, the same prescription is applicable to
courses on administration, on how to organize, systematize,
control implementation, and so on. Courses analyzing situations by whether or not what was planned was realized are
common approaches to such training.

In addition to taking courses, one can learn on the job.
Executive programs should give assignments that enable
teams of five from each company to apply what was learned to
their working environment and to report back on their success or failure. Furthermore, **P** may be abundant in organizations, but not comprehensively shared. Specialized people can
teach one another what their functions are and thus create a
learning environment. It is always surprising to find out how
little people know about their own organizations. MDOR
programs employ an analysis of the entire organization so that
its people will understand the process by which results are
produced. By means of this exercise, these people become
deeply aware of their organizational interdependence. They
learn *from* one another how crucial they are *to* one another,
and this helps each of them to produce the results for which
he or she is responsible.

Training for E and I

Training for **E** and **I** seeks to use programming. The underlying assumption of such training is that the person to be
trained already has **E** and **I**. The purpose of the training is to
systematize his or her **E** and **I** with respect to the specific job
performance needed. Courses in brainstorming and synectics
provide guidelines on how to stimulate one's creativity and
to utilize it systematically.

Training for an ability in **I** is being offered in countless
courses on process facilitation, organizational development,

change agents, sensitivity training, and leadership that are being given at countless universities, institutes, and clinics. The techniques of integration and conflict management can be augmented and improved if the basic personality capabilities exist to begin with. However, it is counterproductive to give I training to people who have a blank in I.

DEVELOPMENT METHODS

In order to develop a capability which may be latent at best, or to which the person who possesses it may be "blind," a necessary prerequisite is an environment which requires and encourages that capability and reinforces and rewards its manifestation. Environment in this case means a task, a job, a position, and an organizational climate.

Before we delve further into this subject, we must clarify the distinction between delegation and decentralization. Delegation is the transfer of responsibility for programmed decisions to subordinates. This means that P and A can be delegated. Decentralization, however, involves more than the transfer of programmed duties. Those to whom power is given by decentralization are expected to use discretion in decision making, to take initiative, and to accept responsibility for being self-starters, as well as to do what they are told. In other words, decentralization requires that E and I be *nurtured* on the lower levels of the organization. The E and I roles cannot be delegated since they are not programmable. They have to be *nurtured*.

Thus, delegation is not synonymous with decentralization. In order to decentralize, freedom to make nonprogrammed decisions must be granted. Decentralization necessarily implies more elbow room for nonprogrammed decisions, which are inherently unpredictable. This provokes a fear of decentralization in people who want to remain in control. As will "decentralize" if they can control absolutely what is done; in so doing, however, they limit the chances for E and I to be expressed and grow and thus end up not decentralizing at all, but delegating a task or two at best. Therefore, decentralization is suggested as one vehicle for developing **E** and **I**.

If a person has a blank on **P**, as do the Bureaucrat, the Arsonist, and the Superfollower, or if he or she has a blank on **A**, as do the Lone Ranger, the Arsonist, and the Superfollower, how can the missing qualities be developed?

Developing P and A

In order to develop **P** and **A** in people, they should be exposed to or delegated a task that requires the performance of **P** and **A** roles. Since **P** and **A** are related to the need to achieve and the need for power, then in order to develop **P** a person should be assigned to a task in which his or her performance is easily accounted for, so that success or failure can be attributed to that person. Sales and production line work are examples of such tasks. The task should have short-term feedback loops—that is, the results should be forthcoming without too much delay.

Developing is painful because it is when we develop that we expose our weaknesses. People with a strong fear of failure will probably find such exposure most terrifying. If they cannot grow, for their own sakes they should probably stay away from managerial tasks, since such tasks will be neither gratifying nor rewarding.

The **A** role requires systematization, order, details, power, operating under certainty, maintaining a certain level of predictability, enduring repetition, and enjoying routine. To develop **A** a person must be exposed to a task that requires and rewards **A** qualities. Such tasks are easily found in production scheduling, in accounting, and in the classical personnel jobs.

An Arsonist could benefit from a short-term excursion into the (for him or her) no-no domain of keeping the system running as a system.

By and large, organizations have been quite successful in

developing **P** and **A**. They have been less successful in developing **E** and **I**.

Developing E and I

Large organizations have either alienated the Entrepreneur type (**E**) or have monopolized tasks which require the performance of **E** at the top of the pyramid and discouraged **E** throughout the rest of the pyramid. Consequently, when chief executives are needed, more often than not they are sought outside the firm because **E** talent has been prevented from growing inside it. It is not strange, then, that many executives find that switching organizations is the easiest way to get promoted.

I is not as endangered or as beleaguered as **E** but its growth and development are not especially encouraged by organizations with exclusive goals. Organizations are goal- and task-oriented. They expect results, and in order to achieve results they depersonify interpersonal relations. Consequently, professional relations rather than person-to-person relations develop in organizations. This impairs the **I** capability.

Developing **I** means being exposed to situations which test one's ability to work with people. One has to hear, to listen, to feel, and to react empathetically (see Chapter 9, page 139). One must develop an inner ear for what is not being said, a sixth sense to interpret how things are said and to compare them to what is actually being said in order to fully understand the situation.

Under any circumstances, development involves growing pains which can be minimized but not eliminated. However, for people who have no **I** to begin with, experiences which require working to overcome that weakness can be so traumatic that they refuse to undergo any further exposure to such experiences.

As a matter of fact, in extreme cases of persons who perform only one role to the exclusion of the other three, exposure to experiences in the other roles cannot yield satisfactory results since such persons will be traumatized by the many new experiences to which they are exposed. These people probably need professional psychotherapeutic intervention if they are to change and become better managers. In milder cases where one role has to be developed, a gradual increase of exposure with fast reinforcing feedback is of value.

Let us take an example from mental health. Some people break down if they have to make decisions under conditions that involve any uncertainty. One therapist has used the production of television shows to rehabilitate such people. Producing TV shows involves different degrees of uncertainty. Thus, a patient can progress from the least uncertain to the most uncertain task. He learns to handle his tasks as a member of a group and receives reinforcement from the group. Similarly, different managerial tasks involve different degrees of uncertainty. Managers should gradually learn to deal with increasingly uncertain tasks.

Extraorganizational activities can be used to teach people to deal with diversity and to integrate people. For example, industrial organizations might sponsor artistic activities in which all of their people could participate. One bank in downtown Los Angeles has a magnificent stage which it uses only for sales meetings. If the workers and managers of the bank used that facility to present a show for the bank's employees and clients and their families, hierarchical barriers could be broken down and a new dimension could be added to the lives of the people in the organization. This could also improve I, and, via diversity, it could probably increase E as well.

The best vehicle for developing E and I is probably democratization and decentralization. The result is participative systems. Yugoslavia, Peru, West Germany, Norway, Israel, Sweden, and the Benelux countries have established such systems. The more people participate in decision making, the more E and I they will develop and use.[14]

E and I might even be developed in schools by giving students tasks to do on their own and by providing experiential education. At the UCLA School of Business, for example, all students have at least one experiential course during the first quarter. The course emphasizes working with others—a process which can lead to a good knowledge of self, in addition to the beginnings of decision making with others. The course is intended to provide experience in making well-integrated decisions.

At Itesm University, Mexico, professors and business executives assist students on a continuing project. The students identify a business opportunity and plan, structure, and manage a business with the help and supervision of the professors and the business executives. Each generation of students passes its results along to the next generation.

Aside from obtaining training, being aware, understanding himself, and knowing the various characteristics and roles of management, an individual working alone can do little to improve himself. Working alone is working in a vacuum. Our own growth occurs as we work with others.

It is also possible to augment an organization's creativity and entrepreneurial resources by hiring people who are strong in E and I. These people are usually found in high creativity businesses such as advertising, and in small expanding firms and organizations. Many have worked as sole proprietors of a new organization.

It is important if one is introducing a creative person to an organization that is very oriented toward P and A, to assure that his integration is successfully achieved. Otherwise, frustration rises both in the new employee and the organization, a subject that will be explored in Chapter 12 when organizational therapy is discussed.

Thus far, we have discussed how to train human managers (as distinguished from textbook managers). But even good managers are not enough to ensure good management. To achieve good management, the good managers must work as a team and each manager must have a task that fits his or her style. The following chapters discuss how to match styles with tasks and how to build teams.

NOTES

1. See, for example, Michael L. Moore, "Superior, Self, and Subordinate Differences in Perceptions of Managerial Learning Times," *Personnel Psychology*, 27 (Summer 1974), 297–305; and Robert N. Carter, "OD Strategy for Today's Training," *Training and Development Journal*, 29 (April 1975).

2. For example, see Leonard Sayles, *Managerial Behavior* (New York: McGraw-Hill, 1964); and Richard C. Hodgson, Daniel J. Levinson, and Abraham Zaleznik, *The Executive Role Constellation* (Boston: Harvard University, Division of Research, Graduate School of Business Administration, 1965).

3. H. Mintzberg, "The Manager's Job: Folklore and Fact," *Harvard Business Review* (July–August, 1975).

4. Hilgert, for instance, offers managers ten suggestions to strengthen their own positive thinking in order to influence subordinates. See Raymond L. Hilgert, "Positive Personal Motivation: The Manager's Guide to Influencing Others," *Personnel Journal*, 53 (November, 1974), 832–34. (The true surge—in fact, avalanche—in this field has come with the advance of sensitivity training.)

5. See Herbert H. Hand, Max D. Richards, and John W. Slocum, "Organizational Climate and the Effectiveness of a Human Relations Training Program," *Academy of Management Journal*, 16 (June 1974), 185–96.

6. William S. Quigley, and Ronald J. Stupak, "An Experiment in Managerial Creativity: The Federal Executive Institute and the Policy-Making Process," *Training and Development Journal*, 28 (June 1974), 22–28.

7. Robert Townsend, *Up the Organization: How to Stop the Corporation from Stifling People and Strangling Profits* (Greenwich, Conn.: Fawcett Publications, 1971).

8. See Ichak Adizes: *Dialectic Convergence for Management of Conflict*, Paper no. 10 (Los Angeles: MDOR Institute, 1977); idem, *A'S/M Method for Diagnosis of Organizations*, Paper no. 7 (Los Angeles: MDOR Institute, 1977); Idem, *Democratization of Organizations*, working paper (Human Systems Study Center, Graduate School of Management, UCLA, 1977).

9. John B. Miner, *Human Constraint: The Coming Shortage of Managerial Talent* (Washington, D. C.: Bureau of National Affairs, 1974).

10. In addition, the phenomenon can be accounted for by the fact that surface streets are generally less safe than highways and that most driving is done within a ten-mile radius of home.

11. Laurence J. Peter and Raymond Hull, *The Peter Principle* (New York: Morrow, 1969).

12. In 1968, I established the first training program for arts administrators (at UCLA). It has been an uphill fight to convince people in the arts that more than a knowledge of the arts is needed in order to manage an artistic organization.

13. Ivan Illich, *Deschooling Society* (New York: Harper & Row, 1971).

14. For more information, see these publications:

(a) Ichak Adizes, *Industrial Democracy: Yugoslav Style* (New York: Free Press, 1971). Idem, "The Developing Nations and Self-Management," Research Paper Reprint No. 1 (UCLA Institute of Industrial Relations Publications Series, 1975), translation of chap. 1 of the Spanish edition. Idem, "Problems of Implementation and the Role of Professional Management," Research Paper Reprint No. 2 (UCLA Institute of Industrial Relations Publications Series, 1975), translation of chap. 10 of the Spanish edition.

(b) I. Adizes and Elisabeth Mann-Borgese, eds., *Self-Management: New Dimensions to Democracy* (Santa Barbara, Calif.: ABC/CLIO, 1975).

(c) I. Adizes, "Industrial Democracy and Codetermination," in *Encyclopedia of Professional Management* (New York: McGraw-Hill, 1977).

(d) J. Zupanov and I. Adizes, "Labor Relations in Yugoslavia," in *Handbook of Contemporary Developments in World Industrial Relations*, ed. A. Blum (Westwood, Conn.: Greenwood Press, in print).

(e) I. Adizes, "On Conflict Resolution and an Organizational Definition of Self-Management," in *Participation and Self-Management, vol. 5: Social System and Participation*, First International Sociological Conference on Participation and Self-Management, Zagreb, Yugoslavia, 1973, pp. 17–33.

Chapter **11**

Fitting a Personal Style to Task Demands: Building the Managerial Mix

Four roles (**PAEI**) must be performed if the managerial process is to be effective and efficient. Each of these roles is a necessary but insufficient condition for effective management. The four roles in combination are sufficient, but no one individual can perform them all at the level of skill necessary for effective management. Whenever any of the roles is not performed, a distinct mismanagement style can be observed.

If no one person can be a **PAEI**, what, then, is good management? We have noted in Chapter 9 that the human manager realizes and accepts the fact that he is not and cannot be a **PAEI**. We have also noted that even if the **PAEI** existed, the "personalitis" that would result from his presence might be dangerous to society in general.

If no one individual can be a **PAEI**, does this mean that organizations are doomed to be mismanaged? The answer is no. The solution is teamwork among people with complementary styles—well-trained people with different orientations and personal needs, who can work together and balance one another's biases.[1] What is needed is individuals who possess the entrepreneurial and integrating qualities that can guide a united organization into new courses of action; administrators who can translate the ideas of the entrepreneurs into operative systems that produce results; and producers who can make the system work and set an example for efficient operation.

Analysis of the history of any successful organization will show that it owed its success to a team of people whose styles, behavior, and needs were different but who could work together. Although organizational success is usually attributed to one person, behind that person is a team that enabled him to perform well.

The December 1972 issue of *Fortune* describes how Arlen Realty and Development became the biggest real estate company in the nation. Arthur Cohen, who formed Arlen Realty, stated that it was by no means a one-man show; "My role is where we are going [entrepreneuring]; Marshall's role is how we get there [administering], and Arthur Levine makes sure it works [producing]." Arthur Cohen was probably also the integrator who brought the group together.

Many people think of the Ford Motor Company as the success story of a person who did it alone. But according to Peter Drucker, at the time of its growth and success, that is, from 1907 through the early 1920s, the company was, in effect, run by a top-management team, with James Couzens coequal to Henry Ford and the final authority in many top-management areas. After Couzens left, Henry Ford became a one-man top management. It is hardly surprising that Couzens' departure impaired the company's competitive capability.[2]

The discovery of organizational teamwork should not be too startling. After all, we are quite familiar with the Mama-Papa store. Traditionally, Papa bought, negotiated, set prices, and provided business leadership (**PE**). Mama kept the books, provided constructive criticism of Papa's Utopian dreams, mollified the clients and the employees, kept morale up, and acted supportively (**AI**).

The traditional family was also "comanaged." The father was the breadwinner, had a global view of society, and pursued a career (**PE**). The mother managed the family, organized the household, and made the house a home (**AI**). In the **PAEI** code, Papa is a **PaEi** and Mama is a **pAeI**

With the feminist movement, a great deal has changed. Women are tired of the supportive role. They want to be **PaEis** themselves. But frequently the husband refuses to take over the supportive role. Thus, in some families both partners act as **PaEis**. In such instances, unless both partners have a big **I** and both wish to share in the **A,** the family will break down. Or it will need a good maid, secretary, and bookkeeper (**A**), and perhaps even a psychotherapist (**I**).

THE MANAGERIAL MIX

A managerial mix is a team, each of whose members is a good manager, as defined in Chapter 9. The team members must complement one another and thereby form a **PAEI**. That could mean a team composed of a **Paei**, a **pAei**, a **paEi**, and a **paeI**. Even better would be a team composed of a **PaeI**, a **pAeI**, and a **paEI**, since all of these perform well in integration. Such teams lead to an effective and efficient organization. But if there are only **PaeIs** on the managerial team, no matter how many of them there are, the organization will be mismanaged.

When there are two men in a business who always agree, one of them is unnecessary.

William Wrigley, Jr.

If any one of the four roles is truly indispensable for an executive, it is that of integration. If an executive does not perform the other three roles himself, there may be others who can; but the executive has to be able to integrate in order to allow the other functions to be performed in a positive fashion. If the integrative function is not fulfilled, the management team will disintegrate.

Some organizations are trying to develop the concept of the chief executive office. They have accepted the view that one person cannot do the management job, so they have several executives sit together to manage the organization. Very often this approach fails, because the executives choose people like themselves to work with them.

For example, an **A** executive will choose other **A** people. But a team can perform a complex task only if differences among its members are accepted.

IS A GOOD MANAGERIAL MIX SUFFICIENT?

A managerial mix composed of a well-rounded, complementary (**PAEI**) team is a good starting point for effective management. The next condition is that the members of the team be placed in positions in which their respective styles can be most useful. Intuitively, we would not expect a person who feels very comfortable in an accounting job to be excited about a transfer into sales, or vice versa.

In one organization, a marketing manager who was exclusively in marketing (sales did not report to him) was a **P** and **A** with very little **e** and **i**. He was almost a Slave Driver. Due to his style, marketing was not very popular in production or in sales. Furthermore, production and sales planning was neither aggressive nor imaginative. Had this person been in sales or even accounting, his assignment would have made *some* sense.

Thus, the style with which a task should be carried out has its own requirements. However, it is essential that managers rather than mismanagers be assigned the tasks for which they are suited.

FITTING TASKS TO STYLES

Four questions must be answered before the requirements of a task can be identified. Then one can search for the person whose style fits the task, thus obviating the need for expensive development and permitting immediate training.

1. What are the characteristics of the task (task demands)?
2. What is the degree of discretion in decision making one will have with the task (freedom tolerance)?
3. What are the styles of the other team members (team requirements)?
4. What is the organizational climate? What style does the organization need (organizational requirements)?

Task Demands

The requirements that a task imposes on whoever will perform it can be analyzed. These requirements correspond to a certain managerial role.

1. Does the task require working under pressure?
2. Does the task require short-term results?
3. Is it relatively easy to attribute the results to the person who performed the task?
4. Is the task programmable, is it easy to train persons to perform it?
5. How much interaction with other individuals is necessary to accomplish the task?
6. Does the task require substantial follow-up?
7. Is the task complex, and does it require detailed orientation and understanding of organizational interdependence?
8. Can the task be systematized?
9. Are organizational policies and rules needed in order to secure compliance and repetitiveness in performing the task.
10. How much initiative is expected in the task?
11. How much ability to abstract, deduce, and induce is required to perform the task effectively?
12. How unstructured is the task?

13. How much uncertainty has to be dealt with in order to perform the task?

14–15. How long does the task's uncertainty last?
14. A long time. 15. A short time.

16–19. Does the task require decisions which involve risk: If yes, is the risk low (17), moderate (18), or high (19)?

20. What is the rate of change in the nature of the task?

21. How much interrelationship with and cooperation from people is necessary to do the task?

22. How controversial can the activities of the task be?

23–25. Does the feedback on success or failure close relatively fast, or almost instantaneously (23), at an intermediate rate (24), or after a long-term, delay (25)?

These 25 questions can be put into a table, and if the answer to a question is positive, a subjective ranking of from 1–4 (1 being the maximum) is made in the appropriate column for each role.

	Style Needed			
Task Demands	P	A	E	I
1. Does the task require working under pressure?	1	4	2	3
2. Does the task yield short-term results?	1	2	4	3
3. Can success or failure in the task be attributed to an individual?	1	4	2	3
4. Is the task programmable?	2	1	3	4
5. Does the task require interaction with other people?	4	2	3	1
6. Does the task require rigid follow-up?	3	1	4	2
7. Does the task entail complexity and detail?	3	1	4	2
8. Can the task be systematized?	2	1	4	3
9. Does the task require compliance?	3	1	4	2
10. Is high initiative required?	3	4	1	2
11. Does the task require capability for abstraction?	4	3	1	2
12. Is the task unstructured?	3	4	1	2
13. Does the task require handling uncertainty?	3	4	1	2
14. How long must uncertainty be endured? A long time?	3	4	1	2
15. A short time?	1	2	4	3
16. Does the task require no risk-taking?	2	1	4	3
17. Does the task require low risk-taking?	1	2	4	3
18. Does the task require moderate risk-taking?	3	4	2	1

		Style Needed		
Task Demands		P	A	E	I
19.	Does the task require high risk-taking?	3	4	1	2
20.	Does the task require a high rate of change?	3	4	1	2
21.	Are interrelationship and cooperation required? ...	4	2	3	1
22.	Can the task be controversial?	2	3	1	4
	Is the feedback on success or failure closes in the performance of the task:				
23.	Fast or instant?	1	2	3	4
24.	Intermediate in duration?	2	1	3	4
25.	Long and delayed?	3	2	1	4

The accompanying table is a sample of an approach that can be taken. Tasks can be evaluated by means of the 25 questions posed in the table. The answers to each question can be assigned various weights, and the total will indicate which style is best suited to a particular task.

If an analysis of a task was done (keeping other factors constant), then a marketing task would probably require more **P** and **E** than **A**, and an accounting task would probably require more **A** and **I** than **E**:

	P	A	E	I
Marketing	2	4	1	3
Accounting (for a stable organization)	3	1	4	2
Sales of consumer goods	1	4	2	3
Sales of industrial goods	1	2	3	4

Discretion in Decision Making

The higher a person ascends in a hierarchical organization, the more power, authority, and influence he has and therefore the more discretion in decision making he has. By the same token, the more decentralized an organization is, the more discretion in decision making will be granted to lower levels of the organization.

Thus, in two organizations the same task will require two different styles of management if one of the organizations is centralized and the other is decentralized. The more decentralized an organization is, the more initiative it will expect and the greater **E** and **I** should be.

Complementarity to Other Team Members

Even if a person has all the abilities that are needed to perform all the necessary roles of management (that is, he or she is a **Paei** or a **pAeI** or is able to perform whatever other combination of roles may be required), and even if that person's abilities fit a team's requirements well, still his or her style may not be adequate. To determine whether or not this is the case, one has to analyze the team members with whom the person in question is going to work. For example, a person with extra **I** may be needed if the other team members are weak in **I**.

The need for complementary styles of management is evident from many news reports. For example, on January 10, 1977, an article in *Business Week* stated that for years Occidental Petroleum had experienced "a revolving-door pattern of executives in the presidential job." The description of Dr. Hammer, the chairman of the board and founder of the company, probably exemplified the founder style mentioned in Chapter 8. Unless a complementary style was found, Occidental Petroleum would have faced major difficulties with the departure of Hammer. When Baird succeeded Hammer as president, financial institutions were willing to extend more credit to the company. Baird was a banker whose conservative style complemented Hammer's style well.

Organizational Requirements

Finally, one has to ascertain what the organizational climate will accept, what style should be matched to what task, what can be done.

A bureaucratic organization may need an entrepreneuring

marketing manager, but its members probably won't give him a chance to perform his or her role until the organization changes its climate.

To summarize, in order to have good management:

1. An organization needs, not one good manager but a group of managers who:
   a. Are capable of performing all four roles.
   b. Know their strengths and weaknesses.
   c. Accept themselves.
   d. Accept persons who are different from themselves.
   e. Can identify excellences they do not possess.
   f. Can work out differences with others.
2. Each member of this group of managers should:
   a. Be able to meet the demands of his or her tasks.
   b. Be capable of discretionary decision making.
   c. Be complementary to the other members of the team.
   d. Be acceptable to the organization in light of its climate.

When the first condition is met, there is a managerial mix. When the second condition is met, there is a managerial mix that fits. Good management will exist when both conditions are met.

CHANGING JOBS—A PROMOTION

A person's style has to change when he or she climbs the organizational ladder (which is hierarchically structured) while remaining in the same discipline (that is, while staying in, say, production, accounting, or sales).

At the very bottom of the hierarchical organization, the major requirement for success is **P**. However, when a good **P** is promoted to first-line supervisor, his or her **A** grows in importance. **E** is still not expected. **I** may be desired, but it is not insisted upon. The organization really expects a **P** as a first-line supervisor who is somewhat of an Integrator (**I**). (Thus,

"*Why, this broth we made is magnificent!*"

Drawing by Dana Fradon; © 1976
The New Yorker Magazine, Inc.

we have the Coach style, which Fiedler and others have found to be the most efficient style at this level of supervision.)

At the next level of management, the departmental level, the orientation must be a little broader. The manager's **P** can be reduced, but his **A** must increase. He must organize his department; set rules, policies, and guidelines; and provide for structure and follow-up. Consistency and routinization are important. His **I** should remain large at all levels. It is *always* necessary to integrate oneself with people.

At the levels which involve strategic decision making, **E** must become larger. This evolution can be shown as follows:

Laborer, worker .... P--- ∂ℓi

First-line supervisor .... PaeI

Departmental manager ...... pAeI

Vice president (in general) .... PaEi

Chief executive .... PAEI

A person is not always able to change his style when he gets promoted. Perhaps he lacks the ability to perform one or more of the managerial roles, or perhaps the organization discourages their expression. E, for example, is discouraged until a person becomes a vice president. Then he or she is expected to develop a large E instantaneously. Since this usually does not happen, it is not strange that many companies seek prospects for top-management positions outside the organization.

Changing one's style is not easy because this means changing one's behavior. In order to reduce his P, a new on-line foreperson must "let others do the work." This entails becoming relatively detached from tasks to which he or she may have been totally dedicated and to accept the fact that others can do the job that he or she did formerly.

Further promotion to becoming a departmental manager requires new capabilities and a completely new managerial style. The promoted person's frustration is greatest when the task begins to require E, because he or she is being asked to make nonprogrammed decisions, to be creative, and to undertake strategic risks. Thus, it is not surprising that studies show middle managers to be more averse to change than any other managerial group in the organization.

A person can change jobs in other ways than by climbing the organizational ladder. That is, he can change his career, not just his level of *power* in the organizational hierarchy.

CHANGING JOBS—A CAREER CHANGE

A person needs to change his style, not only when he climbs the organizational ladder, but when he changes from production to marketing, from marketing to selling, from a line position to a staff position, or from one industry to another industry. Such changes, however, are more demanding than promotions, since the task changes significantly. When task characteristics change, the fit of people changes too, and the demands to change style can be rigorous. Some people find such demands too taxing, and they never really succeed in mastering or feeling comfortable with their new task.

Thus, a promotion or a career change calls for a change in the way we handle ourselves and others. Such a change in style may involve growth pains. The persons who learn and grow most successfully are those who are effective managers to start with. These people probably became well-rounded people because they had already experienced some fruitful change early in their development. They do not feel threatened by change; rather, they seek opportunities to grow.

There are trees which are "trained" to be transplanted when they are still small. They are transplanted every so often, so that they get used to being transplanted.

Many managers have never experienced transplantation. Changing the conditions in which they function might destroy them, for they lack adaptability.

Flexible people are rare. Organizations discourage flexibility by rewarding performance rather than development. Many organizations train people without developing them, or expect society at large to pay the price of development. These organizations may be penny-wise and pound-foolish. Organizations have to *develop* people in order to have promotable "raw material" that can be trained later on. The cost of training people who reject change and are defensive about their deficiencies is many times more expensive than the cost of development. Developing human resources is inexpensive as compared with the costs of turnover, the costs of repetitive training, and the costs of lowered morale.

THE OFFICE OF THE PRESIDENT

For effective management, a managerial mix is needed—that is, a team of effective managers who complement one another and can create a working **PAEI**. This mix is composed of people who have no blanks in their managerial code. Furthermore, the mix is well suited to its tasks and to the organizational climate.

A managerial mix can occur successfully at different levels in the organizational hierarchy. Some organizations have even attempted to establish such a mix in the president's office. This type of participatory top management has been termed the "corporate office." Among the companies which have established this sort of top-management committee are Aetna Life and Casualty, Sears, TWA, ITT, GE, Travelers Insurance, Armco Steel, Honeywell, Heublein, and RCA.

However, these efforts have not always proved successful. At Aetna, the corporate office was disbanded after four years. At RCA, it lasted only two months. I would like to suggest what may have gone wrong.

First, a **PAEI** team does *not* negate individual leadership. All of the team members are *not* equal. Someone has to head every team. What the **PAEI** model suggests is that the head of the team needs the rest of the team in order to help him make decisions. Group decision making without a leader produces a structure "that can lead to delays or impede the decision-making process," as Aetna's management complained. A group management committee whose members are all equal and whose members all consider themselves to be **PAEIs** could lead to stalemate and eventually destroy a company.

Another reason why a corporate office may not work is that the team members or their tasks do not complement one another or that the team members are not well-rounded managers. This would cause the committee to remain in constant conflict.

Finally, a corporate office may not work if all of its members have the same backgrounds, values, training, and styles of management. In this case, the organization might suffer in the marketplace from a lack of successful innovation, and this might cause the management team to disband.

Thus, for the corporate office to be successful, all of its members must be good managers, matched to their tasks, and complementary to one another, and the corporate office must have a leader who is capable of maintaining team environment and team operations.

THE ISSUE OF RESPONSIBILITY

What does the **PAEI** model say about responsibility in organizations? Does it suggest that no individuals have any responsibility, since no one individual can perform all of the managerial roles?

Managers usually perceive responsibility as something undertaken by one person. I would like to suggest another possibility: *Everybody* should be responsible. Each member of the team should be responsible for his or her contribution to the decision made and carried out by the team; each should feel responsible for the specific role he or she excels in. Thus, the **Paei** should feel responsible for the results; the **pAei,** for the way the results are administered; the **paEi,** for ideas, directions, decisions, and so on; and the **paeI,** for the establishment and maintenance of teamwork.

Experience has shown that unless everyone *feels* responsible, no one can *be* responsible. So every manager must work to create an atmosphere of collective responsibility. Managers should beware of falling into the very common trap of assuming all of the burdens themselves, of accepting responsibility for everything that goes on in the office. Since an individual manager cannot be a **PAEI,** he cannot be responsible for everything.

THE NATURE OF CONFLICT

The existence of an excellent managerial mix that is perfectly suited to its tasks does not mean that the organization will run without conflict.

An organization will operate without conflict if it is composed of one individual who makes all the decisions himself and he implements them alone. But in that case there is no organization.

An organization composed of Deadwood can also operate without conflict. No one complains, but no one cares either.

Finally, conflict can be avoided by an organization in which all the members of the managerial team play the same role— all are **As**, or all are **Ps**.

In the organization composed of Deadwood, all of the decisions would be programmed and predetermined, and no one member would want to change anything. The result would be no conflict. In the organization composed of managers with identical codes, the managers would have the same outlook and thus have no conflict. But both types of organizations would not be well managed. They would experience significant problems in meeting any goals in a changing environment. They will be stale.

A situation with unmanageable conflict will exist when the managerial group is composed of managers who do not have the ability to perform all roles, who are "blind" to one or more roles. There will be unmanageable conflict since such managers do not have respect for the managers whose roles differ from their own can contribute to the joint effort.

However, there is conflict even on a complementary managerial team even if the goal, the information, and the reward system are clear. Those are the factors which Herbert Simon believes cause conflict.[3] Such conflict arises from the diverse capabilities of its members. It is salutory but it must be manageable.[4]

APPLICATIONS OF THE MANAGERIAL MIX

To explain the managerial mix further, let us consider two hypothetical organizations. A typical organizational chart is shown in Figure 9. This chart encompasses a typical top-management team. Looking at it, we should ask, "What should the styles of each manager or department be?" In an organization large enough to have several top executives, if we rank-ordered the importance of each role performed by the chief executive officer (CEO), the least important would be **P** and the most important would be **I**. In a small organization that is "fighting for its life," **P** is of crucial importance. But in an organization whose markets and products are well established, a chief executive officer can hire **P**s, **A**s, and even **E**s. What he or she must do, is provide the leadership, which in this case stands for integration. A CEO who provides integration and vision (**EI**) and is somewhat implementation- and results-oriented (**pa**) would be a very effective manager. The opposite case will, above all, be oriented toward results and efficient implementation. This style might be desirable for a young and growing organization, but it should not be the "first choice" for a mature organization. Whenever **P**s and **A**s can be provided on lower levels of the organization, the chief executive officer should concentrate on providing vision and integration.

From this standpoint, we can say that the titles of many books on management give a misleading impression of what the roles of management should be. For example, instead of

FIGURE 9
Organization Chart

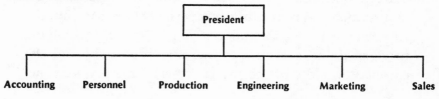

talking about management *by* results, we should be talking about "management *for* results and *by* process"—that is, **EI**. The title Management *by* Objectives also has the connotation of being almost exclusively **P**-oriented, toward objectives which are usually quantifiable and may exclude **E** or **I**.

Now let us look at the most desirable styles for the other members of the managerial team. In accounting, the predominant role should be **A**. In a relatively stable organization, **I** would rank second, **P** third, and **E** last. However, in an organization that is going through rapid changes, **E** would rank second, because in such an organization the ability to change systems is vital. If accounting does not have this ability, it can become an obstruction to growth. In the rapidly changing organization, **I** would rank third and **P** last.

If results orientation (**P**) is too high on the "totem pole" of importance, the accountant might consider himself responsible for results and try to run the whole show. He would work out budgets, approve them himself, set goals for the organization, and measure efficiency. An accountant as a staff person with this type of style will quickly alienate management. Thus **P** is placed last in the rank-ordering of the accountant's roles. Replacing the alphabetical code for the accounting department (**PAEI**) with a numerical code, we would give the department 3142 or (4123), 1 being highest in importance.

In personnel management, many different styles can exist, because many different meanings can be given to the four management roles. The most important role of the personnel department is usually **I**, but the role that ranks second is not always clear, because the function of this department differs in different organizations. If its task is primarily one of "files administration," as is true for many personnel departments, the role that ranks second would be **A**. If personnel is a tool in the hands of the management to increase productivity and efficiency, **P** would rank second. However, if the personnel department is a department of human resources, the second-ranking role would be **E** since in such a department creativity is oriented toward improvement in integration.

For the purposes of this example, let us assume we have a typical "files-administering" Personnel Department (3241), and go on to the next department.

In production, one would expect **P** to rank first. **A** would rank second, **I** third, and **E** fourth This does not mean that **E** is not important to the manager of the production department. Remember that we are ranking the *relative* importance of each role.

The task of the production department is effective and efficient operations (**P**). Naturally, the systems must run smoothly (**A**), and the people must work together (**I**). The production department attaches less importance to change and innovation (**E**). This may be explained by the technology of its task. In production, many variables have to be kept under control for extended periods of time in order to achieve results. Thus, production people resent too many changes because these require painful adaptations on their part.

In engineering, on the other hand, **E** is the most important role. The creativity of engineering should be directed toward results (**P**), should be "sold" to production (**I**), and, finally, should be administered in a highly structured way (**A**). In marketing, the four roles have the same sequence of importance.

Many executives suggest that the most important role of sales is **P**. Next comes **E**, for a salesperson must be highly creative in order to make tactical decisions in his or her field; then **A**, for he or she must understand and abide by the administration; and lastly **I**, for a salesperson can be an individualist, although some integration of his or her clients will be necessary. For this reason, in selling to consumers as compared to industrial selling, **I** and **E** might be given more importance than **A**.

Figure 10 shows the desirable styles for each manager or department. (Remember, 1 represents the most important role.) Looking at this chart, one should be aware that the engineering and production departments do not see "eye to eye." This "difference" arises because engineering is change-oriented, whereas production seeks stability and order. The difference is due not only to the different styles of the individual managers but to the technology of their respective tasks, which causes their styles to differ. In an organization that is managed well, conflict will exist between these two departments.

The marketing and production departments are at odds with each other for the same reasons. Marketing seeks change and flexibility, whereas the flexibility of production is limited by technological restrictions. Marketing and engineering, however, should get along quite well and should share the same distaste for the production department. If marketing and engineering do not get along for a protracted period of time, this conflict calls for attention and corrective action.

In our chart, accounting is in more conflict with marketing and engineering than with production and sales. It gets along best with the personnel department, as long as the latter acts as a "filing" service. If the personnel department becomes a human resources department and requests some human resources accounting, it will get more static from accounting than it ever got before.

FIGURE 10

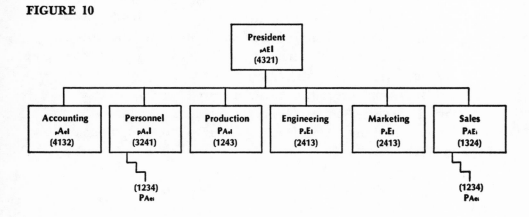

Personnel is generally looked down upon as long as it remains a "filing" service. When it begins taking initiative and acting more as an agent for organizational development (**E**), its sun starts to rise. But that sun could set very rapidly if its innovative efforts do not produce some results.

To illustrate the importance of matching styles with tasks, let us take the same organization and switch its managers around. The engineering manager will keep his style, but he will take over the production department. The accountant will take over engineering; the production manager will take over accounting; the personnel manager will manage sales; and the sales manager will take over personnel. The president will take charge of the marketing department, and the marketing manager will provide the behavior of the salespersons or the line workers. Finally, the style of the salespersons will dominate the office of the president. Can you picture what the new chart would look like and predict what would happen to the organization?

The number and the placement of the departments in the organization remain the same. The same people remain managers—they have merely changed places. Let us assume, moreover, that they are capable of changing departments—that the accountant understands engineering, etc. So what we are asking is whether these people can manage their new departments well, whether their styles and their new departments are well matched? The new organizational chart is shown in Figure 11.

What can you predict about the behavior of this organization? The president is a producer who pays little attention to people and to the direction the organization is taking. He is hardworking and tends to be a Slave Driver. Accounting furthers this tendency, since its manager has a strong results and systems orientation. Personnel also joins in this orientation toward short-term results. However, the production department cannot deliver. It is highly disorganized, and is constantly changing direction. Engineering is stifled under a paternalistic system of **A** and **I**. Marketing has some vision,

FIGURE 11

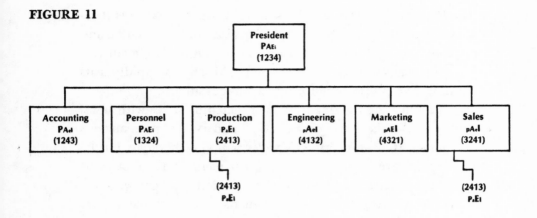

but it is not results-oriented. Sales does the best it can by being results-oriented and by trying to innovate as well.

Figures 10 and 11 describe the behavior of organizations by looking at the behavior of the people who hold manageriaı positions. At the MDOR Institute such charts are called organizational holographs. The charts are used to diagnose how well an organization is performing, where its conflicts are, whether or not there is turnover and where it is located, who will probably succeed the president, and so on.

Given the examples provided in Figures 10 and 11, the diagnosis might begin by noting that Organization X is performing more efficiently than Organization Y. This is because all of the employees, from the president down, are well suited to the functions they perform. Furthermore, the president (of Organization X) is a good integrator, and activities are decentralized throughout the organization. The diagnosis might then be directed towards existing conflicts, the turnover of employees in each department, and the best possible candidates for future management jobs.

AN ORGANIZATIONAL HOLOGRAPH

Let us study a simple organizational holograph to show an example. A small company (annual sales of about $2 million) had three equal-share partners with the following styles:

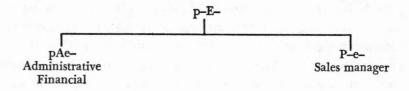

p–E–

pAe–
Administrative
Financial

P–e–
Sales manager

First, it should be obvious that the three partners were not getting along well at all. The president was running ahead at full speed, changing direction all the time. The administrative vice president could not control the president but tried to control the vice president of sales, who was trying to get the job done. Who got the heart attack? The vice president of sales!

One day the partners redesigned and expanded their building and their office space. Who dealt with the details? Who decided where each partner's desk would be? Obviously—the vice president of administration and finance. Where did he place the president? I hope you guessed right. As far as possible from himself. Where did he place the vice president of sales? As close as possible so that he could keep an eye on him.

For almost a year a consultant was unwittingly performing the **I** role. Unfortunately, he performed it badly. Instead of developing the **I** of the partners, he was providing **I** himself. The partners became addicted to the consultant. Finally, the consultant realized his error, and at his suggestion the company hired a **PaeI**. But that did not work either. The **PaeI** could not get his **I** going, since the partners all lacked **I**.

The consultant finally concluded that sensitivity training was indispensable. The blanks in the partners' codes had to be removed before complementary staffing and team buildup could be made to work.

We have discussed what a "human" manager is, how to train him, and how to compose a managerial mix in which people's styles fit their task. In this way we showed how to develop and staff an organization with the management it needs. But that is only part of the picture. Organizations have a life cycle. Merely staffing an organization with well-trained managers who are suited to their tasks and even work well as a team will not necessarily make an organization well managed, at least not in the short run. The organization's climate, the style reflecting its position in the organizational life cycle, has to fit and support its management. Changing an organization's climate is indispensable if one wants to achieve a more rapid improvement in the organization's managerial process and in the organization's results.

The process of changing an organization's climate will be discussed in Chapter 12.

NOTES

1. On the subject of teamwork, see also Rensis Likert, *The Human Organization: Its Management and Value* (New York: McGraw-Hill, 1967).

2. As reported by Ernest Dale, *The Great Organizers* (New York: McGraw-Hill, 1960), pp. 50–51.

3. The commonality of individual goals, the clarity and consistency of the reward structure, and the compatibility of individual rewards are the factors that effect goal differentiation among individuals and subunits in organizations. See James G. March and Herbert A. Simon, *Organizations* (New York: Wiley, 1963), p. 125.

4. On conflict as a manifestation of good management, see also Sol M. Davidson, *The Power of Friction in Business* (New York: Frederick Fell, 1967), pp. 83–139.

Chapter 12

Organizational Therapy

The purpose of organizational change is to reverse the "aging process" of organizations. One method of accomplishing this purpose is "organ transplantation"—that is, top management is fired and new people are brought in to replace it. But how is this "surgery" performed?

Often consultants are secretly called in to redesign the organization. Their planning, hiring, and firing are done secretly. When these measures are carried out, their implementation resembles a coup d'etat. In the course of such "surgery," a lot of "blood" can be spilled. Serious wounds may be inflicted, and the organization could fall into a state of shock from which it will not recover easily. People develop a serious aversion to the word *change*. They become almost paranoid whenever someone mentions that something is wrong with the organization. There are problems that call for organizational change, but people will not publicly disclose what they are. They have learned from experience that while change is certainly painful, it is not necessarily helpful. To avoid change, people deny publicly that any serious problems exist, whereas in private they complain vehemently. Such complaints do not lead to functional change and therefore do not lead to solutions.

How does one go about improving the condition of an ailing organization without inflicting excessive pain? How does one go about performing organizational therapy rather than organizational surgery? In this chapter organizational therapy will be discussed insofar as it utilizes the **PAEI** model.

My organizational therapy varies, depending on what stage of its life cycle an organization is in (some points concerning this therapy were given in Chapter 8). Basically, the therapy consists of a series of assignments that the organization is given to work on. A certain theoretical framework determines who gets the assignments, the sequence of the assignments, and the completion dates. The "classic" solution for organizational change is sometimes used—that is, new management is brought in as needed, and then integrated into the existing structure.

TREATING THE INFANT ORGANIZATION (Paei)

The infant organization needs constant, close supervision in order to keep it out of trouble. It needs attention, nurturing, support, and protection from exposure. Such organizations are often helped on a voluntary basis. They lack funds, yet require a great deal of time.

Because infant organizations have no system, they are constantly getting into trouble, so that all of their needs have to be met almost simultaneously. The therapist must perform at least two functions for the infant organization: First, he must give it a sense of reality, and second, rather than tell it what to do (a very common trap—the therapist becomes a full-time employee), he must help it develop a vision and long-term foresight. An infant organization should become aware of how it can grow. The therapist should teach it how to develop realistic expectations.

Because infant organizations are inexperienced, they often

make unrealistic commitments. Because their resources are slim, they are often overworked. As a result they lose the grand view and their expectations of what can be done are circumscribed by the limited world they get a chance to get exposed to. Since infant organizations get overcommitted to the insignificant and the unfruitful, they waste themselves on the trivial.

Since the resources of infant organizations are slim, to say the least, they live from month to month. Frequently, they run out of working capital.

The organizational therapist has to "hold their hands"— to help them overcome each crisis, and most important, to help them realize what they should *not* do.

Infant organizations are given assignments that orient them toward analyzing the environment, planning future cash flow needs, and forecasting sales, production, and staffing needs. But this should be done sparingly. Attempts to transform an infant organization into a highly structured and specialized organization are usually harmful. Since the executives must often do all the work themselves, spending time on procedures (SOP) would endanger the organization's ability to survive in a highly competitive environment by reducing its flexibility and productivity.

Some infant organizations spend inordinate amounts of time on systems, or buy computerized systems before they really need them. Others establish expensive headquarters before they can afford to. They should reserve such luxuries for the future.

The founder of one such organization bought fancy systems, located the organization in a prime location, and established an organizational routine that severely restricted improvization and required stability and standardization. The organization could not take the expense, and it lost its earlier strengths, which included flexibility and adaptability.

The organizational therapist gives the infant organization assignments that lead it to predict, analyze, and schedule. Individuals are assigned these assignments, because the organization is not big enough to be able to afford teamwork. The deadlines are flexible, because the organization is overworked, and as long as it is on the right track, there is no real need to put more pressure on it.

The infant organization may fail to develop its capacity for E, perhaps because the founder has no E or because the therapist has failed to give the organization a panoramic view of its future. In this case, the organization becomes the Lone Ranger's trap. An owner works very hard but nets very little. Most of the organization's operating earnings go toward paying the interest on its debts.

The owner works for the bank, or for his suppliers, and in some instances he is so busy that he is unaware of what the competition is doing. His prices may be far too low, and he may be achieving "sales success" at the expense of profits. If the company goes bankrupt, the Lone Ranger's trap becomes a graveyard. Otherwise, it will die with the death of its owner or grow under new management.

In any case, while the organization is "alive," its owner works harder for less than he would earn as an employee elsewhere. The only possible benefits for the owner of such an organization are independence and the pride of ownership.

If a new manager can be brought in, he or she should be a strong E, with A second in importance, I third, and P last. Such a manager would be a good complement for the infant organization which is strongest in P. The owner of an infant organization, however, cannot usually afford to hire a top manager. He usually has to relinquish ownership.

TREATING THE GO-GO ORGANIZATION (PaEi)

The go-go organization's biggest goal should be to move on to the adolescent stage. It needs more A—organization and stabilization. Once the direction and strategies that the company will follow are agreed upon, the assignments of the organizational therapist are directed toward systematization.

The therapy appropriate for the go-go organization is to help it realize what *not* to do. This is necessary because the go-go organization tends to spread itself too thin, and tackles too many frontiers at the same time.

The first assignment that the therapist should give the go-go organization is have it list all projects that are in the process of completion—those under way, those just being started, and those only contemplated. Then the organization should be required to estimate the resources and time necessary to accomplish each project. The go-go organization is usually shocked to learn that it is planning to complete a lifetime of projects in one year. The sooner the go-go organization realizes that it will have to set priorities, the faster it will grow. Therefore, the therapist's role in a go-go organization is to facilitate the organization's ability to set priorities. The organization must learn, experience, and accept the fact that resources are limited, and that given limited resources, the law of opportunity costs prevails—doing one thing means that one cannot do something else, and the cost of doing one thing is the price of not doing something else.

This simple law of economics, known as the law of butter and guns, was popularized by Paul Samuelson in his textbook *Economics*. It usually comes as an unpleasant revelation to the go-go organization, whose members want to have their guns and their butter too.

After the go-go organization has set its priorities, it is given the assignment of establishing detailed objectives and guidelines. The next step is "hand-holding" to facilitate the implementation of whatever the organization plans. One must constantly watch to see how new assignments are added and make the organization realize that it is violating its priorities. The go-go organization is usually restless and jumpy. It says one thing, but as soon as one is not looking, it is back to its old tricks, trying to do everything.

The go-go organization is quite difficult to handle, and the therapist is usually on the verge of being dropped since he makes it realize its limitations. The organization basically has to mature at its own speed. Its members are so excited with their results and their ideas that they do not want to heed to any doomsday prophecies about "the price that will be paid tomorrow for the mess of today."

The members of the go-go organization are simply too busy to spend any time getting organized, and they do not see the *short-term* benefits of such an investment of time. Typically, the go-go organization rewards performers. Thus, it is contemptuous of administrative tendencies and shows little, if any, desire to have the external facilitator implement change.

One simply has to wait for such an organization to "grow up." If, however, it cannot get organized by itself and it does not call for help from the outside, the organization becomes a "founder's trap" (**P–E–**), as described in Chapter 8.

The teams to which assignments are given in the go-go organization are small: two or three people at most. The assignments have to be short and doable in a short period of time (thus, many small tasks have to be assigned in succession). This is necessary because the people in the go-go organization do not have the patience for postponed gratifications. If they do not see immediate relevance and benefit, they lose interest and usually discontinue the treatment.

In its advanced stages, the go-go organization could obviously benefit from a good **pAeI**. (In its early stages, a **pAeI** might become a burden to the organization.) A **pAeI** is to the **PaEi** what Mama was to Papa in the traditional Mama-Papa store. He or she introduces some order, some stability, some direction, and some routine. At the same time, he or she provides a smile and a friendly personality.

In the advanced stages of the go-go organization, it is not too difficult to introduce and integrate a solid **pAeI**. This person is usually well accepted and appreciated. However, if the **pAeI** is brought in early, prematurely, the go-go organization has no time for him and will put him in the "storeroom" to wait until it is ready. He may feel neglected, forgotten, and unappreciated. When he indicates a desire to leave, the go-go organization reacts reassuringly: "Just wait a little longer, until we are ready . . . it will come . . . we *will* do what you say . . . but don't be in such a hurry," and so on, and so on. The therapist must try to integrate the **pAeI** into the go-go organization as soon as possible.

TREATING THE ADOLESCENT ORGANIZATION (pAEi)

The adolescent organization, as was pointed out in Chapter 8, is somewhat schizophrenic. It wants stability, yet it also wants an escape from the mess of development, the superficiality of projects, and the despair of getting involved in useless, expensive investments. It therefore seeks to establish policies, routines, standards, systems, and the like. At the same time, however, it wants to keep the freedom of irresponsibility, of trying out untested methods. It wants to set as many records as possible.

The therapist is caught in a double bind in such an organization. If he facilitates stabilization and systemization, some members resent him, and if he does not systemize, other members may resent him. Hardly anything that the outsider can do will be accepted gracefully by the *whole* organization. The adolescent organization is a pain in the neck. The therapist must have enormous patience to live with it. He has to maintain a very delicate balance between flexibility and systemization, and to change direction and assignments rapidly and with good timing.

For example, he may follow an assignment about future planning with an assignment about the system necessary to implement the future planning. While maintaining an optimum tension between structure and process, the therapist should help the organization to focus on the desired results and on the process for achieving them. Thus, the schizophrenia of the adolescent organization is in a sense resolved by treating the process and the desired outcomes simultaneously by assigning short-term doable problems.

When the adolescent organization clearly identifies and achieves commitment, it becomes a prime organization. If an adolescent organization is incapable of such a focus, it can become either arsonous or rigid. It becomes arsonous if it loses all interest in systemization. It gets involved in too many projects and fizzles away like a meteor. If it loses its **E**, it becomes rigid and disappears, since it cannot adapt or produce results (–**A**––).

The assignments for the adolescent organization are usually given to a multidisciplinary group (from production, marketings, sales, etc.), so that there is an adequate balance between **A** and **E**. The therapy leads to commitment to **P**.

Strict deadlines are necessary. Leniency permits organizational schizophrenia to play a bigger part than it should. The therapist is tossed from **A** to **E**, becoming the victim of their incongruence.

A simple managerial transplantation does not work very well for the adolescent organization. The therapist has a hard enough time. A new person would have even more difficulty. A good possibility for improvement arises, however, when a **PAEi** joins the organization if one can be found or afforded. This type of person gives the organization the sense of direction it needs, and at the same time is able to cope with the inconsistencies in its behavior.

One typical mistake is a sort of "marriage" between an adolescent organization and an aristocratic organization. The former is looking for stability, direction, and peace of mind. The latter is looking for a vitalizing influence. In the long run, such a marriage can be a very costly disaster for both organizations.

The aristocratic organization sees in the adolescent organization its go-go past and its potential for becoming a prime organization. The adolescent organization does not realize that the aristocratic organization is past its prime and wants "to marry" the aristocratic organization for its name, fame, and money. The two organizations appear to satisfy each other's needs, and they enter into a merger or an acquisition scheme. Their decisions are based on the wrong assumptions, however, and neither realizes what it will take to keep the marriage going.

The aristocratic organization is not capable of giving direction, and the adolescent organization lacks a focus for the production of results. Thus, the adolescent organization becomes too unpredictable for the aristocratic organization. Eventually, the management of the acquiring company fires the management of the acquired company, and we have major surgery. If the adolescent organization obtains a **PAEi** as a manager, he will probably in due time become the president of the aristocratic organization. If the adolescent organization finds itself instead with a **pAei**, he will fit the style of the aristocratic organization (**pAeI**), but neither organization will really benefit from the merger. In the long run, the marriage may not be consummated—that is, the merger or acquisition will not produce the anticipated and desired synergetic outcomes.

TREATING THE PRIME ORGANIZATION (PAEi)

The **I** of the prime organization tends to be smaller than the other roles because its members are working by and for results. The prime organization pays little attention to interpersonal relations; it views results in the marketplace as really what counts. Consequently, the prime organization grows faster than its capacity to train its managers; thus, it is in great need of management training and management evaluation systems.

Above all, the prime organization needs to decentralize, in order to keep its growth rate high. The major task of the organizational therapist, then, is to facilitate this process of decentralization. Decentralization—the maintenance of **E** accompanied by the development of teams (**I**)—can create the **PAEI** organization in the long run.

The therapist's assignments involve identifying boundaries for decentralization. This includes simulating the new organizational structure (so that individuals feel comfortable about the new system) and training the management (so that it can perform the new tasks).

The groups to whom these assignments are given consist of those people who can be expected to lead the new profit centers. The deadlines for the completion of the assignments are neither stringent nor lenient.

There is usually no problem with managerial transplantation in the prime organization. Since the pie is continually growing, the employees welcome newcomers and fear nobody. The prime organization is therefore the best candidate to buy other companies or to be bought by them.

If the prime organization does not decentralize, it will become a stable organization. This can happen as management grows older, sales grow larger, and the staff gets bigger. The prime organization simply becomes too "heavy."

TREATING THE STABLE ORGANIZATION (PAeI)

Consciousness-raising is the most indispensable task of the stable organization. Its members must realize that **E** has declined and **I** is growing. The members of the stable organization agree on everything, and they are too close to everything that happens around them.

The assignments here are to forecast the future, analyze the environment, foresee the threats *and* opportunities, and *stretch* in setting goals. Once the members of the stable organization recapture a panoramic view of its future, the next step is to reorganize and rapidly decentralize the company in order to stimulate and stabilize **E**. If **E** is allowed to grow without disturbing **I** or affecting **A**, a **PAEI** organization can again be achieved.

The assignments in the stable organization are given to a large group of people. Stringent deadlines are imposed in order to "wake them up" to the coming of age, and the group must be multidisciplinary in order to obtain the highest **E** possible.

For the stable organization and organizations at later stages in the organizational life cycle, management transplantation becomes a problem. The stable organization is set in its ways; a new style of management might well be too trying. The older an organization becomes, the more it will resent different individual styles in managers.

The stable organization needs a capacity for **E**. If a **paEi** manager is brought in from the outside, he will most likely experience difficulties because he is different. The difficulties, however, are not so great as to preclude integration.

TREATING THE ARISTOCRATIC ORGANIZATION (pAeI)

It is a bit more difficult to help out the aristocratic organization than to help out organizations in other stages of the organizational life cycle. The aristocratic organization needs an awakening, especially from its "Finzi-Contini syndrome." The first step I take here is to conduct a "group diagnostic session," a methodology of synergetic participative diagnosis (Syndag) which takes three days to complete. A Syndag is a deep consciousness-raising session at which all participants share information about the problems a company is facing. Viewed in this way, the problems are seen to be truly overpowering. The need for change becomes obvious. Frequent Syndag sessions are necessary in order to remind people of the state the organization is in, as opposed to the state it wants to be in. The therapist must constantly call attention to manifestations of the Finzi-Contini syndrome.

Once a strong commitment for change has been created, the organization's **E** capacity must be "pumped up." Assignments are given to analyze the mission of the organization according to another model of mine. This model helps members of the group to analyze the technological, political, economic, legal, social, and physical environments of the organization. It teaches them how to analyze their markets, product scope, and values. All of this enables them to derive the opportunities and threats that face the organization.

Realizing what the future will bear leads them to design a strategy of dealing with it. A decentralized organizational structure is designed to implement this strategy. Once decentralization has been decided upon, training can start which will enable behavioral change as well. In the short run the organization becomes a pAEI and people begin to wonder whether all of this activity will actually produce results. My experience has been that, within a year of decentralization, the organization will become a PAEI.

In order to stimulate E without affecting I the assignments of the therapist are given to a multidisciplinary and multilevel group. The deadlines must create pressure and a sense of urgency.

Bringing a person with a large E into an aristocratic organization is not recommended. The members of such an organization constitute a mutual admiration society in which detail and maintenance, not growth, are the major orientations. In such a setting, a predominantly E person will experience difficulty in expressing himself and exercising creative leadership. Success would be more likely with a PaEi or a PaEI. A PaEi has a better chance for success than a paEi since he is goal- and results-oriented, qualities which the aristocratic organization needs and will encourage. A paEi can only be integrated by way of a bypass system.

When a person whose style alienates the organization is brought in, the aristocratic organization will try to discourage his style. The A rejects the E, since the latter injects turbulence which the A cannot control well. The outcome is that the E is either rejected or absorbed into the organization as a benign substance. (It loses effectiveness.) In other words, the organization develops immunities to odd, strange, or different substances, thereby rejecting qualities which may be significant and functional to its growth and survival.

To integrate an E into an aristocratic organization, the therapist begins by looking throughout the organization for anyone with an active E. Such persons are easy to find, since they are the ones who are complaining that one thing or another is not what it should be. They are also usually people whom the organization is trying to get rid of. The therapist insists that they be retained. In a sense, this stops the "bleeding" of E.

Next, the therapist establishes a task force to work on a new project that can be completed in a short period of time (such as a new product, a new market, or a new system). The therapist recommends that a newly hired E chair this task force, which is composed of the organizational "deviants." Since the latter are Es from several disciplines and levels of the organization, they constitute a bypass of the A channels of the organization. The latter have already developed "arteriosclerosis"—that is, they resent and reject change. Thus the scope and tasks of the deviants are enlarged, and P is created which rejuvenates the organization somewhat. It again believes that change is possible. More such teams can then be established, and the outsider E will soon feel comfortable in his new climate.

When a bankrupt aristocracy develops, the task becomes much more difficult, since the e has been replaced by a blank, and there is a total rejection and resentment of change. "Surgery"—a change of management—may be the only viable alternative for such an organization; since it is on the brink of bankruptcy. Surgery in itself, however, it not sufficient, and "recuperation,"—organizational therapy—is needed later on.

TREATING BUREAUCRACY (–A–i; –A––)

Bureaucratic organizations usually do not have the nerve to ask for an eclectic consultant, prefering a systems analyst to increase the **A** which they already have in overabundance.

Such organizations probably need "surgery" and a long period of "rehabilitation." The surgery would be a type of bypass—an addition of **E**. The **E** would probably have to be forced on the organization since the organization would probably fight it with all its might.

Rehabilitation would be needed in order to get **P** back into action again. Shock treatment (threats of firing, unrealistic demands, etc.) is inadvisable, because it would simply scare people, making them go frantically through any steps that they are required to make. But the results would be very short-lived, and eventually, the organization would fall back into apathy. In fact, a series of such treatments might spur the remaining good managers to leave, forcing the organization into a coma.

What is needed is multiple, simultaneous managerial transplants, with close monitoring of their integration into the system.

As for restoring dead organizations to life, this is probably a capability reserved to saints.

FIGURE 12
Recommended Treatments

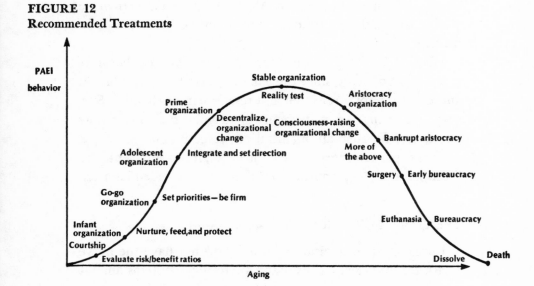

CAN AN INTERNAL CONSULTANT DO THE JOB?

It has become fashionable for large organizations to develop their own consulting departments, often called OD (organizational development) departments.

Such departments can be functional during the early stages of the organizational life cycle. However, older organizations —stable organizations and their successors—will have less success with OD departments. In a young organization, **A** and **I** are the needed capacities. These can be provided from within easily enough; the consultants would not have to fear losing their jobs. However, as an organization approaches its zenith, **E** is what is called for, and that requires "insultants" more than "forsultants." An internal consultant might not be willing or able to make the necessary "waves" and create the consciousness and desire for change.

Organizational development specialists appear to have been trained and to be inclined to perform only the **I** role. Most frequently they are ----**Is**. At *best,* they are **paeIs**. Such a style is of no use for an organization which needs serious therapy and rejuvenation. A **paeI** or ----**I** style only maintains what exists. OD specialists operate more as establishment agents who make the existing fare seem palatable than as agents of change who create the needed new dish.

Throughout my method of therapy, A'S/M, as presented above, integrators who act as agents of change are trained and developed. For at least the beginning stages of therapy, I have found that external "pacing" is necessary to create the impetus and direction for change, and to buffer any negative short-term reactions that the organization may have. For organizations at and beyond the stable stage, a more potent "medication" than simple advice is needed, and it must usually be administered externally.

SUMMARY OF THE MAIN POINTS

We have come to the end of our descriptions, analyses, and prescriptions. The main points have been:

1. No one can be an outstanding manager.
2. Thus, a complementary team composed of people with *different styles of behavior* is called for.
3. People's styles should fit the tasks they perform.
4. Conflict is inevitable and desirable.
5. A learning environment to transform conflict into a functional force is needed;
6. To maintain long-term rejuvenated organizations, periodic, timely, and therapeutic organizational changes are required.

Part IV

OUT OF THE TRAP

Chapter 13

Once Again and for the Last(?) Time: What IS Management?

> We, the willing,
> led by the unknowing,
> are doing the impossible
> for the ungrateful.
> We have done so much,
> for so long,
> with so little,
> we are now qualified
> to do anything
> with nothing.

WHAT IS MANAGEMENT?

We often take it for granted that things will get done. We expect—and we greatly want—organizations to perform. We are not surprised by changes in the world, in our cars, in the foods available on our grocers' shelves. When we consider how things happen we may think of management as playing an

215

important role in our changing society. In fact, Peter Drucker has stated that "management is the success story of the twentieth century."

Pause for a moment to consider: What is "management"? At seminars throughout the world people from different organizational levels and different disciplines (administration, finance, marketing, etc.) were asked to suggest synonyms for the verb *manage*. They came up with a variety of meanings. Before seeing what they think, pause for a moment and write your own synonyms on this page. What does the verb *manage* mean to you?

To *manage* is to:

The following list contains many of the words that people commonly selected as synonyms for the verb *manage*. Do you share their views and understanding of the concept? To *manage* is to:

Plan	Make happen	Listen
Direct	Train	Communicate
Execute	Monitor	React
Implement	Integrate*	Make and keep
Decide	Govern	submissive
Effect	Judge	Treat with
Husband	Coerce	care
Administer	Utilize	Alter by
Guide	Regulate	manipulation
Control	Mold	Run
Do	Manipulate	Supervise
Rule	Develop	Operate
Organize	Teach	Accomplish
Coordinate	Educate	Contrive
Lead*	Cooperate	Connive
Motivate*	Inspect	Conduct
Achieve	Inspire	Dominate
Handle	Review	Evaluate

These are not all of the words that have been suggested, but they are a good sample. We can check the completeness of the list by looking at the definitions of *manage* in several dictionaries.

The *Random House Dictionary*[1] defines *manage* as to bring about, to accomplish, to take charge, to take care of, to dominate, to influence, to handle, to direct, to govern, to control, to wield (a weapon), to contrive, to conduct business, to conduct commercial affairs, to be in charge, to handle or train, as a horse.

The *Funk and Wagnall's Dictionary*[2] adds new synonyms to those we already have. It defines *manage* as to guide or restrain, lead, keep in a desired state or mood by persuasion, render subservient, control, make tractable, break in, or train.

The *Oxford Illustrated Dictionary*[3] adds "to gain one's end with flattery, etc., contrive, succeed in one's aim, cope with," and *Webster's Third New International Dictionary*[4] offers the following concepts: to render submissive by delicate treatment, treat with care, steer carefully, direct, govern, order.

Let us analyze the synonyms that have been suggested. If we put aside for the moment the words marked with asterisks in the above list—*lead, integrate,* and *motivate*—we can see a common thread among the synonyms. Each synonym creates a distinction between persons who manage and persons who are managed. Each of these terms implies that person A performs some process on person B. That is, A husbands, directs, controls, and plans for B. The converse, that B processes or performs a process on A, does not hold. The common denominator of these synonyms for *manage* is the existence of a hierarchy in which one person, A, tells another person, B, what to do. Person A is the independent agent, and person B the dependent agent. B acts or should act in a manner which will satisfy A.

Commanding Compliance

Many of the words on the list, particularly the latter ones, suggest an intent to secure compliance. It is assumed that the manager knows where he or she wants to go. The purpose of the management process is to see that those who are managed, the dependent agents, will act in a manner which insures their full compliance with the manager. That is why he directs, decides, trains, governs, educates, supervises, evaluates, inspects, administers, and so on.

The common denominator is the origin of the word *manage.* The word comes from the Italian word *manegg(iare),* which means to handle, train (horses) and is derived from the Latin *manus,* for hand.

Consider the process of handling or managing a horse. If

the skilled rider can put the horse through maneuvers, we say that he or she is a capable rider or handler (manager) of the horse. With increasing skill, the rider becomes more of an independent agent and is better able to secure full compliance from the horse. In this way the distinction between which of the two gets the other to do what becomes increasingly clear. We expect and even assume this, because the rider knows what he or she wants to do and is capable of securing the compliance of the horse. Although the horse is a great deal stronger than the rider, the nature of their interaction is such that the rider makes choices with which the horse complies, and not vice versa.

Another example, though less parallel, is the handling or managing of an automobile. To manage a car, the driver makes movements with his or her hands and feet, and expects prompt, consistent, instantaneous, and proportionate response from the machine. Many people wish to manage an organization as they would manage a horse or a high-performance car. Most managers would love to have a well-handled organization, one that responds like a well-tuned machine or a well-trained horse. They want an organization to respond instantaneously and without argument to all the decisions they make. Most managers evaluate themselves as managers by how well they decide and by how well they are able to make an organization act in accordance with their plans.

The assumption is that the rider or driver knows where he wants to go and what he wants to do. A good driver or rider knows how to make the car or horse perform best. The things he handles have no intent of their own. They are basically tools that enable a controller to achieve his or her goals.

To achieve such a high level of predictability and responsiveness, the manager of people wishes to narrow the gap between what can and what should be done. He performs the managerial functions of planning, organizing, and controlling, but he is trying to achieve instant compliance, not from horses or cars, but from people, who have their own wishes, ideas, and needs. And on the whole people do not comply well to the wishes of other people; at least they do not comply automatically, as machines do.

Directive Motivation

The synonyms *lead, motivate,* and *integrate,* which we put aside earlier, can have the same connotations. The verb *lead* can actually mean "to manipulate." A manipulative leader gets people to follow him wherever he wants to go, regardless of what the interests of the followers might be. *To lead,* then, really means to find out how to get followers to go where the leader wants them to go.

The contingency theory of leadership may be an example of this approach. In a certain form this theory holds that the leader should change his style, depending upon the conditions the organization faces, in order to secure the compliance of the followers and achieve his goals. The goals are given; the question is how to make the followers get to them. In this connotation the closest synonym to the verb *lead,* in my opinion, is Webster's "to steer carefully."

The concept of motivation can also be manipulative. A widely used training film on motivation opens with the statement, "This movie is about motivation, or *how to get the maximum out* of your people." If control and punishment do not work, perhaps motivation and incentive plans will. The manipulative content of motivation is quite apparent from the title of such books as *Management of Organizational Behavior* and *Utilizing Human Resources.* (The word *utilize* has obvious exploitative connotations.) The decision has been made. The only question is how to achieve it—by control or by motivation? Frederick Hertzberg begins his famous article "One More Time: How Do You Motivate Employees?" as follows: "How many articles, books, speeches, and workshops have pleaded plaintively, 'How do I get an employee to do *what I want* him to do?'" (italics added). Read it again. Is

Hertzberg speaking about motivation or manipulation? In this connotation management motivation is synonymous with Webster's dictionary: To render submissive by delicate treatment.

As an administrator, you need to give ten pats on the head for each kick in the butt. This is the reason for having a fairly small number of people report to you. Otherwise, you will run out of hands but still have an overcapacity in feet.

From Thomas L. Martin, Jr., *Malice in Blunderland* (New York: McGraw-Hill, 1973), p. 32.

Motivation can be seen as a tool for securing compliance, a tool that managers use to achieve their goals or the goals that they set for the organization. Indicative of this bias is the literature on motivation. In that literature, motivation is said to yield increases in productivity and profits, and these are goals of management. But are they necessarily goals of all members of the organization? No one asks why workers should be interested in increased productivity. Where in the literature on motivation is improvement in morale for its own sake treated as a measure of success? If morale is mentioned at all, it is usually as an afterthought, after due consideration has been given to the real test of success—profitability.

It is not strange, therefore, that some trade unions in the United States oppose systems of motivation, job enlargement, and the like. They perceive these as managerial schemes for manipulating workers' productivity, and thus as exploitation of workers.

As taught and practiced, the classical process of management relies upon the *utilization* and control of human resources. Look at the language employed—span of control, unity of command, and so on. Why not span of *motivation* and unity of *direction?*

Personnel are trained in order to increase their ability to

> A story that appeared in the *New Yorker* sometime ago described a conversation between a mother and her son. The mother was a psychologist, and one day, she asked her son to take out the trash. She began saying something more, but before she could, her son interrupted, "OK, Mom, I'll take out the trash, but *PLEEEASE don't* motivate me!"

contribute to the organization, to implement organizational goals.

Classical management theory—planning, organizing, motivating, and controlling—is basically a theory of how a trained elite should make decisions *for* an organization and then secure the efficient implementation of those decisions by the rest of the organization.

Classical management theory is *elitist,* since management constitutes only a small minority of the organization. It is undemocratic, since it assumes that those managed will have hardly any say on who will manage them (that is, those who lead them were imposed on them) or on what is to be done (that is, the goals they are to work toward were set for them).

IS MANAGEMENT NECESSARY?

If management has these drawbacks, why can't an organization identify and achieve its goals without management? In some systems, management is a rotating call to serve the community rather than a professional career. The Israeli kibbutz is an example. In other systems, efforts have been made to abolish management altogether. In Yugoslavia, for example, the goal of the self-management system was to have people manage themselves.[5]

Despite such efforts to rule out management or to weaken it, management emerges as a dominant force to which the organization has to listen.[6] Why? What factors make management indispensable? What role does it play in organizations?

It has been suggested that management is an unnecessary remnant of the preindustrial era, that organizations would be much better off without all those layers on top of each other. The literature is replete with discussions of organizations that are managed by incompetent people whose smart, committed secretaries and assistants keep them out of trouble. But somehow all attempts to rule out management seem to fail. Management, like the phoenix rising from its own ashes, continually reemerges as the dominant force. What makes management indispensable? Perhaps we can answer this question by analyzing what management does.

WHAT DOES MANAGEMENT DO?

In *The Managing of Organizations,* Bertram M. Gross states: "Whenever people want to accomplish a difficult social task, they must strengthen existing organizations or build new ones. But organizations do not run themselves. They must be administered [managed]. If people want to undertake still more difficult tasks, they must build larger or stronger organizations. This leads to still more administration [management]."[7]

In this century, management has become a field of study in its own right. It is associated in our minds with organizations and with professionalism. We think of management as the identification of problems and the application of a range of particular skills to their solution.

Ordinarily, we think of an organization as having a hierarchical structure in the shape of a pyramid and as being run by the managers or executives at the top of the pyramid. We might be better advised to think of an hourglass shape. The top executives are caught in the middle of the hourglass. Above these top executive are the stockholders, the board of directors, the executive committee, and a wide range of external entities, such as advisers, regulators, competitors, suppliers, clients, supporters, and special interest groups.

Management is held responsible for producing results while under pressure from these forces. In order to produce maximal results in what appears to be a hostile environment, it naturally tries to control as many variables as possible. The variables that appear to be the easiest to control are the internal variables, the people who are supposed to carry out directives. Consequently, the greater the turbulance of the external environment, the more hierarchical (control-oriented, power-based) an organization becomes.[8] Bennis laments that although he had expected organizations to be more flexible and more open in a turbulent environment, in actuality they become more bureaucratic. "I can now compare what a specialist, a theorist, blithely believed *should* be done, with what in an imperfect world, *can* be done." Instead of giving rise

FIGURE 13

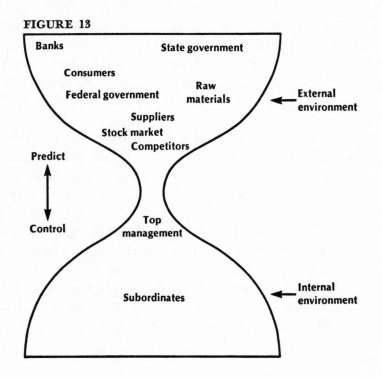

to temporary leadership, temporary groups, temporary authority, Bennis feels that a turbulent environment makes bureaucracy inevitable.

Increase in control appears to be a normal reaction to threats. The more unpredictable the threats, the more tightly we cling to our weapons. It is not strange, then, that management by and large has been opposed to participatory systems. Participatory systems increase the magnitude of the uncertainty with which management must deal, thereby adding to the turbulence that management is already experiencing.

Management, then, handles uncertainty and decides how the organization will exploit the opportunities that emerge in a changing environment. It also decides how the organization will react to environmental threats. The indispensability of management stems from the fact that an organization needs to react to threats and opportunities and that greater turbulence signifies greater uncertainty and greater risks. The greater the risks, the more control management is able to exercise. In a situation without change and therefore without the need for discretionary decisions, management would lose its role.

Management is necessary to provide predictable, effective, and efficient organizational responses to environmental conditions. But at the same time management is an elitist, exploitative, undemocratic process. Does it have to be the exclusive domain of an exclusive group (or of any one individual)? I maintain strongly that it does not—and this entire book is my argument that it *must* not.

The typical mistake of those who believe that management is necessarily elitist is that they assume that "management" as a group of people and "management" as a process are *necessarily* one and the same. But management is elitist only if a group of people monopolizes the managerial process—that is, the determination of what environmental threats and opportunities exist and how to react to them.

Since no individual is a **PAEI,** any individualistic elitism leads to mismanagement. Furthermore, the entire social class of managers cannot manage. The **P** component of the **PAEI** model is typically the people on the line, those who produce the results, that is, the salespersons, the workers, the book-keepers, and so on. To get a true **PAEI** team, one needs workers who will *comanage* with the management: the workers playing the **P** role, while management plays the **A**, the **E** and the **I** roles. One aspect of the mismanagement trap is to believe that managers are **PAEI** (Supermen) and the workers are **----** (Deadwood).

The elitist distinction between those who manage and those who are managed has historical roots, but the distinction is being and should be reexamined in today's society.

THE ORIGINS OF MANAGERIAL ELITISM

Perhaps we can trace the hierarchical nature of management and the exclusivity of managerial prerogatives back to the time when the owner and the manager were one and the same. The owner knew (or was supposed to know) what he wanted. He hired a worker and told the worker what to do.

Drawing by W. Miller; © 1976
The New Yorker Magazine, Inc.

He allocated, organized, and coordinated the work of his employees. The workers were an extension of the plant machinery, "hired hands."

When ownership and management separated and professional management emerged, the theory developed that management represented and was responsible to the owners. Presumably, management defined goals and sought compliance in achieving them on behalf of the owners. However, management became more and more powerful as organizations grew into large bureaucracies. The owners became distant shareholders whose only recourse if they opposed corporate policies was to sell their equity. The board of directors, which was supposed to supervise management and express the interests of stockholders, frequently lost the ability to control management effectively. More often than not, it was nominated and effectively controlled by top management.

An aura of elitism evolved around these independent agents —the managers. It was argued that those who managed knew or should know what ought to be achieved. The components of the managerial process—organizing and controlling—developed as a means of securing compliance from those who were managed so that the manager could achieve the goals he had defined for the organization.

This book has focused on the organizational consequences of a nonteam approach to the management process. However, the hierarchical nature of most of today's management has extraorganizational consequences as well. A hierarchical, exclusively compliance-seeking industrial system creates real dangers for democracy. How much participation in political life can we expect from an individual who is dominated, manipulated, passive, and complying for most of his working hours? How can a person who cannot control his work environment perceive himself as being able to control his political destiny? Individuals who are passive in their working life are also likely to be passive in their political life.

Because of the nonhumanistic, mechanistic aspects of the

managerial process, management has been under increasing attack in recent years. There has been hostility toward big business, big bureaucracies, and powerful managerial elites. This is not strange. Why should people want to be on the receiving end of the managerial process? And why should they want to be on the receiving end of the decision-making process? Would you like to be planned for? directed? executed for? implemented? decided for? husbanded? administered? guided? controlled? ruled? organized? coordinated? governed? dominated? manipulated?

Many students of our society (for example, Mason and Galbraith) feel that the technostructural managerial elite needs to be socially and politically controlled. The members of this elite hardly represent the stockholders; they mostly represent themselves. It has been suggested that such a powerful self-interest group is politically unacceptable in a democratic society. The political pressure to make management more responsible has expressed itself in different theories on the social responsibility of management.

It has been suggested, for example, that managers have to be responsible not only to the stockholder but to the worker and the consumer. Although the power of management has increased, management is still viewed as a top-down elitist process on the assumption that management still represents the owner and that the subordinates are still "hired hands." The responsibility of management to different constituencies, including the subordinates, has not expressed itself in management theory or in management tools and techniques. The language, the tools, and the organizational systems that facilitate the top-down managerial process must be changed if the process of management is to effectively reflect the changes in our society.

THE MANAGEMENT TEAM

We have already said that management is a social, systemic, proactive, and purposeful process.

It is social because it involves interaction among people who have to work together in order to produce the results for which an organization exists.

It is systemic, that is, both systematic and comprehensive. Since management is systematic, its decisions are sequenced, timed, applied, and methodical. Since management is comprehensive, it encompasses the organization in its totality. Management tries to control the relevant variables, the inputs and the throughputs, to produce the desired result.

The management process is proactive. That is, it is goal-oriented behavior based on what is expected to happen rather than a reaction to what has already happened.

But can the proactive activities of management be implemented by one individual alone? For proactive behavior, **E** is needed; to make proactive systems work, **A** is called for; to make them socially acceptable, **I,** and to make them effectual, **P.** Clearly, proactive activities require complementary teams. Thus, while the managerial process is indispensable, the elitist managerial structure (in which an individual manager of a group of managers monopolizes this process) can and should be questioned. For the managerial process to be successful, the entire organization should participate in it: "Every employee a manager," as Scott Myers put it.

But the desirability of participative management can hardly be considered a new idea. How can participative management be achieved? Thus far, I have discussed *why* we need participative, team management. In the next and last chapter, let me *introduce* my methodology for making participative management work.

NOTES

1. *The Random House Dictionary* (New York: Random House, 1967).

2. *Funk and Wagnall's New Standard Dictionary of the English Language* (New York, 1963).

3. *Oxford Illustrated Dictionary* (Clarendon Press, 1962).

4. *Webster's Third New International Dictionary* (Springfield, Mass.: Merriam, 1954).

5. Ichak Adizes, *Industrial Democracy: Yugoslav Style* (New York: Free Press, 1971). Reprinted, paperbound edition, Los Angeles: MDOR Institute, 1977.

6. I. Adizes and Elisabeth Mann-Borgese, eds., *Self-Management: New Dimensions to Democracy* (Santa Barbara, Calif.: ABC-CLIO, 1977).

7. Bertram M. Gross, *The Managing of Organizations* (New York: Crowell Collier, 1964).

8. Adizes, *Industrial Democracy*, chap. 7.

Chapter 14

An Introduction to the Adizes Management Method

THE LIMITATIONS OF THE CLASSICAL PYRAMIDAL STRUCTURE

Let us look at a typical organization and analyze it according to the **PAEI** model.

The typical organization is structured pyramidally; it is hierarchical in nature. Hierarchical organizations have certain characteristics. One of them is that the higher one rises in the hierarchy, the more one gains in authority, in responsibility, and in rewards. Thus, the top of the hierarchy has maximum authority, responsibilities, and rewards. The bottom (that is, workers on the line) has little or no authority, little responsibility, and little rewards.

Viewed from the standpoint of the **PAEI** model, the pyramidal organization looks as if it were structured in layers. The bottom is almost all **P**; then there is a layer of **A**; and at the very, very top there is an **E** layer. There is no **I** layer. In hierarchical organizations one is expected to go through the chain of command and not violate the formal channels. If there is some responsibility for integration, it is usually dele-

FIGURE 14

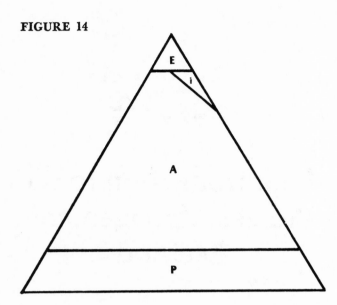

gated to an organizational development department which is tucked away in some corner or the middle level of the organization.

A hierarchical organization is structured to secure control and predictable results. The **E** at the top is in command. He plans, decides, develops scenarios of what should happen. The **A**s administer his ideas (that is, translate them into operational systems), and the **P**s implement them.

The purpose of the pyramidal structure is to see that what the "boss" wants done, is done. The boss is the brain—his subordinates are his hired hands. (Notice that in describing their subordinates, people will often say, "XYZ is my right hand," "ABC is my eyes and ears," and the like, but that they are very unlikely to say, "So-and-so is my brain.")

The pyramidal structure is intended to ensure that the lower layers of the organization, **A** and **P**, will faithfully carry out the decisions of the higher-ups, **E**. The structure is for a follow-up: for efficiency, effectiveness, and control. Notice that the expressions we use are "unity of command" and "span of control" rather than "unity of direction" and "span of motivation."

In pyramidal organizations **E** and **I** activity is encouraged only at the top; the top makes plans and decisions. The rest of the organization carries them out (**A** and **P**).

This structure in **PAEI** layers impairs *long-term* organizational effectiveness, since **A** behavior, which is programmed and efficiency- and detail-oriented, stifles the expression of **E**. Under this structure, integration (**I**) is discouraged throughout the organization, since it might break down the formal channels of communication and thus reduce the predictability of outcomes.

It is not strange, then, that organizations that want efficiency (**A**) and result orientation (**P**), are high programmed (**PA**) and thus very resistant to change. If a person on lower levels of such an organization has an idea, the chances that the idea will be accepted by the organization are very slim. An **E** idea that starts "floating" up the organizational hierarchy threatens **A** and **P**, thus, there is a very good chance that someone will see the idea as a threat to the system that he is trying to control and will "kill the idea" either by ignoring it or by saying that "it won't work."

Many companies realize that the **PA** structure clogs the channels of communication and cuts off the flow of good ideas. Thus, to circumvent the **PA** structure they organize a president's coffee hour, or establish an open-door policy that enables people to visit and express themselves to executives, or nail up suggestion boxes. But there is very little evidence that these methods really work. The stronger the **PA** orientation of an organization, the less variation in behavior it permits and the less chance there is for anyone at the bottom to win acceptance for his ideas.

The deficiency of **E** in large organizations is manifested in various ways. One manifestation is that older organizations usually import top managers (pirating), as if to admit that creativity and aggressiveness are extinct within them. A second manifestation is the "fast-track" phenomenon. To obtain **E**, organizations hire graduates from leading business schools and put them on a fast track to the top. A third manifestation is the fantastic growth of the consulting industry. What consultants offer is **E**, ideas of what changes organizations should make.

To nourish **E** and **I**, what an organization needs is an **EI** structure that complements the **PA** structure. In my opinion many mistakes have been made by well-intentioned organizational behavior professionals who have tried to shake up the **PA** structure and to make it more **EI**. In the process they have ruined the **PA** structure. One leading university has eliminated all departments in order to encourage flexibility and interdisciplinary fertilization, that is, **EI**. Under the new system, however, it takes about three times as long to make a decision and people do not know who makes them or how they are made.

In an effort not to be bureaucratic, many organizations establish a highly flexible participative structure (**EI**), but within a year or two the people in such organizations are exhausted by the lack of predictability of the new system. They almost yearn for a strong leader who will take over and tell them what to do. In the long run such a nonstructured and nondisciplined participative system fails.

I suggest that we should neither try to convert a **PA** structure into an **EI** structure nor "run for cover" to the security of **PA** from the anxieties of **EI**. Both a **PA** structure and an **EI** structure are essential to the effective and flexible long-run operation of an organization.

But how can we create an organization embodying both of these structures?

I have spent the last ten years trying to build parallel and complementary **PA** and **EI** organizational structures that operate with a growthful participative decision making process. The purpose of this chapter is to introduce the method.

THE ADIZES SYNERGETIC MANAGEMENT METHOD (A'S/M)

The Adizes Method is first of all synergetic. A synergetic process is one in which the combined effect of the component parts of the process is greater than the separate effects of those parts. In other words, the interaction among the parts has a value. **PAEI** is larger than **(P)** + **(A)** + **(E)** + **(I)**. **PAEI** is a synergetic process in which each participant learns from the others. Everyone grows in a learning environment, and what is learned is the value added or created.

In synergetic management, workers **(P)** and management **(A** and/or **E)** can create more by working together **(I)** than by working separately.

S/M as a symbol has a meaning. It means that given S (synergy), M (management) will occur. Management will occur if there is synergy, or to put it in other words, if there is no synergy, there is no management. The role of management is to create an environment for synergy.

This means that the function of the managerial process is to create an environment in which people can share ideas openly, cooperate rather than compete, learn from one another, and share the responsibility for the outcome. Thus, the Adizes Method differs from traditional management theory, where the manager plans and then is responsible for seeing to it that his plans are carried out (that is, organizes, controls, motivates, disciplines, etc.) by or even with others.

The letter A in A'S/M stands for my last name. I put it in in order to differentiate this method of management from those that already exist. I have observed that, at least in the United States, fashion dominates. If any system achieves minimal success, or if there is a new catchword, within a very short period of time everyone is using it. Some of those who indiscriminately jump on the bandwagon are not qualified or trained, and within a few years a highly acclaimed concept becomes so adulterated in practice that few dare to use it anymore. That, I believe, has been the fate of "participative management," "open systems," and "sensitivity training," and that is what I believe is going to happen to "sociotechnical systems," "contingency theories of leadership," and the "quality of working life."

To avoid this fate, I have added my name to the system and I have registered it as a service mark, so that only people trained by MDOR Institute in the latest A'S/M techniques can claim to be using it. I have established MDOR Institute for this explicit purpose of training A'S/M facilitators and for research and development of materials to support the A'S/M method.

What, then, is the A'S/M method? It consists of a structure and a process and it operates with phases to accomplish a set of goals.

A'S/M STRUCTURE

The A'S/M organizational structure has two parts. The **PA** part needs no introduction: it is the hierarchical system that exists in most organizations.

FIGURE 15

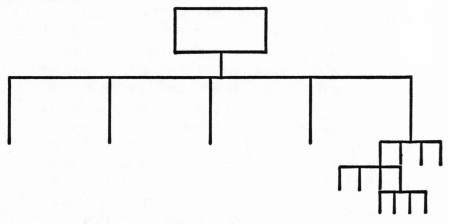

The **PA** part can be presented as a half-circle: at the top is the president, and at the bottom are the workers.

FIGURE 16

As I have suggested before, it would be very difficult if not impossible for **E** or **I** to "float up" this **PA** half-circle since it is structured for **P** and **A**. This would be like having blood flow in opposite directions and in the same vein. Obviously, a blood clot could be generated that would stop the circulation altogether. Anyone along the line who feels threatened by an **E** or **I** suggestion can stop it. Thus, for bottom-up floating of **E** and **I** we need a separate **EI** structure.

FIGURE 17

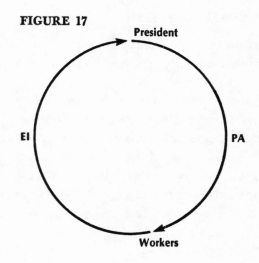

The **EI** structure is composed of synerteams and a POC (Participative Organizational Conduit) System.

The synerteams are ad hoc groups of people that are assigned to solve specific problems. They are disbanded when their problems are solved. They meet for a maximum of three hours per week. POC is basically a permanent synerteam for a certain organizational unit in the organization.

There is a POC for every level and organized unit of the **PA** structure. These POCs reflect the **PA** structure. Thus, we may have corporate, divisional, departmental, plant, shift, and working unit POCs. A POC can appoint any number of task synerteams, depending on how many problems it wishes to solve.

The **EI** structure is complementary and not a substitute for the normal, hierarchical top-down **PA** structure. It is a parallel structure, participative in nature to enable a bottom up flow of ideas, problems, solutions, etc.

The parallel structure has been tried before, especially in General Motors, and it has been called the "collateral organization."[1]

In A'S/M it is of permanent nature. It meets once a month and has a plan of action, eleven phases to go through in order to maintain its proactive character (see below).

Synerteam: A PAEI + capi Team

1. Synerteams are created to solve a problem that is not well defined and that can only be solved by means of a *new* system, **EI**.

2. A synerteam will also be established when the person in charge of the relevant **PA** structure does not have *capi*.

Managers in organizations have authority, power, and influence or a combination of the three. These three sources of "organizational energy" overlap. If a person has *capi* over a problem, he should not create a synerteam. He should be able to implement his decision effectively without one.

FIGURE 18
The Elements of *capi*

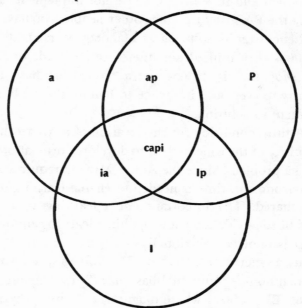

a	= *Authority:* A manager's legal right to make a decision—embedded in his position in the organization—which the manager has no power to enforce.
ap	= *Authorized power:* The authority to punish or reward.
p	= *Power:* The ability to punish and reward without authority.
ip	= *Indirect power:* Exists when a person appears to be influencing, but there is an attributed threat to what the person is saying, and people do what the person tells them to do, not because they believe in what he is saying (*i*), but because they fear the repercussions of refusing to comply (*p*).
i	= *Influence:* The *ability* to make another person do something without using either power or authority—that is, we truly convince the other person. Pure influence occurs when the focal person (the one we are influencing) believes in the activity himself—that is, he is coopted enough to do whatever needs to be done on his own volition.
ia	= *Influencing authority:* The authority we accept, frequently called professional authority or authority by acceptance.
capi	= *Coalesced authority, power, and influence:* When a person has *capi* he has authority to make a decision, he can legally punish those who refuse to comply with the decision, and he is able to argue the merits of his decision convincingly.

Very frequently a manager realizes that although he knows the problem and its solution, he cannot implement his solution via the **PA** structure, since other people who have power or influence over his solution will sabotage it. He realizes that his *capi* is very limited and therefore he needs to create a group *capi,* that is, to coalesce a group that has sufficient authority, power, and influence to handle the problem and implement its solution.

3. A third condition for the creation of a synerteam is the availability of the time needed to develop a team approach to solving a problem. Since the Adizes Method requires a learning environment, time is needed to enable learning to occur or be shared. The importance of a learning environment should be self-evident by now; within a learning environment conflict is resolved functionally.

Thus, a synerteam is created: (1) to solve a specific problem for which no *one* individual has *capi;* (2) to diagnose and/or solve an **EI** problem whose diagnosis or solution requires a participative design; and (3) to handle problems within a learning environment.

The synerteam assignment sheet (Figure 19) is an example of the degree of structure and discipline which is required in using the method. It states *what* is to be done. Next the assignment sheet states when the team is to start working and when it has to finish. It must meet *regularly* for a *fixed* period of time. This is done to simulate as closely as possible a seminar, classroom atmosphere.

The assignment sheet identifies the members of the task synerteam. These members constitute a *capi* group. First, we look for a team member who has authority to make a decision concerning the problems being analyzed. A synerteam is *not* a study group or a recommendation committee; it is a decision-making team. Next, we try to identify those who have power over a possible solution—those who can sabotage the solution. A nonrepresentative sample of this group is part

FIGURE 19

ADIZES
SYNERGETIC MANAGEMENT METHOD

WHAT
SYNERTEAM _____

PIPS:

(see over)

WHO

CAPI	NAME	PAEI	ROLE
C		pael	INTEGRATOR
a		PaEi	IMPLEMENTOR
p		pAEi	ADMINISTRATOR
p		paEl	FIRST OBSERVER
p		pAEi	CONDUIT
p		paEi	RESOURCE
P		paEi	RESOURCE
p		paEi	RESOURCE
i		paEi	RESOURCE

HOW

BUDGET ALLOCATED_____

TIME ALLOCATED:

   DAY _____

   TIME _____TO_____

   FREQUENCY:
   EVERY_____

MEETING PLACE:
   _____

OTHER:

WHEN

STARTING DATE _____

FINISH PHASE _____ ON _____

FINISH PHASE _____ ON _____

FINISH PHASE _____ ON _____

SOLUTION IMPLEMENTATION COMPLETED: LATEST DEADLINE _____

FIGURE 19 (*continued*)

WHAT: (continued)

PIPs:

PAEI	ROLE	RESPONSIBLE FOR:
ael	INTEGRATOR	Synerteam operation in accordance with A'S/M method. Facilitating growth of synergy and integration.
PaEi	IMPLEMENTOR	Synerteam producing results by fixed deadlines. Implementing solution. Punctuality of attendance. Mutual respect (e.g., no smoking).
pAEi	ADMINISTRATOR	Scheduling of meetings and meeting space. Information and minutes. Updating absentee members. Opening and closing meeting. Announcing beginning and end of breaks. Posting synerteam charts and nametags. Appointing a mirror. Guarding that A'S/M rules are being followed. Distributing minutes.
paEI	OBSERVER	Reflects at end of meeting how synergetic integration of group is progressing.
pAEi	CONDUIT	Reporting to higher OS/T ideas and action taken and all problems being experienced with implementation of A'S/M.
PaEi pael pAEi	SYNERCORE	Fixes agenda. Appoints a synerteam to have CAPI.

of the synerteam. ("Nonrepresentative" means that the most powerful, and active people are called in.) Last, we look for persons who are professionally knowledgeable about the problem. These persons could come from within the organization, or they could be brought in from the outside.

When a synerteam is a *capi* group, this means that it can solve the problem with which it is dealing. If it cannot do so, this means that it needs more authority, power, or influence. If a problem is totally out of the control of the synerteam, the synerteam is disbanded.

A synerteam has *capi* and has to perform like **PAEI**. Each member of the team has to perform in a certain style depending on the component of *capi* he or she brings in (see Figure 19).

The person who has the authority to decide has to undertake the **P** responsibility, i.e., he is responsible that the team solves the assigned problem. The people who were appointed due to their power to sabotage a solution have to undertake the responsibility to **E**: be entrepreneuring about how to solve the problem ("tell me how *yes* to solve it rather than why you *won't* do it"). A person who neither has authority, nor power, nor influence (professional bias) over the problem is appointed to coalesce the group. He is the integrator.

By composing a team that has *capi* to act as **PAEI**, several goals are achieved:

1. Planning is linked to implementation.
2. Those who possess negative energy (power) are asked to create a solution, rather than sabotage it. Power is converted into a positive force.
3. People have to act out a role which makes the system developmental to the individuals.
4. Cross fertilization of know-how is achieved: a person from Marketing integrates a team in Production and a person from Production integrates a team in Marketing.

POC

A POC is composed of:

1. Permanent members.
   a. The head of the organizational unit.
   b. All those who report to him directly.
2. Members who serve for one year as conduits of directly reporting lower level POCs who report to this organizational unit in the **PA** structure.
3. Ad hoc members who serve until the synerteam dissolves. Those are the conduits of each synerteam created by the POC.

Thus, a hierarchy of permanent POCs is created, each of which has its own synerteams which are working on specific problems. If a synerteam runs out of *capi*, it goes to the corresponding POC to which it pertains. If that POC lacks enough *capi*, the problem is presented to a higher POC until it achieves the necessary *capi*.

What should be clear is that change (**E**) is generated in the **EI** structure of POCs and synerteams. In organizations that apply A'S/M a person who has a significant recurrent problem that needs *nonprogrammed* solutions will go to his synerteam or POC. If the problem were brought only to the boss, there is the danger that he would apply a **PA** solution to it for reasons of expediency.

This, in short, is how the **EI** structure complements the normal **PA** structure. The **EI** structure meets periodically to deal with specifically defined problems. Once the **EI** structure makes a decision, the **PA** structure is assigned to carry it out.

THE ADIZES METHOD AS A DECISION-MAKING PROCESS

Basically the process of the Adizes Method follows the phases of the creative process:

1.	Defreeze.	5.	Illuminate.
2.	Accumulate.	6.	Accommodate.
3.	Deliberate.	7.	Finalize.
4.	Incubate.	8.	Reinforce.

In individual decision making one person usually goes through steps 1–5 and then brings his decision to his superiors for evaluation; in other words, he recommends but they may finalize. That might be called the short-long way. It does not take too long for a person working alone to reach the illumination stage. It takes quite a long time, however, for the person to "sell" his idea and see that it is implemented. This is especially true if the person has no *capi* and especially if the problem was not **PA** in nature but an **EI** one, i.e., calls for systemic change.

In the Adizes Method, for **EI** problems that require group *capi* the long-short way should be taken. The synerteam integrator leads the group *together* through steps 1–5. The group takes much longer to go through these steps than would one individual working alone. However, once a *capi* group illumination has been reached, the accommodation is swift.

TABLE 2
Nonprogrammed Decision-Making Process

	Traditional Management	A'S/M
1. Defreeze		
2. Accumulate		
3. Deliberate	Alone } Short	Group } Long
4. Incubate		
5. Illuminate		
6. Accommodate		
7. Finalize	Group Approval } Long	Group } Short
8. Reinforce		
Total Time:		Shorter

The philosophy of the Adizes Method is to provide a wholistic, synergetic, cooperative teamwork for **EI** type of problems and individualistic top down decision making on **PA** type of problems.

The cooperative **EI** teamwork, however, should avoid the fate of participative management where committees are created.

Management by committees is a disaster and by no means do I recommend that. The Adizes Method attempts to build teamwork and avoid management by committee. What is the difference?

In a committee the different roles that people are inclined to perform lead them to focus on and emphasize one stage in the creative process more than another. The **A** type of individual usually has difficulty illuminating. He appears to be accumulating forever. He wants to think things over; he deliberates, incubates, and then goes back to accumulation. On the other hand, the **E** illuminates at the slightest provocation. The **I** accommodates. The **P** rushes to judgment, that is, he shoots from the hip—he wants to finalize as soon as possible.

Thus, when there is an unstructured participative decision-making process like in a typical committee, the people in the group "spread" all over the creative phases of decision making. While an **A** is trying to identify the problem and is asking for more data about it, an **E** already is suggesting what can be done before he even knows what the problem is. The **E**'s suggestion is often only tangential to the problem at hand. At the same time, a **P** is pressing for a conclusion "so we can get back to work for heaven's sake." The **A** is highly annoyed by the pressure and holds back making a decision; the **E** comes up with a slew of ideas and can't understand why the **A** finds fault with all of them. The **P** bursts with motions to call the question and take a vote. At the same time the **I** tries to accommodate as well as he can. Meanwhile, time is running out. Finally a decision is forced on the group by the chairperson. Most of the members are unhappy with it, since they are still at different phases of the creative process. Someone will then say: "We got manipulated. Participative management doesn't work." It doesn't, I agree, because participative management should not mean that anyone can say anything he wants to say anytime he wants to say it. It is a mess and there is no reason why it should work. There is no discipline or system to it.

In the Adizes Method, the role of the integrator is to lead the discussions of the team in a manner that almost assures that its members will move *together* from one phase of the creative process to another. The Adizes Method has "rules of the game" (what can and what cannot be done during a discussion) that prevent jumping from one phase to another. The Method prevents going on to accumulation before defreezing has been completed, and it then prevents the Es and the Ps from rushing through accumulation into deliberation and premature illumination before all relevant information has been accumulated.

As the group proceeds together from one phase to the next, a cooperative learning environment is created and maintained. This process takes time, but it should be viewed as an investment that yields results. The improved results stem from improved communication, a supportive environment, and better decision making.

In the Adizes Method there is no voting. The Adizes Method is a learning environment in which one of the important results is what was learned from the discussion in addition to what was decided. All participants express opinions, but the final decision is made by the P (the person with the authority) who is responsible for its implementation. Since no meeting is held unless the P attends it, and since the entire team proceeds together from phase to phase in the decision making process, it is most improbable that the P will make a decision that the synerteam will not accept.

In ten years of experience with the method in over 100 companies, we have never had a case in which the manager has vetoed the teams conclusions. The problems solved were of major and minor importance, from a total reorganization to a change in production processes. In a year, an average 40 percent of the problems identified are solved, the condition of 40 percent more improved; 20 percent are left to be dealt with in the second year.

The synerteam integrator keeps the group together as it moves from phase to phase of the creative process. In a synerteam the integrator is chosen from outside the unit which he is integrating and he is chosen from among the people who have the least bias on the subject being discussed. Thus, in the Adizes Method there is cross-pollination of knowledge. People from marketing integrate people in production; people in production spend up to 20 percent of their time working with their colleagues in engineering; and so on.

But there is specialization in roles too. The synerteam integrator sees to it that the climate is conducive to learning. The synerteam implementor sees to it that meetings yield results. The synerteam administrator is responsible for seeing to it that the team has all the information that it needs in order to be productive.

The purpose of the Adizes Method is to achieve the process of management described in this book. People participate on subjects which either affect them or to which they have something to contribute. Via synerteams and the POCs, they can change whatever can and needs to be changed. And the structured, disciplined decision-making process of the Adizes Method enables people to feel responsible for the decisions that are made cooperatively.

PHASES OF THE ADIZES METHOD

The Adizes Method has been applied to about 100 organizations. There are several phases to the method (see Figure 20), and different organizations have reached different phases.

Companies that have gone through more than five stages

FIGURE 20
A'S/M Phases

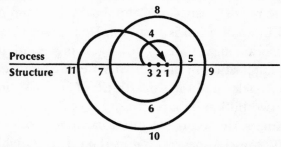

"Intervention to establish an organization that can redesign itself . . ."

1. Syndag (synergetic diagnosis).
2. Synerteams formation and training.
3. POCs established.
4. Defining organization's mission with the Adizes Method.
5. Cascading the method to lower levels of the organization.
6. Reorganizing the **PA** structure.
7. Redesigning information flows to fit the reorganized **PA** structure.
8. Detailed planning via synerteams on marketing, production, finance, and human resources strategies.
9. Resource allocation: dollars, people, space, time (via synerteams).
10. Finalization of the POCs all the way to the bottom of the organization until a full "circle" (**PA–EI**) has been created.
11. Incentive systems that reinforce the previous ten phases and reinforce repeating them (wholistic synergetic).
12. Resyndag—redo diagnosis and start circle again.

find that communication is easier, problems are attacked faster, turnover is almost nil, morale is higher, and productivity, profitability, and market share are on the rise. People's attitudes change in a positive direction, and cooperation is easy to obtain. People truly try to help each other. In some companies the Adizes Method has been cascaded to the workers on the line.

The change does not happen without growing pains though. All the behavioral manifestations of organizational change occur when the Adizes Method is introduced.

It has had, however, an impact on organizations since it is a method that, once mastered, becomes part of the normal way of managing an organization.

The longest experience with the Method in a company that

went beyond four phases is with CBI, Atlanta. The smallest company that applied it consists of 50 employees and two million in revenues (Doody Co., Columbus, Ohio), and the most advanced in application is Inspiron, Division of C. R. Bard, Rancho Cucamonga, Calif. The largest organizations to attempt its application in the United States are Northrop Aviation, Los Angeles, and the Department of Social Welfare, Los Angeles (two billion dollars in size).

The Adizes Method is not just a participative system or a sensitivity, consciousness-raising method. It is a highly structured method on the what, when, how and who in participative managerial decision making.

GOALS OF THE ADIZES METHOD

The Adizes Method has four goals that it attempts to achieve *simultaneously*:

1. Solve the actual organizational and managerial problems of the company.
2. Establish team building.
3. Provide for individual growths.
4. Provide for managerial training.

Among the problems that get solved are communication, morale, productivity, awareness to company problems, organizational structures, almost any problem that management as a team can relatively decide on and control.

The Method differs from other systems in that it attempts to be *comprehensive*. The Syndag, which is the first step of the 11 phases, has some similarity with the Japanese K.J. Method and with Kobayashi's Method, but it goes beyond both of them. In A'S/M, teams are built to solve the identified problems in a way that improves the teamwork. In this phase OD takes over,[2] and the method borrows heavily from structured small group dynamics. Once teams know how to identify and solve problems, a network of teams, the **EI** system, is established (similar to Likerts' overlapping structure). Then strategic management and policy making theory is introduced and teams focus on the setting of the mission, goals and objectives that can be and are communicated downward—a method which is similar but not identical to Management by Objectives. Once diagnosis has been completed in a cooperative, participative way, teams have been set up to work together and actually solve problems and once jointly the goals are set, the organization structure is designed participatively in synerteams. Information flows are designed again by synerteams to reflect the structure, mission, and definition of the problems and eventually the incentives reflect a structure that is designed to achieve the mission and the necessary information and resources to accomplish them.

Going through the 11 phases in the sequence as designed achieves the four goals of the Adizes Method simultaneously.

The A'S/M method is an accumulative synergetic and wholistic integration of different theories and practices of organizational change to provide for balanced growth for organizations on the ascending part of the life cycle or/and for organizational rejuvenations for organizations on the declining part of the life cycle.

It maintains balanced growth since the organization **PAEI**s with *capi* making its decisions jointly, so they are balanced and the results are implementable. The individuality cult of the traditional management theories and the founder's trap is avoided.

The method rejuvenates since synerteams and POCs, the **EI** structure, introduce a significant amount of integrated Entrepreneurship to solve actual company problems.

It provides for negative entropy since diagnosis is repeated annually. Thus, a new source of energy is created to move the organization from one equilibrium to another. It is an open system because the organization analyzes where it is, where it wants to go, and makes the necessary changes to adapt in its structure, information, resource allocations, and reward systems to the changing mission and environment.

This was an introduction to the Adizes Method which is applied in the USA, Ghana, Mexico, Sweden, Denmark, Israel, and other areas in the profit and not for profit sectors of society. In the Ministry of Health of Ghana, it has been applied to design the planning of the health delivery system of the country. In Baja California, Mexico, it has been applied to plan the socio-economic future of the state. At Doody it has been applied to design store planning of department stores. At Northrop it has been applied to plan the future generations of their airplanes.

My next book will dwell in depth on how the system works and what are its promises and pitfalls.

NOTES

1. "The Parallel Organizations Structure at General Motors— An Interview with Howard C. Carlson," in *Personnel* (September-October 1978), 64–69.

2. Dale E. Zand, "Collateral Organization: A New Chance Strategy" in *Organizational Development: Theory, Practice, and Research,* edited by French, Bell, and Zawacki (Dallas, Tex.: Business Publications, Inc., 1978).

Appendix

Variations on the Theme (Performing Several Roles— But Not All of Them!)

It isn't necessary that the **PAEI** code always be made up of capital letters. A **P** may be a superstar salesperson, but an average salesperson with some producer characteristics is a **p**. Thus, in the discussion of mismanagement styles in this appendix, people who have some measure of **PAEI** will have codes of uppercase and lowercase letters to show their qualities.

We have seen what happens when one managerial role is performed exclusively. When **E** is the only role performed, one gets the style of the Arsonist (--**E**-). That is, we get a person who is solely interested in creating new plans and new projects. However, when such a person's **E** is coupled with another managerial role, his creativity is focused on that role. For example, if the person is a **P**-**E**-, he becomes an inventor who is so creative that he improves his innovations all the time. But since this person is not capable of performing the **A** and **I** roles, we have a new style of mismanagement.

When a person's **E** is coupled with **A** his creativity is oriented toward administrative systems. He could be a -**AE**- or a **pAEi**. The former gives us the Pain in the Neck, whom we will soon discuss. The latter could give us a consultant, a person who uses his creativity to improve the control systems of an organization, a systems analyst. The – A E – is a mismanager because of the blanks in his managerial code. The **pAEi** is a manager who has strengths (**AE**) and weaknesses (**pi**).

When **E** and **I** are coupled, the Superfollower disappears. His **E** is oriented toward the integration of ideas. If he performs these two roles exclusively, we get the Demagogue, or cheap politician.

The ways in which managerial roles are often combined give us ten new styles of mismanagement. These styles will be the subject of this chapter.

THE SLAVE DRIVER (PA––)

The Slave Driver is oriented toward achievement, results, and control. He is interested in efficiency and effectiveness; in *what* is done, *and* in *how* it is done. However, he is neither creative nor people-oriented.

This very autocratic individual is a taskmaster. We call him the Slave Driver because he has a very mechanistic view of the organization. His plans and work are highly organized and systematized. He relies heavily upon precedents and past experiences. Due to his **P** he is oriented to the particular task on which he may be working: he is a tactician who makes everyone work hard. Due to his **A**, he is efficiency-oriented and tries to create effective controls over processes. He is concerned with what people do *and* with how they do it. He prefers top-down communication. The Slave Driver is found quite frequently in the military. Proliferation of this type of manager can lead to a stagnant company.

The Slave Driver differs from the Long Ranger (**P–––**) in that he excels in putting things in order and has institutional-style staff meetings. He differs from the Bureaucrat (**–A––**) in that he always emphasizes the results that have to be achieved. Similar behavior is exemplified in this statement,

"I've never concerned myself with the issues; I'm a political mechanic. I work programs, not issues, not speeches, not phrases. . . . I'm simply putting it all together."[1]

The Slave Driver is inflexible and opinionated. There is basically one way to get things done: the right way, his way. He pays careful attention to details, deadlines, and procedures. He has no sympathy, and he accepts no excuses. Getting the job done right is all that is important.

The Slave Driver is very impersonal. His businesslike approach makes him always appear distant, and it gives him a machinelike personality. His behavior is highly predictable. This makes him easy to cope with as long as one is willing to be enslaved. One knows exactly where one stands with him. His subordinates fear him, but at the same time they learn to live with him.

One should never ask the Slave Driver for favors. One should always accept the fact that one is a tool in the Slave Driver's hands.

But interestingly enough, the Slave Driver is himself a tool in the hands of others. He hardly manages anything for himself. He carries out orders efficiently. He is basically a loyal, dedicated, and hardworking servant of his masters. He drives his slaves for other people's goals.

The Slave Driver is often a "slave" who was promoted and became a supervisor. In order to please his bosses, he accepts tasks blindly and he carries them out blindly. In Hebrew such a person is called "eved ki yimloch," which means "a slave who became a king."

The Slave Driver is frequently despised by those who possess any spark of independence and self-respect. The stifling, inhumane, work-only atmosphere created by the Slave Driver causes some people to quit. Others find the security and certainty acceptable, and they accept enslavement willingly. After some time, they even resist being freed, because this would introduce uncertainty into their lives.

How does a person become a **PA--**? Perhaps with a promotion, for such a person is a strong achiever to begin with. He works hard and achieves results (**P**). His success as an individual could easily lead to a managerial position. As a manager, he is still dominated by his results orientation, except that he adds to it the role of administering or controlling so that other people achieve results as well. His need to exercise power, which was latent before he was promoted, comes into full bloom when he is given an opportunity to manage others. Without the promotion, he would have remained a pure **P**.

The Slave Driver is impatient with himself and others. "Keep moving" is the feeling he imparts to those around him. His speech tends to be brief; his penetrating eyes are "steel cold"; his movements are abrupt. He cuts people off in the middle of their sentences and finishes the sentences himself. If he is prevented from interrupting, he exhibits his displeasure by "freezing out" or interrupting behaviorally. By "freezing out," I mean that he fixes his eyes on the person who is talking, does not move a muscle in his body or face, locks his jaws tightly together, and waits for the other person to "get the message" and shut up. If the Slave Driver is talking to a person who is of higher status and cannot be frozen out, the Slave Driver interrupts him behaviorally. That is, the Slave Driver moves his body in an up-and-down motion: first up on his toes, then down on his heels. While the Slave Driver is up on his toes, he looks as though he might jump or fall forward. When he lands on his heels he clicks them together, and for emphasis he may also smack his lips or make a clicking noise with his tongue. This body language is meant to exhibit the Slave Driver's high impatience and to interrupt the other person. All of this time the Slave Driver is somewhat angry with himself for having lost control of the conversation.

A model in managerial literature of the **PA--** is the "Commander" style described by Bell.[2] This person attempts to control his environment so that he can regulate all of the events that occur within it. He blames mistakes on problems with the subordinates. He dislikes ambiguity and uncertainty, and therefore he categorizes the world. It has been said that there are "two types of people in the world: the type who dichotomize everything, and the others." They tend to stress short-term goals, almost as much as ultimate objectives. Their communication is one way: down! They will tell you what to do and talk about getting the job done, but that is all.

Bell claims that Commanders perform best in situations in which the environment is relatively stable. Given clear-cut tasks that can be accomplished in an orderly, precise manner, a person using the Commander style will assert his control, dominate the routines, dominate the subordinates, and concentrate on the means to the end.

My observation has been that **A, E,** and **I** deficiencies that were latent and benign when the Slave Driver was an employee, or "slave," became dysfunctional and malignant when he was promoted to a managerial position and became a Slave Driver.

The Slave Driver style makes the organization very inflexible. The organization lacks creativity and does not readily adapt to changes in the environment. Although it will normally be very efficient in the short run, morale is low and turnover is high. Individuals who do not cause problems are promoted, so that the growth of creativity is hampered.

When the **PA‑‑** leaves an organization, there is a noticeable difference in results. People would break the machinery if they could. They are apt to strike, produce less, and show similar manifestations of rebellion and relief.

The Lone Ranger's change in position required a change in behavior. The Lone Ranger (**P**) added an **A** to his style, but this change was not sufficient.

What happens if the Slave Driver is able to integrate ideas and people, as well as produce and administer? We would then have our next combined style of mismanagement (**PA–I**), the Benevolent Benign Prince.

THE BENEVOLENT BENIGN PRINCE (PA–I)

The Benevolent Benign Prince combines the three managerial roles: those of the producer, the administrator, and the integrator. He is involved with producing short-term results (**P**), he focuses on effective systems of control (**A**), and he is capable of integrating people. Whereas the Slave Driver (**PA––**) gets people working, the Benevolent Benign Prince allows others to present and discuss ideas, but then he makes the final decision. In one organization the **PA–I** would listen to ideas, decide what was desirable, obtain agreement, then proceed as a Slave Driver toward the goals. Since the ideas were acceptable to the people in the organization, this Benevolent Benign Prince was powerful and effective.

The Benevolent Benign Prince is distant and impersonal. His subordinates worship him and work hard to get the job done in the way he wants it done. The subordinates have no

Drawing by Chas. Addams; © *1976*
The New Yorker Magazine, Inc.

ideas of their own, but neither does he. He is not a king. He is just a prince who is able to get people to do the job amicably.

The Benevolent Benign Prince is not charismatic. His **P** is basically short-term in orientation, whereas a charismatic leader would possess a large **E.**

As a small-time implementation integrator, the Benevolent Benign Prince exerts a positive impact in the short run. But when he leaves the organization, the followers will continue to work in the way that they have been used to working, and they will slowly disintegrate as a group. This happens because the subordinates have no ideas (**E**) to integrate them, but only an implementation system which becomes obsolete over time.

We have said that the Benevolent Benign Prince has no ideas of his own (no **E**). He functions as a team member (**AI**) who brings the ideas of others to fruition (**P**). A description of Cyrus Vance is interesting to analyze:

> In the Pentagon he developed a reputation as a good manager, an implementor of policy [A], and a man able to get along with the military [I] even when the defense secretary McNamara's relations with the military began to sour. . . . Some of those who worked with him in the past consider him to be too much of a consensus man, waiting for positions and pressures to develop before taking a stand [I]. He does not jump in right away, but comes in before the outcome is clear, particularly on an issue with moral aspects [I]. . . . Some maintained that Mr. Vance is not imaginative [no E]. . . . He is described as a good technician [P], a loyal team player [I]. . . . His style in the past has been to let the White House take the lead [no E]. . . . the professional diplomats who know Mr. Vance expect him to run a well-organized department [A], but to maintain a low profile [no E]. . . . Mr. Carter stressed [Vance's] competence rather than his conceptual brilliance or policy innovation [no E]. . . . Vance is a superb technocrat [P] with an incisive executive mind who executed presidential policy [A]. . . . Mr. Vance immediately indicated that he would shun what Mr. Carter derisively termed the "Lone

Ranger diplomacy of Mr. Kissinger" (*New York Times,* December 4, 1976, p. 13).

The role mentioned most frequently (four times) is **I**. **A** is mentioned three times, **P** is mentioned two times, and the fact that Vance has no **E** is noted four times. Vance's code then appears to be that of a **PA–I** (Benevolent Benign Prince) or a **PAeI** (Shepherd).

What happens if a Benevolent Benign Prince is not oriented or inclined to produce? In that case, we get the Paternalistic Bureaucrat, our next combined style of mismanagement.

THE PATERNALISTIC BUREAUCRAT (–A–I)

A nondirective manager who is concerned with form and with people, but not with ideas and results, performs only the **A** and **I** roles. We will refer to such a person as a Paternalistic Bureaucrat. We might also call him an Open-Door Manager. Whatever function he manages, he will work in a more participative manner than most managers. The Paternalistic Bureaucrat seeks to establish controls which are agreeable to his people. His concern is with implementing an established system and following established processes. His **I** enables others to work under him more easily than they would under the Bureaucrat.

The Paternalistic Bureaucrat listens, agrees, and accepts, but only as long as you do not violate any rules! His door is always open, but like the Superfollower, he is not really sincere in his expressed willingness to accept ideas that come through that door. This is because he has no orientation toward results, no inclination to change anything, and because he refuses to introduce conflict.

The Paternalistic Bureaucrat is concerned with forms and with people. He calls meetings and lets people talk; he shows concern and interest; he encourages and motivates. Yet his dominant message is always "We must make the system work the way it's designed to work." Subordinates must get to work on time, and must get along with everyone—including, of course, the Paternalistic Bureaucrat.

Training, explanation, and help are more abundant under the Paternalistic Bureaucrat than under the Bureaucrat, but under both the orientation to produce is missing. For a while one tends to like the easygoing atmosphere in an organization headed by a Paternalistic Bureaucrat. The organization seems to run efficiently, and people are very friendly to each other. It is a kind of mutual admiration society. But soon one begins to realize (especially if one comes from outside the organization) that the management style is making the organization stale. The organization has no excitement, no goal orientation; no ideas that make life different, no pending changes. Deep disagreements are submerged and cannot be dealt with publicly. The organization looks somewhat like a resort town for retired people.

The Paternaltistic Bureaucrat can only survive in a noncompetitive, nonchanging environment. In government bureaucracies, for example, he is probably considered the most successful type of manager, since he does his job without rocking the boat, thereby minimizing friction. He is basically a friendly Bureaucrat.

But let's change the role combinations around again. When a manager produces results and gets along with people (but without vision or a system), we get our next combined mismanagement style, the Small-Time Coach (**P--I**).

THE SMALL-TIME COACH (P--I)

The Small-Time Coach is a manager who excels both at producing results and at integrating his subordinates. He is an excellent process facilitator, and he is excellent at using compromise to produce results, particularly in the short run. Although he may be somewhat idealistic and critical, he is a developer of teams. A **P--I** could be a people-oriented, first-line supervisor. He does not concern himself with the externalities of the system, and he does not stand on formality. He encourages and supports the people who do the job.

The Small-Time Coach resembles the youth leader and the small-time politician. He seeks to generate excitement, and then he channels the energy he generates into the production of results. Results produced in this manner can be expensive to an organization. They are always short-term-oriented, and they often fail in the long run since there is no system to follow them through and since their goals are tactical in nature.

Unlike the Lone Ranger (P---), the Small-Time Coach seeks agreement and is people-oriented. He rarely establishes a top-down command, as the Lone Ranger does. Unlike the Superfollower, he produces results. He has no system, and he has no large ideas. Thus, he is not a major league coach, but rather a tactical integrator of people for some short-term activity.

If we take away the integration orientation of the Small-Time Coach and make him an entrepreneur instead, what style will we observe?

THE SPROUTING FOUNDER (P–E–)

We refer to the manager who performs only the producing and the entrepreneuring roles as the Sprouting Founder, because this type of individual usually founds an organization. However, he never really gets beyond the "sprouting" stage— he loses the organization when it gets too large. He is tremendously energetic—a self-starter who sees his projects through to the end. Because he is task-oriented, he is at his prime when the firm is small and growing. In the long run, however, the organization often outgrows his capabilities. When more formal controls are required, his style loses effectiveness. It becomes dysfunctional, since he has no administrative or integrative capabilities, both of which are required for long-term organizational growth.

The Sprouting Founder is a creative risk-taker and a results-oriented individual. He is usually very outgoing. He sees farther than the Lone Ranger, since he has the **E** orientation, and unlike the Arsonist, he is goal-oriented.

The Sprouting Founder starts his own fires and then tends them. He has followers or subordinates, but basically he runs a one-man show, with no time left to integrate or delegate. His ideas are exciting. He knows how to produce results, and his subordinates simply try to emulate his style. However, they are not integrated into a team. They follow him as individuals, and he may have as many as 30 subordinates reporting to him.

Since the Sprouting Founder neither administers nor integrates the organization, it only grows up to the level of his personal managing capability. Furthermore, since he is not an integrator, the organization usually crumbles and disappears when he leaves or dies.

In addition to the Sprouting Founder, there is another type of **P–E–**. This is the Mismatched Director of Professionals. He may be the director of an artistic organization, the medical director of a hospital, or a department chairman in an academic institution.

He is mismatched because he does not particularly care for administration or for integrating people. He got his job because of his production or entrepreneuring capabilities, or both. That is, he was promoted because of his individual professional excellence. But managing an organization requires more than the ability to dance, cure, or teach.

As a result, he becomes frustrated and constantly reminds himself and others that he really has another task in life. His present occupation is a career mistake or a temporary assignment (perceived by him as a big sacrifice or as the consequence of a masochistic tendency on his part). He plays the part of a martyr, never forgetting to let the sympathetic listener know how much he hates administration and how demoralizing it is. In actuality, he never returns to producing art, practicing medicine, or doing research. He gets too hooked on the power game. He also appreciates the instant feedback that the administrative process gives, which is much more gratifying than the feedback that results from professional activity, whose extrinsic gratifications, such as recognition, may take forever to come, if they come at all.

To be a good artist one needs the **P** and **E** orientations. However, administrative and integrative capabilities are not very necessary. We think of writers and painters as persons who have to come up with ideas, put them into a medium for communication, and see the process through to completion. The real artist needs **E** to create new things and **P** to see his projects through. The artist's achievement orientation permits him to disassociate himself from his labor of love and to let it go when it is completed. An artist without a **P** will either never finish his work or will never let go of it when it is done (which is equivalent to never finishing).

A person with **P** and no **E** could be a commercial artist. He repeats himself constantly. An artist with an **E** and no **P** might be a bohemian—he has ideas about what should be done, but he doesn't do anything.

Why are **P–E–**s mismatched? A great actor may wish to be a director. The best doctor becomes the chief of staff. The most respected researcher is asked to head a university. But the **P** and **E** of such people won't always fill the bill. An actor cannot direct unless he can integrate an ensemble (**I**). An artist who becomes an artistic director may be unable to handle the board of directors, plan systematically, raise funds, or even plan the next tour (no **A**).

The brilliant doctor (**P–E–**) who is appointed chief of staff may have endless fights with his colleagues (no **I**). He may also fail to control the budget, to hire the most qualified nurses, or to supervise the handling of medical information (no **A**).

In universities, alas, uncountable **P–E–**s are in the saddle. Faculty hiring policies shift with the ever-changing objectives of new chairmen. The changes that are introduced by each new chairperson implement no long-range policy or plan. Courses multiply—the names are new, but the content remains unchanged. Academic cross-fertilization within a department is often a myth or a mirage cherished by aspiring new faculty members.

Both the Sprouting Founder and the Mismatched Director of Professionals fail as administrators, and therefore they tend to alienate the groups with which they work. They are respected in their profession, but disorder in their departments causes them to be despised for the way they are running things.

To be a good manager of professionals, one needs **P** and **E**, but also some **a** and **i**. In professional organizations, **A** and **I** are usually provided by administrative directors.

This leads us to another question: Could an **−A−I** run a professional organization? It seems to me that he could not, because he needs **P** and **E** to understand the organization. But even if he could, the professionals would probably not allow him to. They wouldn't trust him, and they would despise him because he was not an artist, doctor, teacher, or researcher.

The **−A−I,** however, would do a better job as the leader of a professional organization than would the **P−E−.** This is because he would spend a good deal of time trying to please the professionals (**I**) and would serve them as a support system (**A**). But he would be mistrusted, disliked, ignored, ridiculed, criticized, and so on. The **P−E−** mismanages much more significantly, but he is forgiven for his administrative failures because of his professional accomplishments. He is considered a martyr who should "get the hell out of there" before "it gets to him."

A professional organization should have **PaEi** as a professional director (artistic, medical, or academic) and a **pAeI** as an administrative director. Both are needed.

One might ask, "What would be wrong with having a **P−E−** and a **−A−I**?" The answer is that these cannot work together because each is insensitive to the contributions of the other. The professional director lacks the time and the inclination to pay attention to people's aspirations and organizational needs. The $-A-I$ does not care about the results being achieved (**P**), and he has no professional aspirations or creativity (**E**). But he needs both in order to back up his professional director and to gain some respect from the people he manages. Over time, his **I** disappears because he doesn't use it.

In addition, if a **P–E–** and a **–A–I** have no respect for each other, they probably won't cooperate with each other. What is needed, then, is the ability to perform in more than two roles. Thus, the most desirable of professional managers is the **PaEI**. However, the **PaEi** is acceptable, since very few great professionals are capable of performing an **I** role. They are to individualistic (**E**) for that.

What is important is that the professional director not be completely lacking in **I**. This can easily happen, since a professional organization tends to single out the person whose **E** is largest for the position, and such a person's **E** usually develops at the expense of his or her **I**.

THE SOLO DEVELOPER (PAE–)

The master at putting together a complex project is the Solo Developer. He nurtures the project until results are forthcoming. Because of his **E**, he sees the big picture. He identifies what results can be achieved. His **P** makes him results-oriented. His **A** is employed in creating a system to obtain the desired results. But the developer has no **I** and he is therefore another example of a one-person show.

In comparison to the Sprouting Founder, however, the Solo Developer's organization can grow beyond his individual contributions (due to his **A**). The organization will still experience difficulty when the Solo Developer leaves, because he was its only producer, administrator, and entrepreneur. The subordinates were mere followers. He did not build a team of producers, administrators, or entrepreneurs that could maintain the previous rate of growth. **PAE–s** could be systems analysts or classic consultants. They have ideas on how to produce results or on how to organize the system to achieve results, but they cannot create an environment in which subordinates generate such programs.

A variation of the Solo Developer is found in the construction industry and in investment banking. The people who exemplify this variation have good ideas, know how to produce results, and can organize everything into a nice, neat "package." But there is no continuity. The deal is made, and it must stand on its own. A person who manifests this style is also a one-man show whose departure will leave the organization in a difficult position.

THE DEMAGOGUE (––EI)

This type of mismanager excels only as an integrator and an entrepreneur. He might be a convincing salesman or a run-of-the-mill politician. Although he is creative and adaptive, he is unconcerned about consequences of his efforts: he has no **P**.

As a politician, the Demagogue identifies the ideas that will appeal to his constituents and integrates these into his own style in the form of promises. But he has no system for keeping these promises (no **A**), and no ability to deliver what he promises (no **P**). He relies on his **E** capabilities to identify the messages (any messages) that will unify people.

The Demagogue will make irresponsible promises. He does not let one know (because he must not know) what the precise results will be. His aims are to generate excitement and interest and to rally support for himself. He worries about the results of the next election. What happens afterward will have to take care of itself.

The Demagogue differs from the Arsonist (––E–) in that he does not generate ideas solely to satisfy his ego. He listens to what people want, need, and expect. As an **I**, he is able to detect social undercurrents. His **E** capability allows him to formulate a message that will give expression to those undercurrents. He makes the promises that people want to hear. He differs also from the Superfollower (---**I**). Whereas the Superfollower can integrate only a small group of people because his personal intervention is required, the --**EI** can integrate by means of his ideas alone.

There is yet another difference between the Demagogue and the Arsonist. The subordinates of the Arsonist do not follow him, although they claim that they do. Those who work for the Demagogue, however, are so stirred up by his message that they will go all-out for him.

A subordinate of the Demagogue goes through a hot and cold emotional bath. While in the Demagogue's presence, the subordinate can find his ideas exciting and the right thing to do. But afterward the subordinate wonders where to begin or what to do. "What exactly did he want?" he may ask. The Demagogue told the subordinate what he wanted to hear and built up the subordinate's aspirations to achieve something—but what?

In Mexico, such a leader is called an Alka Seltzer. He relieves you of your anxiety, but only for a few hours. Then you feel lousy again. Bell calls this type of leader the Performer.[3]

Typically, the Performer is a smooth operator and a shrewd politician. He has developed the social graces to a T. The Performer is a dynamic person who frequently does several things at a time. Bell suggests that "to reach great successes, the Performer develops special talents in maneuvering others." These skills include pseudoparticipation, making special deals, cooperating with other performers, taking credit for successes, and parceling out compliments.

Let us explore now what happens when a Demagogue works with another mismanager. One potentially dangerous combination is the Demagogue (--**EI**) as a manager with a Slave Driver (**PA**--) as his subordinate. The Demagogue has ideas that he expects his subordinates to support totally and unequivocally. The Slave Driver looks for opportunities "to get things done right," and he is more than willing to be dedicated, enslaved, and enslaving.

However, the Demagogue's ideas and directions are very vague, whereas the Slave Driver want to run a "tight ship," so he picks up what he believes he understands and proceeds to do it or to get it done. The Demagogue doesn't see any problems because he doesn't care what the Slave Driver does. Like the Arsonist, the Demagogue enjoys the fact that someone is totally committed to his ideas. In the meantime, the uncreative Slave Driver may be cooking up a disaster.

The result might be a situation such as Watergate. Nixon was on top of his White House staff, with Haldeman and Ehrlichman under him. Nixon had a great vision of what he was going to do as a statesman (E), and he badly needed to be accepted (I), as was indicated by his unhappiness about the nonsupportive media. So he found himself a few Slave Drivers, such as Haldeman, to serve him blindly. The result could have been a fantastic misunderstanding—the ––EI's directions were too general, and they were being interpreted by a PA–– in detail, without any real vision (E) or ethics behind the P.

Thus, there are workable and nonworkable combinations in management. We have seen the combination of a PA–– and a ––EI as a potentially dangerous partnership. We have also seen that the combination of a PaEi and a pAeI could be a workable partnership as long as the pAeI does not mind being in a supportive role. Hospitals, operas, theaters, and universities are often run by such a partnership.

Our next combined style of mismanagement occurs when we add the ability to organize to the already enthusiastic Demagogue.

THE FALSE LEADER (–AEI)

This type of manager generates ideas, integrates people behind his ideas, and establishes a system to implement ideas.

However, the system does not produce results. People follow the False Leader and carry out their assigned tasks, but their beliefs are shattered in the long run since what is promised never materializes. The False Leader *does* organize, he *does* provide for an integrating mission, but the activities that he organizes ultimately fail.

A typical False Leader is a Communist leader in the eyes of a realistic nonbeliever. While such a leader's goals (**E**) may seem humanistic and attractive, their integration and implementation produce results that are nightmarish for all who experience them (no **P**).

A person can easily find himself without any **P** orientation. He can lose his **P** by getting carried away with power and thus losing whatever social judgment is necessary for **P**. Or he can lose it by trying to "run a war from a map while ignoring any information from the field," as Hitler did. Without knowledge **P** is fruitless.

An industrial example of the False Leader is the manager who is brought in to save a failing company. Such a person is expected to produce results almost instantaneously; everyone looks up to him as a savior. He may be very achievement-oriented, but perhaps his **P** is weak because he has not yet learned the technology of his new company, its market, "what makes it tick." However, without know-how his achievement orientation is useless. He turns out to be a False Leader. People expect too much too soon, and their expectations are not met. Such a person may be a great entrepreneur, administrator, and integrator, but he just doesn't understand what he has to do.

There are endless examples in industry of this type of manager—eager to succeed, good administrators, entrepreneurs, and integrators, but without knowledge of a particular field and without the time they need to acquire it. These managers are therefore incapable of producing results.

George Steiner describes such a manager in his *Top Management Planning*.[4] He tells what happened to the Winchester

Company in the 1920s and 30s. The president appointed managers who had had no previous experience in the field to key positions.

He boasted that the company had added about 1,000 new products in 1923–24. But to improve sales, these new products competed with Winchester's bread-and-butter products and Winchester merged with its major competitor. The results were more than disappointing. Salesmen had to sell products that they had previously criticized. Sales declined from $18 million in 1923 to $7 million in 1931.

It is obviously not enough to innovate and change. A manager has to have intimate knowledge of the field in which he innovates. He must know the discipline, the function, the market, and the product in order to make adequate judgments. Change for the sake of change can have disastrous effects.

Consequently, those who say "A manager is a manager is a manager" are mistaken. Any organization can be managed well, but only after some time. It is necessary for every manager to spend time learning and understanding the **P**, developing the **A**, experiencing the **E**, and working for the **I**. The **P** must be gained by learning the technology, the market, the customers, and other crucial factors that make a specific organization successful. No two organizations are alike; each has its own peculiar personality. A manager must understand what produces results (**P**) before he can perform the rest of the roles.

Our next combined style of mismanagement has neither a **P** orientation nor an **I** orientation. It is creative (**E**) and control-oriented (**A**). This gives us a unique style of a mismanager whom we classify as the Pain in the Neck.

THE PAIN IN THE NECK (–AE–)

The Pain in the Neck is really not concerned with what is done or produced. Furthermore, he is insensitive to other people and incapable of integrating their ideas into a cohesive whole. However, the Pain in the Neck is full of ideas on what should be done, and he wants to control in detail all aspects of what is being done.

The Pain in the Neck differs from the Bureaucrat (–A––) in a number of respects: he frequently generates new ideas; he holds impromptu meetings; and he is irregular in his desire to put things in order, to control the system, and to hold regular, organized meetings. His communication style tends to be top-down.

He behaves somewhat like a schizophrenic. He is ridden with internal conflicts. He wants to control, and at the same time he wants to change things. He sees opportunities and threats and he becomes excited about what needs to be done. Yet he relizes all the implications of what he wants to do. He sees all of the complications that will prevent it from being done.

The Pain in the Neck's frustration with his own "impotence" makes him brooding, dissatisfied, unfriendly, and nonsupportive. In meetings he is always on the other side of the fence. If the discussion concerns the details of operational control, he will bring up the "big picture" and complain that "we are not adapting to the changing needs of our markets." If the discussion is on long-term future trends, he will insist that it is dangerous to make changes.

The –AE– is controversial, and he makes it impossible to be on the same side that he is on. He is not popular in organizations since he permanently plays the Devil's advocate.

If the Pain in the Neck had even a little of a **P** orientation, he would be a good problem solver. He would take a complex problem (**E**) and structure it so that it was controllable (**A**) and produced results (**P**). However, since he has no **I**, he can't be a consultant. As a p**AE**–, he is at best a highly creative systems-oriented staff person.

Our –**AE**– resembles Bell's Attacker.[5] The Attacker, according to Bell, rebels against authority, social customs, and the like. This is the **E** orientation in him. However, as an Attacker (the **A** orientation in him), he tends to be a nitpicker. Nonetheless, he avoids responsibility (lack of **P**) by acting uncommitted and failing to show interest in projects. Since he has no **I** he transfers his internal conflicts to others and thus alienates them. When he is given a project, he expends a good deal of energy finding mistakes and problems with it.

To shield himself from responsibility to the environment, the Attacker will form a group of Attackers around him. This group will develop cynical perspectives and reinforce these perspectives in one another. They will attack anything and everything that is presented to them. In one situation they will argue that a certain task needs to be controlled (exhibiting their **A**). In another situation they will argue that not enough is being done. "You should always be moving" (**E**).

So whatever approach one takes, the Attacker goes to work and presents the other side. Since he often changes his mind, he is constantly at odds with himself. This makes him a bitter, bitchy, critically oriented, frustrated Pain in the Neck! As a consultant, the −**AE**− is dangerous because he has no **P** and no **I**. That is, he will offer ideas on how to change a system for better control, but he does not understand what the system is for, and he fails to consider integration and the need for teamwork.

THE CHARISMATIC GURU (P–EI)

The effective leader creates new directions (**E**), motivates his fellow workers (**I**), and produces results (**P**) with a system (**A**). The Charismatic Guru creates these results with his charisma. In contrast to the Demagogue, the Guru *does* produce results. He also identifies the big picture, both now and in the future. He integrates people and sets out to make effective changes. He will worry about the next generation, and not necessarily the next election.

The Charismatic Guru's creativity is results-oriented. He

has a commitment to certain goals, and he focuses his entrepreneurship on them. Furthermore, he is a capable persuader, and he is able to communicate his ideas and the desired results in a manner that integrates people. That is what makes him a Guru.

However, there is no system to follow (**A**), because it is the Guru's personal style that his followers admire. The Guru does not institutionalize himself, so that when he dies, his followers must systematize and ritualize his teachings, or his influence will disappear.

One of the **P–EIs** I analyzed was charismatic, produced results, and was head and shoulders above his peers. But when he died his organization found it difficult to survive because it had not been set up for effectiveness and efficiency. Its past achievements had depended too much on the personal intervention of its late leader. It had not become systematized, and it was like a ship that had lost its navigator and could not be oriented without him.

The Charismatic Guru may be considered a type of False Leader in the sense that he appears to be the perfect manager but does not come through in the long run. He provides **A** with his personality, but when the person disappears, the latent **A** deficiency expresses itself fully. The integration he achieved may soon be eroded. Subsequently, results diminish, and without integration and results, the **E** he bequeathed has no chance of expressing itself or of being carried out.

What I am suggesting here is that charismatic leadership is also a type of mismanagement, because the life span of organizations is longer than that of any individual. If an organization's success depends on the life span of its Guru, in the long run the organization will not survive.

NOTES

1. Theodore H. White, *Breach of Faith* (New York: Dell, 1975), p. 139.

2. Gerald Bell, *The Achievers* (Chapel Hill, N.C.: Preston Hill, 1973), chap. 2.

3. Ibid., chap. 6.

4. George Albert Steiner, *Top Management Planning* (New York: Macmillan, 1969).

5. Bell, *Achievers,* chap. 3.

Index

A

Ablon, Ralph, 78, 85, 135
Achievement, need for, 82, 83, 84
Adizes Synergetic Method (A'S/M),
    124, 153–54, 211, 235
Administrator, 4, 5–6, 24–25
    attitude toward other managers,
    35
    Deadwood, 76–77
    development, 168
    managerial practices, 34
    Paternalistic Bureaucrat, 260–61
    staff meetings, 31–32, 34
    style, 33–35
    subordinates, 34
    time management, 34–35
Adolescent stage of organization,
    100–102
    treatment, 119–20, 203–5
Affiliation, need for, 82, 83
American Indians, 135–37
Argyris, C., 142
Aristocratic organization, 106–12
    bankrupt, 111–12
    managerial uniforms, 106
    meeting place, 109
    mergers and acquisitions, 110–11
    mode of address, 106–7

Aristocratic organization—*Cont.*
    mode of speech, 107–9
    rejuvenation, 124
    treatment, 204–5, 207–9
Arlen Realty and Development,
    175
Arsonist; *see* Entrepreneur
A'S/M; *see* Adizes Synergetic
    Method
Attacker, 272–73
Avoider, 74

B

Balzac, Honoré de, 140
Behavioral science, 164
Bell, Gerald, 61, 74, 141, 256, 257,
    268, 272
Benevolent Benign Prince, 258–60
Blake, Robert, 59, 84
Blanchard, K. H., 85
Boren's Laws, 74
Bureaucracy, 113–16
    Early, 112–13
    treatment, 209–10
Bureaucrat; *see* Administrator
Burnham, David, 83
Burns, Robert, 139
Business administration, 163

Business school, 133
  behavioral science, 164
  management training, 149, 152,
    161–65

C

capi (coalesced authority, power,
    and influence), 238, 239
  group, 245
  task synerteam, 240, 243
Career changing, 184–86
Cervantes, Miguel de, 138
Charismatic Guru, 273–74
Chief executive office, 177
Coalesced authority, power, and
    influence; *see capi*
Cohen, Arthur, 175
Collateral organization, 238
Committee, 246
Conflict, 144–45, 188
Consciousness-raising, 206, 207
Consulting, 211
  external or internal, 211
Courtship stage of organization,
    93–94
  treatment, 118–19
Couzens, James, 175
Creativity, 38
Culbert, S., 139

D

Deadwood
  Administrator, 76–77
  attitude toward other managers,
    80
  conflict, 188
  Entrepreneur, 77
  Integrator, 77
  managerial practices, 80
  origins, 75
  Producer, 76
  staff meetings, 80
  style, 72–75, 79–80
  subordinates, 79–80
Decentralization, 120, 121, 123, 167,
    205, 208
Decision making
  Adizes Method, 244
  Administrator, 65
  group, 186

Decision making—*Cont.*
  nonprogrammed, 245
  participative, 246
  Producer, 65
  programmability, 156–59
Delegation, 125–26, 167
Demagogue, 267–69
Drucker, Peter, 10, 85, 86, 216

E

Eichmann, Adolf, 28, 29
Elitism, 222, 225, 226–28
Engineering department, 191, 192,
    193
Entrepreneur, 4, 6, 56
  attitude toward other managers,
    54
  bureaucracy, 155
  Deadwood, 77
  managerial practices, 53–54
  role, 37–39
  staff meetings, 53-54
  style, 39, 52–53
  subordinates, 41-52, 53
  time management, 53–54
  training, 166-67
Entrepreneur-Integrator, 57
Executive training programs, 162

F–G

False Leader, 269–71
Feminist movement, 176
Finzi-Contini syndrome, 108, 124,
    207
Ford, Henry, 56, 175
Ford Motor Company, 175
Founder's trap, 99, 125, 202
Go-go stage of organization, 98–100
  treatment, 119, 200–203
Gow, Charles, 105
Gross, Bertram W., 223
Group diagnostic session, 207
Group entrepreneurship, 56

H–I

Hammer, A., 181
Hersey, Paul, 85
Hertzberg, Frederick, 200, 221
Hull, Raymond, 71n
Illich, Ivan, 165

Infant organization, 95–98
  treatment, 119, 199–200
Integration, 56
  lateral, 58
  training, 166–67
  upward-downward, 58
Integrator, 4, 6–7
  active, 58
  Adizes Method, 247, 248
  attitude toward other managers,
    69
  Deadwood, 77
  exclusive, 58, 59
  managerial practices, 68–69
  passive, 58
  staff meetings, 68–69
  style, 58–68
  subordinates, 68–69
  time management, 68–69

J–L

Job changing
  career change, 184–86
  promotion, 182–84
Kami, Michael, 86
Kroc, Ray, 146
Law of butter and guns, 201
Law of opportunity cost, 201
Leadership, contingency theory of,
    220
Learning environment, 145–46
Lone Ranger; see Producer
Lord Acton's Law, 86

M

McClelland, David, 82, 83, 84
Management
  committee, 246
  definition, 215
  elitism, 222, 225, 226–28
  hierarchy, 227
  motivation, 220
  necessity for, 222–23, 225
  roles, 4, 5–7
  social responsibility, 228
  teamwork, 174–76, 228–29
  training and development, 149–
    71
Management by Objectives, 190,
    251

Management styles, 66, 132, 144,
    192–95
  complementary, 181
  exclusive, 67
  hierarchy, 160, 161
  Integrator, 58–68
  programmed, 160, 161
  task fitting, 177–82, 193
Management theory, 9, 10, 133
  elitism, 222, 226–28
Management training and develop-
    ment, 149
  administration, 168
  behavioral science, 164
  decision making, 156–59
  entrepreneurship, 166–67, 169–
    71
  integration, 166–67, 169–71
  methods, 165–66, 167–71
  obstacles, 151
  participative, 246, 247
  production, 168
  program content, 161–65
Manager, 131
  characteristics of good manager,
    134–47
  teamwork, 174–76
  theory, 133
  training and development, 149–
    71
Managerial mix, 176–77, 186, 189–
    95
Managerial practices
  Administrator, 34–35
  Deadwood, 89–90
  Entrepreneur, 53–54
  Integrator, 68–69
  Producer, 22–23
  Textbook Manager, 89–90
Managerial teams, 88, 228–29
Managerial transplantation, 197,
    204, 207
Mark, Charles Christopher, 48
Marketing department, 192, 194
Martin, Thomas L., Jr., 45, 74, 86,
    221
Maslow, Abraham, 140, 141
Maturity and immaturity, 142
Mayo, E., 9
MDOR, 8

Medicine wheel, 135, 136
Mergers and acquisitions, 110–11, 123, 205
Mintzberg, H., 159
Mismanagement styles, 132
Mismatched Director of Professionals, 263–64, 265
Morale, 221
Motivation, 220, 221
Mouton, Jane, 59, 84
Myers, Scott, 229

O

Occidental Petroleum, 181
Organization
  hierarchy, 231, 232
  PAE model, 231, 232–34
  roles, 154–56
  styles, 92
Organization chart, 121, 122, 189, 193–94
Organizational development, 211
Organizational holograph, 194–96
Organizational life cycle, 92, 93
  Adolescent stage, 100–102, 119–20
  Aristocratic, 106–12, 123–24
  bankruptcy, 116
  Bureaucracy, 113–16
  Courtship stage, 93–94, 118–19
  Early Bureaucracy, 112–13, 124–25
  Go-go stage, 98–100, 119
  Infant organization, 95–98, 119
  Prime organization, 102–4, 120
  rejuvenation, 120, 124
  Stable organizational stage, 104–6
Organizational passages, 92, 103
Organizational therapy, 197

P

PAEI model, 150, 198, 253
  organization life cycle, 93
  organizational analysis, 231–34
  Textbook Manager, 81
Pain in the Neck, 253, 271
Parkinson's Law, 30
Participative management, 246, 247
Participative Organization Conduit (POC), 238, 244, 246, 247

Paternalistic Bureaucrat, 260
Performer, 268
Personality, 135–37
  maturity, 142
  self-actualized, 140–42
Personnel management, 190–91, 193
Peter, Laurence J., 71n
Peter Principle, 19, 71, 161
Pleaser, 61, 62
POC (Participative Organizational Conduit), 238, 244
Polanyi, M., 38
Power, need for, 82, 83
President, office of, 186–87
Prime organization, 102–4
  treatment, 120, 205–6
Producer, 4, 5, 13–23
  attitude toward other managers, 22–23
  Deadwood, 76
  development, 168
  management practices, 22
  staff meetings, 22, 31
  style, 21–23
  subordinates, 21–22
  time management, 22
Production department, 191, 192
Promotion, 182–84
Public administration, 163

R

Rangnekar's Rules for Decision Avoidance, 74
Rayburn, Sam, 59
Reich, Charles, 27
Responsibility, 187
Riklis, Meshulan, 165
Risk-taking, 39
Rogers, Will, 40
Ross, Joel, 86

S

Sales department, 191, 192, 193, 194
Samuelson, Paul, 201
Self-actualization, 140–42
Shaw, George Bernard, 38
Simon, Herbert, 188
Slave Driver, 152, 254–57

Small-Time Coach, 261–62
Solo Developer, 266–67
Sprouting Founder, 262–63, 265
Stable organizational stage, 104–6, 206–7
Staff meetings
  Bureaucrat, 31–32
  Deadwood, 80
  Entrepreneur, 53–54
  Integrator, 68–69
  Producer, 22, 31
  Textbook Manager, 89–90
Steiner, George, 270
Storm, H., 135
Subordinates
  Administrator, 34
  Deadwood, 79–80
  Entrepreneur, 41–50, 53
  Integrator, 68
  Management styles, 144
  Producer, 21–22
  Textbook Manager, 89
Superfollower; see Integrator
Synergetic participative diagnosis (Syndag), 207
Synerteam, 238, 240, 245
  assignment sheet, 240, 241, 242
  capi, 240, 243

T

Tasks
  demands, 178–80

Tasks—Cont.
  managerial styles, 177–78
Taylor, F., 9
Team management, 174–76, 229
Technology, 14
Textbook Manager, 14, 15, 81
  attitude toward other managers, 90
  incompatibility of characteristics, 86
  managerial practices, 89–90
  myth of, 132–34
  nonexistence, 82, 85
  staff meetings, 89–90
  style, 88–89
  subordinates, 89
Textbooks, 163–64
Time management
  Bureaucrat, 34–35
  Deadwood, 80
  Entrepreneur, 53–54
  Integrator, 68–69
  Producer, 22
  Textbook Manager, 89–90
Townsend, Robert, 152

V–W

Vance, Cyrus, 259, 260
Weber, Max, 33
Weiner, N., 9
Wilson, Flip, 38
Wouk, Herman, 29